TEACHER EDUCATION CURRICULUM

About the Book

The book provides a holistic view of the National Curriculum Framework developed through consultations held with public, employers, educational experts and practitioners in the field of education and development in general, and school education in particular. The coverage includes all aspects of school curriculum ranging from conceptualization of school education with its link to the task of national development, its implications for school practice, and the challenge preparing efficient teaching force.

The ideas presented in the book are the outcome of individual thinking of the professionals and practitioners tempered by interaction with experts in respective field. Synthetic view presented in the beginning and towards the end adds value to the book. Implications for practice of school education and teacher training will be quite helpful to teachers and teacher educators to refine their thoughts and practice. The outcome will be the well equipped citizens of tomorrow. This book is a modest attempt in provoking the improvement in the Teacher Education Curriculum in the context of NCF–2005.

About the Editor

Dr Mahabir Yadav is presently serving as Principal of Army Institute of Education, Delhi Cantt. An intellectual with versatile personality, he has served for twenty-six years in Army Education as an officer and has been closely associated with teacher's training for last seven years at AIE. A keen worker who is involved in best practices in teaching learning processes, developing research competencies in teacher trainees and in developing learning resources to stimulate academic growth.

TEACHER EDUCATION CURRICULUM

Edited by

Mahabir Yadav

Principal

Army Institute of Education, Delhi Cantt.

2010

Kaveri Books

New Delhi - 110 002

First Published in 2010

ISBN : 978-81-7479-110-8

Published by
Kaveri Books
4832/24, Ansari Road, Darya Ganj
New Delhi-110002 (India)
Tel: 011-23288140, 23245799
Telefax: 011-2382 8140
E-mail : kaveribooks@vsnl.com
web : www.kaveribooks.com

Typeset in Times New Roman at
Delta Book World, New Delhi - 110 002

Printed at
Chawla Offset Printers, Delhi - 110 052

Published by Rakesh Goel for Kaveri Books, New Delhi in collaboration with Army Institute of Education Delhi Cantt, New Delhi - 110 010.

PRINTED IN INDIA

Preface

Pre-service teacher education lays foundation of teacher quality. It is a pity that this foundation input is the weakest link in the educational system of our country. Various Education Commissions have called for teacher education reform, including curriculum restructuring. National Curriculum Framework formulated by nationwide debate under the leadership of Prof. Yash Pal in 2005 provides a fresh look at the school as well as corresponding teacher education curriculum. This approach encourages reflection, discussion and knowledge generation. Creativity and innovation are the in focus. It is against this background that the Army Institute of Education at Delhi organized a National Seminar on Teacher Education Curriculum in the Context of National Curriculum Framework–2005 on April 02, 2009. This book is the outcome of this laudable effort.

The book has been divided into the following four thematic sections:

1. Perspectives on National Curriculum Framework–2005.
2. Innovative Practices in Teacher Education.
3. Curriculum Transaction.
4. Reflections on the Current Curriculum.

The issues raised during the papers presented in the Seminar will carry the process forward towards implementing the emerging ideas. The participants surely benefited from the reflecting thinking of creative minds.

A word of caution is in order here. Education reforms can be classified into three categories relating to structure, content and process of education. Structure reforms refer to division in stages of education and duration of studies; administrative structure at different levels; single or multiple stage wise directorates; etc. If funds are available and authority over the system to prescribe the structure can be exercised, it is not so difficult to implement the desired changes. Content related reforms are subject and discipline related. If there is access to new knowledge in different discipline and experts in different disciplines are available, curriculum renewal can be carried out with reasonable effort. Process reforms address curriculum transaction. Implementation of reforms in this area is most demanding since it requires dynamic human relationship involving very diverse group of adults and children. Heavy dose of human effort is required. Even if resources and expertise are available, without adequate preparation of highly imaginative and skilled persons, it is very difficult to implement curriculum transaction reforms. In order to ensure implementation of integrated and holistic reform package the Army Institute of Education will have to look beyond this Seminar. The work will not be confined only to operationalize the curriculum, but will also be extended to its transaction area, which is a challenge indeed!

The Army Institute of Education, Delhi Cantt. deserves a pat for the laudable effort. The faculty, particularly the Principal of the Institute, Dr Mahabir Yadav, have done commendable work in collating papers and organizing the Seminar. Needless to say that success of the event would not have been possible without patronage and involvement of the management leadership. It is very encouraging to note that the team wishes to carry the frontiers of knowledge generated in the Institute further. The present book entitled "Teacher Education Curriculum" will stimulate thinking on the subject in readers and will result in creative responsiveness to the needs of the emerging school curriculum. It may be a small but very significant contribution to teacher education in the country! It will certainly be a contribution towards producing better teachers for developing better educated youth of tomorrow.

N K Jangira
Ex. Professor NCERT
& Education Expert World Bank

Contents

SECTION – II
Innovative Practices in Teacher Education

SECTION – III

Curriculum Transaction

SECTION – IV

Reflections on the Current Curriculum

SECTION-I

Perspectives on National Curriculum Framework–2005

Chapter–1

Organizational Structure

School Education and NCF–2005

School learning is viewed as burden creating stress on children and their parents. This results in deep distortion in quality of education in our schools. There is a deep disquiet about several aspects of our educational practice. The school system is characterized by great rigidity that makes it resistant to change. Learning has become an isolated activity which does not encourage children to link knowledge with their lives. Schools promote a regime of thought that discourages original thinking and creativity. What is presented and transmitted in the name of learning in schools undermines the great human capacity to create new knowledge. The "future" of the child has taken centre stage at the cost of child's "present" which is detrimental to the overall growth of the child as well as the society. The seem to lose their childhood.

The National Curriculum Framework (NCF)–2005 was formulated to over the comprehensive deficiencies of the system annulated above. The NCF identified certain broad aims of education. These include independence of thought and action, sensitivity to others. Well-being and feelings, learning to respond to new situations in a flexible and creative manner, predisposition towards participation in democratic processes, and the ability to

Dr. Mahabir Yadav, Principal at Army Insititue of Education, Delhi Cantt.

work forwards and contribute to economic process and social change. To overcome the burden and stress on children and their parents, the NCF–2005 proposes the following five guiding principles for curriculum development:

1. Connecting knowledge to life outside the school.
2. Ensuring that learning shifts away from rote methods.
3. Enriching the curriculum so that if goes beyond textbooks.
4. Making examination more flexible and integrating them with classroom life; and,
5. Nurturing an overriding identify informed by caring concerns within the democratic polity of the country.

Knowledge is constructed by the child through interaction with his/her physical/social environment. This implies that curriculum, syllabi and textbooks should enable the teacher in organizing classroom experiences in consonance with the child's nature and environment. Teacher should not aim rote memorization and developing unhealthy competition. Rather it should aim at enhancing children's natural desire and strategies to learn. Knowledge needs to be distinguished from information; Teaching needs to be seen as professional activity. Activity is the heart of child's attempt to make sense of the world around him/her. NCF–2005 recommends that every resource must be deployed to enable children to express themselves; handle objects; explore their natural and social milieu, and to grow up healthy. In this context, out teacher education system requires substantial systemic reforms and re-conceptualization of curriculum areas and resources to improve the quality and efficiency of teachers.

Teacher Education and NCF–2005

Most of the teachers education programmes in today's context train teachers to adjust to a system in which education is seen as the transmission of information. Attempts at curriculum reform have not been adequately made so far.

Existing teacher education programmes neither accommodate the emerging ideas in content and pedagogy nor address the issue of linkages between school and society. There is little space for engagement with innovative educational experiments, experience in the practice of teacher education indicate that 'knowledge is treated as given' like commodity embedded in the curriculum and accepted without any question. Most teacher education programmes provide little scope for student teachers to reflect on their experiences and thus fail to empower teachers as agents of social change.

NCF–2005 feels that teacher education must become more sensitive to the emerging demands from the school system. For this it must prepare the teacher for the roles of being as:

- Encouraging, supportive and human facilitator in teaching –learning situations to enable learners (Students) to discover their talents, realize their physical and intellectual potentialities to the fullest, and to develop character and desirable social and human values to function as responsible citizes; and,
- Active member of a person who makes conscious effort for curriculum renewal so that it is relevant to changing societal needs and personal needs of learners.

To be able to realize this vision, NCF–2005 recommended that teacher education must comprise the following features to enable student-teachers to:

- Understand the way learning occurs and to create plausible situations conducive to learning.
- View knowledge as personal experiences constructed in the shared context to teaching-learning, rather than embedded in the external reality of textbooks.
- Be sensitive to the social, professional and administrative contexts in which they need to operate.
- Develop appropriate competencies to be able to not only seek the abovementioned understanding in actual situations, but also be able to create them.

- Attain a sound knowledge base and proficiency in language.
- Identify their own personal expectations, perceptions of self, capacities and inclinations.
- Consciously attempt to formulate one's own professional orientation as a teacher in situation-specific contexts.
- View appraisal as a continuous educative process.
- Develop an artistic and aesthetic sense in children through art education.
- Address the learning needs of all children, including those who are marginalized and disabled.
- In the context of change perspective, it is imperative to pursue an integrated model of teacher education for strengthening the Professionalization of teachers.
- Develop the needed counseling skills and competencies to be a 'facilitator' for and 'helper' of children needing specific kinds of help in finding solutions for day-to-day problems related to educational, personal and social situations.
- Learn how to make productive work a pedagogic medium for acquiring knowledge in various subjects, developing values and learning multiple skills.

NCF–2005 has already been implemented in most of the states for last three years. Accordingly, new textbooks have been developed by NCERT and SCERTs. But a National Curriculum Framework for Teacher Education is yet to be developed based on NCF–2005. Several attempts have been made by NCTE and NCERT to frame/reframe curriculum of teacher education but they are mostly peace meal in approach. They however do not the needs in the context of NCT–2005. Teacher education institute have a great role to play towards preparing curriculum for teacher education. There are many ways to contribute in this area. Forum for inter action among teacher education's teachers ICT professionals can contribute to rethinking of teacher education to make it responsive to emerging needs. A seminar was Organized to discuss to present papers and discuss issues which can enhance teacher education curriculum practices. Organizing seminars may be one of the many ways of providing proper feedback to the experts and policy making bodies towards making essential reform. The recommendations of the experts, paper presenters and participants of the seminar could be very useful for the national level bodies like, NCERT, NCTE, UGC and affiliated Universities etc, towards developing a curriculum for teacher education.

Objectives

The broad objectives of this work are to:

- Review the National Curriculum Framework–2005 in the present context.
- Study the dynamics of implementing NCF–2005 in the present day School education.
- Discuss the various possible modes of Teacher Education in the country.
- Share experience, contribution, achievement and problems of teacher education in India.

Themes/sub-themes

Themes provided to the participants included:

- Perspective on National Curriculum Framework–2005.
- Teacher Education Programme vis-à-vis NCF–2005.
- Curriculum Transactional issues in the light of NCF–2005.
- Reflection of present day Teacher Education Curriculum.
- Teacher education curriculum in the context of Globalization, liberalization and privatization.
- Innovative practices in Teacher Education.
- Strengthening linkage among School, Community and Teacher education institutions.

The book is based on the papers presented in the seminar on Teacher Education Curriculum in context of NCF–2005 organized by the Army Institute of Education, Delhi Cantt. on 02 April 2009. The book of Teachings in Teacher Education curriculum in the context of NCF–2005 will stimulate further thinking and help in evolving improved practices. This will help in preparing in better Teacher for tomorrow.

Chapter–2

Teacher Education in India: Issues and Concerns

Introduction

Teacher education system plays a vital role in improving the quality of school education. It inculcates the necessary pedagogical skills and competencies among the teachers and makes them professionally competent. Many reforms were brought out in this area on the basis of recommendations made by various Committees and Commissions set up particularly after independence. A Centrally Sponsored Scheme was formulated in the light of National Policy of Education, 1986. It has improved the quality of teacher education programme. However, there are many challenges in teacher education which need deep thinking and action on implementation. Teacher education institutions are working in isolation. There is no integration of theory and practice, content and methodology in teacher education Programme. The ICT is not used in curriculum transaction. No mechanism of management in information system has been evolved so far. The curriculum of teacher education is developed by different agencies and there is no coordination among them. No permanent mechanism for updating the teachers on continuous basis has been evolved so far.

Dr. S K Yadav, Professor in Deptt of Teacher Education and Extension, NCERT, New Delhi.

Teacher Education: Future Challenges

Teacher Education System is an important vehicle to improve the quality of school education. The revitalization and strengthening of the teacher education system is, therefore, a powerful means for the upliftment of educational standards in the country. It inculcates the necessary pedagogical skills and competencies among the teachers and makes them professionally competent to meet the demands of the society. The teacher education system in our country have large dimensions in terms of administrative and organizational structure at different levels, policymaking, academic inputs, regulatory mechanism, financial powers etc. The Govt. of India realized the importance of teacher education as a result of which many reforms were brought out particularly after independence. During 1947-48 only 51 institutions existed at the secondary stage where as the number of these institutions have increased more than 8000 at present. The same way more than fifty lakh teachers and thirty five thousand teacher educators are working in schools and teacher training institutions. Over a period of time some structural changes have also been visualized in this field. The teacher training has been replaced by teacher education, training college has been replaced by college of education and the department of teacher training replaced by department of teacher education. Like wise many Committees and Commissions were set up for strengthening the system of teacher education during this period. Some of the recommendations are discussed in this paper.

Education Commission (1966) recommended that quality of training institution and of teacher education programme should be implemented. Isolation of teacher training colleges from the mainstream on national life, from the academic life of the universities, from the schools, from other teacher training colleges and from the very community which they are suppose to serve should be removed. A substantial allocation of funds should be made available to the UGC for improvement of teacher education in the universities.

The University Education Commission (1948) recommended that theory and practice of pre-service teacher education must support each other. The theory courses must be flexible and adaptable to local circumstances. The teachers should also be kept alive and fresh through in-service education. To consider the recommendations of University Education Commission, the first conference of All India Association of Principals of Training Colleges was organized in 1950 at Baroda on teacher education. In the light of the recommendations of this conference, many Universities revised their courses. The Secondary Education Commission (1952-53) recommended the adoption of new techniques of evaluation and suggested that more capable and intelligent persons should be attracted to the teaching profession. There should be two types of training institutions;

(i) two years training for those who have taken the school leaving certificate and,

(ii) one year training for the graduates.

One significant event during sixties was the formation of National Council of Educational Research & Training (NCERT) by amalgamation of various central and national institutions. Soon after the Department of Teacher Education was set up within NCERT. Four Regional Colleges of Education of NCERT were established at Ajmer, Bhopal, Bhubaneshwar and Mysore aimed at preparing teachers for the multipurpose schools with a focus on science, technology, arts, language and commerce and improving the quality of secondary teachers by adopting the pattern of four year integrated courses of general and professional education after higher secondary education. Another important landmark was setting up of the State Institute of Education (SIE) in 1964 for providing greater coverage and regional specificity in the programmes of in-service education and training of teachers and other educational personal concerned with primary education.

In the year 1973, the Government of India constituted the National Council of Teacher Education (NCTE) to act as a National Advisory Body on all matters relating to teacher education and review the progress plan scheme to ensure adequate standards in teacher education. The Secretariat of NCTE was set up in the department of teacher education, NCERT, New Delhi. In 1976, the NCTE recommended four measures;

(i) University to give due recognition to carefully designed short term courses for in-service education of teachers,

(ii) network of extension services to cover school teachers,

(iii) teachers' centers should be established in each district or region for building up human resources, and;

(iv) correspondence-cum-contact programmes should be started for in-service education along with use of modern technological aids.

During 1978 and 1988 curriculum for teacher education were developed by NCTE. The Chattopadhyay Committee Report in (1983-85) recommended that minimum length of secondary teacher training to five years after class XII. Reiterating the need... "to enable general and professional education to be pursued concurrently", the commission recommends that... to begin with we may have an integrated four-year programme.

The National Policy on Education (NPE) and Programme of Action (PoA), 1986, 1992 (revised) calls for overhauling the teacher education system. NPE (1986) made three recommendations i.e.;

(i) teacher education as a continuous process and its pre-service and in-service components are inseparable;

(ii) the need for new programmes of teacher education to meet the thrusts envisaged in policy, and;

(iii) the need for creating new structures and strengthening institutions to concretize the vision of NPE.

In the light of the recommendations of NPE (1986), a centrally sponsored scheme of restructuring and reorganization of teacher education was taken in 1987, to create a viable institutional infrastructure, academic and technical resource base for continuous up gradation of knowledge, competence and pedagogical skills in school teachers by organizing orientation and training programme.

Under this scheme 38 Institutes of Advanced Studies in Education (IASEs) and 88 Colleges of Teacher Education (CTEs) were established so far. The Department of Education in Universities were also strengthened under the scheme.

In 1990, the Acharya Ramamurti Committee suggested that the training programme should be competency based and there should be integration of theory and practice. The first degree in teacher education should not be given through correspondence education. The recommendation visualized for in-service and refresher courses to be specific and related the specific needs of the teachers. A strong distance education system of in-service education system should be developed using television, radio and print media, which can be further, strengthened by occasional contact programmes.

The Yash Pal Committee Report (1993) on Learning Without Burden noted "The content of the programme should be restructured to ensure its relevance to the changing needs of school education. The emphasis of these programmes should be on enabling the trainees to acquire the ability for self-learning and independent thinking". The National Council for Teacher Education (NCTE) was established as a statutory body in 1993 by an Act of Parliament for maintaining norms and standards in the country. In 1998, NCTE brought out Curriculum Framework for Quality Teacher Education, which provides guidelines for the organization of curriculum for different stages of teacher education. The curriculum reflects the realities of the national life, strives to realize the interdisciplinary goal of education, attempts to establish a viable integration of theory and practice of education and provides varied educational experiences needed by a teacher in his work place. It has also suggested two years; duration for all levels of teacher education courses. It has emphasized in service education for to upgrade professional competencies of teachers, prepare teachers for new roles, and provide knowledge and skills to emerging curriculum change. The University Grants Commission (UGC) initiated revision of curriculum framework of teacher education in

1990 at secondary stage. Again in 2001, UGC developed model curriculum. The NCERT has also brought out teacher education curriculum during 2004. The National Curriculum Framework for School Education (2000) has also reiterated that the in-service education should be provided to teachers continuously updating their knowledge and skills. The National Curriculum Framework (2005) recommended that teacher education programme to be recast to reflect professionalism in the process of training and teaching. It must become more sensitive to the emerging demands from the school system. From, this, it must prepare the teacher for the roles of being an:

- Encouraging, supportive and human facilitator in teaching-learning situations to enable learners (students) to discover their talents, realize their physical and intellectual potentialities to the fullest, and to develop character and desirable social and human values to function as responsible citizens, and;
- Active member of a group of persons who makes a conscious effort for curricular renewal so that it is relevant to changing societal needs and the personal needs of learners.

Future Challenges

Though many reforms are brought in teacher education particularly after independence yet there are many more challenges that need urgent attention in future for improving the quality of teacher education. Some of these are as follows:

- The centrally sponsored scheme of restructuring and reorganization of teacher education launched by Govt. of India could not realize the objectives. It needs revision and updating. The Programme on Mass Orientation for School Teachers (PMOST) could not reach to the field in its real spirit. The institutions like CTEs, IASEs, SCERTs are not functioning according to its role and functions. The scheme needs revision and reformulation. It requires to be strengthened in terms of manpower and other resources.

A strong mechanism for monitoring, evaluation and follow-up should be developed and it should be strictly adhered for regular feedback and effective implementation. Besides this, other private and government training institutions at secondary levels need updating and the capacity of these institutions should also be strengthened.

- At present, three models of teacher education at secondary level are prevalent in the country. Four years B.Sc. B.Ed. and two years B.Ed. programme are being run in Regional Institute of Education (RIEs) of NCERT in the name of innovative programmes. One year B.Ed. programme is prevalent mostly in all the universities and teacher training institutions in the country. Besides this two year B.Ed programme through distance mode is also run by Indira Gandhi National Open University (IGNOU), New Delhi. In all the models, issues like integration of theory and practice, integration of content and pedagogy, use of ICT in transaction of curriculum have not resolved so far. These pertinent issues and concerns are to be resolved on the basis of researches and experiments.
- Both teacher education and school curriculum are working in isolation and does not have relationship between two. The pre-service teacher education curriculum does not reflect the needs and demands of students and teachers. It needs to be revised and redesigned keeping in view the new thrust areas of the National Curriculum Framework for School (2005).
- There is no mechanism of Management Information System (MIS) on Teacher Education. The data related percentage of untrained teachers, unemployed trained teachers, number of teacher educators and their specialization, curriculum and syllabus at different levels, frequency of curriculum revision, innovative programmes etc in teacher education are not available at one place. The networking of different institutions both at state and national level to be made by using latest Information and Communication Technology. It will help in formation of

policy planning and decision making.

- The Curriculum Framework for Teacher Education is developed by three national agencies namely NCTE, UGC and NCERT. It has created lot of confusion in the field. There should be effective coordination and linkages among all the three agencies. Accordingly, the curriculum for teacher education should be developed with coordinated effort of all the three agencies by involving field level agencies and institutions.
- In existing system in India, the teachers with general degree of B.Ed. have been teaching from elementary to senior secondary stages. Even at some places, they are teaching subjects which they have not studied at graduation and post graduation levels. It resulted into many complicated problems like dropout, absenteeism & low achievement among the children. There is a need to evolve a policy, under which B.Ed. degree with specialization with stage wise i.e. secondary and senior secondary and also areas wise like special education, physical education, etc should be prepared.
- In case of higher education there is no provision for pre-service education. Teachers are working without professional degrees in colleges and universities. However, teacher educators who are working in training colleges are having the M.Ed. (general) degree. It does not meet the requirement of different stages. Therefore, the degree of M.Ed. should be awarded with specialization both stage wise and area wise.
- There is no permanent mechanism for the in-service education programme for about twenty lakhs secondary teachers and thirty five thousand teacher educators who are working in schools and teacher education institutions in the country for their continuous growth and development. The training programmes are being organized in ad hoc manner. It requires systematic and comprehensive policy by strengthening and coordinating

the national level institutions–University Grants Commission, National Council of Educational Research & Training (NCERT), National Institute of Educational Planning and Administrators (NIEPA), National Council of Teacher Education (NCTE) and state level institutions–State Council of Educational Research & Training (SCERTs), University departments, College of Teacher Education (CTEs), Institute of Advanced Studies in Education (IASEs) and Academic Staff Colleges for continuous and re-current training.

- The traditional face-to-face training modality fails to provide regular training to teachers. Alternative mode of distance education needs to be used. It will not only minimize the transmission loss but also solve the problems of non-availability of Resource Persons at smaller places. Tele-conferencing and use of interactive television will be effective mode for coverage and recurrent training.
- The training methodology should focus on local specific activity based training approaches and IT/ET integration to training transactions. The transactions of training should also focus on audio/video demonstration of skills, competencies, interventions and strategies followed by group discussion, group reflection; panel discussion; brain storming sessions etc. There is need for social sensitivity to socio-cultural, economic and political issues confronting the emerging Indian society.
- Lot of training material is available both with the national and state level institutions. But there is no mechanism to make it available among to teachers and teacher educators at the field level. It should be disseminated/distributed among them for self-learning and their growth. More and more need based training and instructional material should be developed following the modular approach. It can be used both for self-reading as well as in the training programmes.
- Policy research, innovations and experimentation are

largely not encouraged in teacher education programme. These should be promoted for improving the quality of teacher education programme. It will also help in streamlining the practical problems like entry qualifications, admission policy, recruitment and transfer policy etc.

- Monitoring and evaluation should be made an integral part of teacher education programme both including pre- and in-service training programme to know the strength, weaknesses and outcome of the programme with corrective measures for optimising the effectiveness of the programme. The outcome of the training can be measured through pre-and post-tests, participants reactions, observations, focused group discussion and reaction of the resource persons. Therefore, a clear-cut plan with detailed activities is needed for monitoring and evaluation of the programme.
- The follow up activities should be planned in the teacher training programme itself. A regular two-way communication between the trainees and trainers through newsletter, reports, seminars and workshops could be maintained. Visits to the field may be planned. Besides this, some studies may also be conducted.

In the end, it can be concluded that many reforms took place in the area of teacher education from time to time in the light of recommendations made by different Commissions and Committees set up by Govt. of India. But the Future Challenges raised above still need deep thinking and action on the part of both policy planning and implementation at micro and macro level.

Key Words:

- **Education Commission 1964-66** was set up under the Chairmanship of Dr. Kothari to improve the quality of education covering all stages and aspects of education as a whole.
- **University Grants Commission** (UGC) is a statuary body to improve the quality of higher education.

- **University Education Commission** (1948) recommended to improve the quality of teacher education.
- **Secondary Education Commission** (1952-53) recommended to improve the quality of education.
- **National Council of Educational Research and Training** (NCERT) set up in 1961 to improve the quality of school education.
- **State Institute of Education** (SIE) was set up to improve the quality of teacher education in the states/ union territories.
- **National Council of Teacher Education** (NCTE) is a statuary body to improve the quality of teacher education.
- **Chattopadhyay Committee Report** (1983-85) recommended to improve the quality of school and teacher education.
- **National Policy on Education** (NPE) 1986, revised 1992 laid down the principles for improving the quality of education in India.
- **Programme of Action** (POA) 1986, revised 1992. Action points evolved in the light of NPE for its implementation.
- **Acharya Ramamurty Committee** 1990 made several recommendations to reduce the academic burden on students.
- **Yashpal Committee** (1993) recommended learning without burden in school.
- **State Council of Educational Research and Training** (SCERT) is an apex body in the state to improve the quality of school education.
- **IASE**: Institute of Advanced Studies in Education.
- **CTE**: College of Teacher Education.

References

1. Ministry of Education (1948): *Report of the University Education Commission*, New Delhi, Govt. of India.

2. Ministry of Education (1952): *Report of the Secondary Education Commission*, New Delhi, Govt. of India.

3. Ministry of Education (1964), *Education and National Development: Report of the Commission (1964-66)*, New Delhi Govt. of India.

4. Ministry of Human Resource Development (1983). *The Teacher and Society, National Commission on Teachers–I* (1983-85), New Delhi.

5. Ministry of Human Resource Development (1986): *National Policy on Education*, New Delhi, Govt. of India.

6. Ministry of Human Resource Development (1990): Committee for Review of NPE 1986, *Towards on Enlightened and Human Society (Part-I)*, New Delhi, Govt. of India.

7. Ministry of Human Resource and Development (2000): *Selected Educational Statistics, Department of Secondary Education and Higher Education*, Planning Monitoring and Statistics Division, New Delhi, MHRD, Govt. of India.

8. National Council for Teacher Education (1998): *Curriculum Framework for Quality Teacher Education*, New Delhi. NCTE.

9. National Council of Educational Research and Training (2000): *National Curriculum Framework for School Education*, New Delhi, NCERT.

10. NCERT (2005): *National Curriculum Framework*, New Delhi, NCERT.

11. Yadav, S. K. (2001): *Quality of In-service Teacher Training Under SMART-PT in Maharashtra State*: *An Appraisal Study*, DTEE, NCERT, New Delhi.

12. Yadav, S. K. (2003): Research Perspective in Teacher Education, University News, 41, 22, June 02-08, 2003, New Delhi.

13. Yadav, S. K. (2003): Quality Improvement of Teacher Education Programme, *University News*, Vol. 41, No. 40, October 06-12, 2003, New Delhi.

14. Yadav, S. K. (2007): Professional Teacher in Higher Education, *University News,* 45 February, 26-March, 2004, 2007, New Delhi.

15. Yadav, S. K. (2008): Innovations in Elementary Teacher Education, *University News*, 46, 45, November10-16, 2008, New Delhi.

16. Yadav, S. K. and Singh Shruti (2009): *A Comparative Study of Pre-Service Teacher Education Programme at Secondary Stage in Bangladesh, India, Pakistan and Sri Lanka* (Report), DTEE, NCERT, New Delhi.

17. Yadav, S. K. (2009): *Two Year Bechelor of Education (Secondary) Programme of RIEs: A Status Study*, DTEE, NCERT, New Delhi.

18. Yadav, S. K. (2009): *A Study of Pre-Service Teacher Education Programme (B.Ed.) at Secondary Stage in Different States in India* (Report), DTEE, NCERT, New Delhi.

Chapter–3

Learning Together to Achieve Excellence

The Theme Context

Demands on education increase with the global development level, including India's, ranging from the oral tradition and family and guild apprenticeship in an agrarian society through in industrial society to knowledge based post-industrial society of the 21st century. Rapid changes and racy globalization have further added to the complexity of the rising demands. Special skills are required to meet the challenges of the current and future development perspective.

The theme has been selected with this perspective in view. Despite Teacher's Day, the focus is on learning. Learning is the primary element in schooling. Teacher and teaching as learning resource is relatively restrictive in nature. Learning can take place without teacher and teaching. Teacher is one of the many resources of learning. This is not to belittle the role of the teacher in student learning. It merely points to the changing role of the teacher. Effective learning depends on how efficiently he/she involves students in selecting and using various learning resources. Hence, focus on learning!

Learning together is the key phrase in the theme title. Cooperative and collaborative learning is of special significance in

---

Prof. (Dr) N K Jangira, formerly Professor, Head and Dean at NCERT, New Delhi.

the context complex learning skills to develop creativity and problem solving. Again, it is not to ignore the claim of individual learning. This is simply to highlight the enhanced role of teamwork to carry out innovative and creative acts.

Learning to achieve excellence is the ultimate goal of education. Learning should ultimately lead to generating new knowledge, creating innovating structures and producing quality products. Development of cutting edge quality ideas and products can be possible by matching learning practices in learner friendly environment.

Skills to Learn

What are the skills in young learners to meet challenges of tomorrow? Suggestive core skills for school graduates for 21st century development scenario could be:

Digital-Age Literacy: Basic language, scientific, mathematical, and technological literacy; visual and information literacy; and cultural literacy and global awareness.

Inventive Thinking: Adaptability/ability to manage complexity; complexity; curiosity, creativity, and risk taking; higher-order thinking and sound reasoning.

Effective Communication: Tearing, collaboration and interpersonal skills; personal and social responsibility; interactive communicative skills.

High Producivity: ability to prioritize, plan, and manage for results; effective use of real world tools; and ability to create relevant, high quality ideas, structures and products.

Some of you may be surprised at not mentioning knowledge in the above list. Knowledge *per se* is missing because of the rapid pace at which it is multiplying. It is impossible to store even a fraction of it in memory. If we are forcing young minds to do this, it is nothing short of child abuse. The focus has now shifted to location of knowledge resource to research and generation of new knowledge from early years. That is why emphasis is now on *"learning to learn"* and generation of new knowledge. Basic learning tools required for this are mentioned above. These tools will have to be mastered to accomplish the task. These basic tools enable the learner to locate knowledge for application to different tasks leading to generation of new ideas and practices.

Futuristic leaning requires the use of multiple intelligences. Broad intelligences include: Intellectual intelligence, emotional intelligence, spiritual intelligence. Categories based on these four intelligences are:

Linguistic intelligence: understanding phonology, syntax and semantics of language, its pragmatic use to persuade others, remember information, communicate with others.

Bodily-Kinesthetic: Intelligence-the ability to control one's bodily motions and the capacity to handle objects skillfully.

Spatial Intelligence: the ability to perceive the visual world accurately, to perform transformations and modifications according to perceptions.

Musical Intelligence: ability to understand and express components of music through figural and intuitive means.

Logical-Mathematical Intelligence: understanding and use of logical structures, patterns and relationship through quantification, conceptualization and classification.

Intrapersonal Intelligence: ability to access one' own emotional life through awareness of inner moods, intentions, motivations, desires, etc.

Interpersonal Intelligence: ability to notice and make distinction among individuals with respect to moods, temperament, motivations, and intention, and to use this information in pragmatic ways to persuade, influence, manipulate, mediate, counsel individual or groups towards some purpose.

Natural Intelligence: capacity to notice and classify numerous species of flora and fauna, natural phenomena and the ability to interact subtly with living creatures or the whole ecosystems.

All individuals have some level of the above mentioned intelligences but some have higher level of intelligence in certain categories. Learner who aspire to excel in a particular work area either has higher intelligence related to the aspired work or has to develop it. Aptitude testing is based on this assumption. I would like to mention here that the myth that intelligence cannot be learned and improved has been exploded. You can now learn and improve intelligence through focused learning with special efforts and practice.

At this stage, I would like to request to follow up this interaction. You may identify the work area or profession that requires related dominated intelligence. You can also make a three dimensional chart representing Intelligence category, specifications of abilities, and work area for which it is most relevant. It will be very helpful to you in applying the concept to student learning, including counseling. It will also be helpful in guiding students for preparation for competition for respective choices. These intelligences are very relevant for developing curriculum, both for schools as were as teacher training.

Learning Together

Learning Together receives special attention in may scheme of things. Cooperative learning with active collaboration tends to develop team work skills which are required in pursuing innovative and productive work in real life situations. Observation of teaching indicates very restricted use of this approach in most of our schools and colleges. Considering the overriding importance of using skills of cooperative and collaborative skills, I will dwell on using these as a major learning recourse.

I accept that individual learning and large group learning in the classroom will continue to be used. Teacher directed presentations and self directed learning will go on. However, I strongly feel that more time is allocated to learning in small groups to be shared in larger group for further reflection for refinement of the product. Team work to meet challenging situations will form the core of learning. Logic is simple. Each group member has different perspective on the learning task at hand. Each has personal strength. The solution of a problem or creation of a product will be better by pooling more than one talent. Participatory skills are useful for developing democratic outlook.

The concept of one teacher and forty learners has limitations. In multidisciplinary curriculum and accomplishment of tasks require a team. Time available to a students particularly, those who require more assistance to learn, is conspicuous by its absence. This approach considers 40+1 teachers and learners because each one is contributing to learning and teaching. Everyone learns bit higher than what he does in a conventional classroom since each one is getting more attention to learning from other member of the group.

Cooperative Learning

What is cooperative learning? Cooperative learning provides a task structure in which the students are required to work together in small groups to achieve a shared academic goal. They are accountable not only for their achievement but also the performance for other group members. It is useful for the heterogeneity of student population and encourages learning among student with different abilities and socio-cultural variations.

The five defining elements of cooperative learning are: Positive interdependence, face-to-face interaction, individual and group accountability, interpersonal and small group skills, and group processing. Cooperative learning involves active learning, structured problem solving through collaborative working.

Principles of effective participation essential for cooperative learning are:

- Listen to views of others which is itself a learning process that will develop individual's ideas.
- Share ideas and experiences with others as it helps discussion in the learning area.

- Challenge and speak if you hear something with which you disagree or do not fully understand in the same way as you understand. In the same way you must accept your ideas to be challenged by others.
- Relate discussion to your learning area.
- Have fun since there is no evidence to suggest that learning has to be painful.
- Refine through reflection and further work to improve learning to excellence.

Cooperative learning group formats

- **Peer tutoring**: In peer tutoring one student helps another student to overcome a learning difficulty or mastering a particular task.
- **Group work format:** Each group is required to complete a group task and inter-group sharing is used to enrich the learning outcome.
- **Jigsaw format** : Here each group member is assigned a task that is to be completed. After completing their parts, the group is required to put them together which is shared in the group.

In order to optimize learning gains to all students each group is assigned students with different ability levels. Every member has the opportunity to learn in addition to his own level. Sharing contributes to enriched performance which is a progression step towards achieving excellence.

Themes for cooperative learning selected from the syllabus or social and environmental issues, worksheets are prepared, small groups are formed, ground rules form management to ensure participation by all group members are accepted, group reports are prepared and shared, and finally product is obtained though reflection and consolidation.

At the end, I acknowledge that I have touched the fringe of learning together. The attempt was just to stimulate you thinking and motivating you to find more about it. You may like to add this concept to your teaching. That is the best tribute to our philosopher king size teacher, Dr. Radhakrishnan.

References

1. Jangira, N. K. (1992). *Effective Teacher Education: Cooperative Learning Based Approach*, National Publishing House, Delhi.
2. Jangira, N. K. (1992). *Responsive Teaching*, National Publishing House, Delhi.
3. Jangira, N. K. and Pinki Jangira, (1995). *Effective Teaching: Child Centered Approach*, National Publishing House, Delhi.

Chapter–4

Teacher's Empowerment *via* National Curriculum Framework

Introduction

The competence and quality of the teacher educators has its share in the quality of teachers trained by an institution. Education is a process, curriculum is a means to the process. Education is learning, curriculum signifies situations for learning. Education deals with "how" and "when" and curriculum deals with "what". Education is the product curriculum is the plan for the best product we must have an excellent plan.

As an apex national agency of education reform NCERT reviews the school curriculum periodically ensuring the highest standards of rigor and deliberative openness in the process, NPE 1986 and PoA 1992 assigned a special role to NCERT for preparing and promoting a National Curriculum Framework. NPE 1986 proposed a NCF as a mean of evolving a national system of education capable of responding to India's diversity of geographical and cultural milieus, while ensuring common core values along with academic areas.

Significance of National Curriculum Framework–TEP

The NCF–2005 reform was initiated by NCERT in November 2004, led its formulation emerging from deliberations in 21 major groups. This NCF–2005 has been translated into twenty-two

1. Dr. Nakhat Nasrin is Reader, Deptt of Education, A.M.U, Aligarh.

2. Mrs. Sarwat. F Usmani is Lecturer, Deptt of Education, A.M.U, Aligarh.

languages listed in the 8th Schedule of the Constitution for wider dissemination. It has a tremendous potential for guiding long terms reforms in the system of school education. It is a positive achievement for educational issues and on the nature of curricular reforms. The area in which the change is not up to the expectation is the teacher education and examination reforms. "The teacher education programme is the back bone of National education". A perfect teacher produces a perfect student.

Teacher's responsibilities have greatly increased but statutory reforms for improving the available provision for teachers have remained neglected. Prof Krishna Kumar, Director, NCERT said, "The profession is in deep crisis, today and in certain parts of the country it is in shambles, with unqualified, part time, para teachers are serving in place of professionally committed teachers."

Objectives

(1) To develop the ability of in-service teachers to understand the behaviours peculiar to the concerned age group and different learning processes.

(2) To develop fundamental skills of a present day teacher.

(3) To develop basic insights in a teacher.

(4) To develop training of a teacher which can implement inclusive education.

(5) To develop competencies in the teachers to design curriculum according to individual needs.

(6) To develop scientific attitude in teachers like "peace education" touching present issue.

(7) To promote innovations and experimentations in the field of teacher education.

(8) To develop habit of physical exercise in a teacher.

Present Scenario

The concept of teaching is itself is changing, teaching now a days is considered more than imparting knowledge and communication information. A teacher is not merely a communicator of knowledge he has to be a director of learning, so there is an urgent need to think in this direction, teacher education is the most crucial input for improving the quality of school education in the country. Since the policies prepare for the schools are to be implemented by the teachers, there needs should be addressed suitably. we now need a teacher who can fulfill our present needs here the question arises:

(1) What is the expected role of a teacher?

(2) What type of training should be given to in-service teachers so that we get a best quality of teacher?

(3) How does the training of teachers affects the quality of education in our country?

(4) Which new technological skill should he possess?

Shortcomings of Present Curriculum

(1) It is not integrated in terms of theory and practice.

(2) It is not Indian in character and composition it cannot fulfill the needs of different states.

(3) It is out dated in courses and superficial in methods of training.

(4) It is not flexible and is not based on the current educational research.

(5) It's practical aspect is inadequate and perfunctory.

(6) The staff of the teacher training colleges is not very competent.

(7) They lack behind in technological skills.

(8) Libraries of teacher training colleges are not rich.

National Curriculum Framework for Teacher Education Programme:

(1) There is a need for flexibility in pre-service teacher education programme.

(2) Programmes need to be designed to fulfill the requirements of desired conditions and context such as rural multigrade schools, tribal areas, linguistic diversity.

(3) The duration of practice teaching should be at least one year.

(4) Peace education, concept of globalization should be replaced by outdated problems which are still in curriculum.

(5) Outdated topics should be removed from the curriculum.

(6) Inclusive education should be included in a curriculum.

(7) Computer literacy programme should be made compulsory for every pre-service teacher's.

(8) Action research based on the curriculum should be conducted in teacher training colleges.

(9) Provision of continuing education or distance learning programmes should be there via ICT.

(10) There is an urgent need to take Information and Communication in a main foundation courses so that these students will be able to apply different technologies like power point, Audio conferencing, video-conferencing, use of interactive board etc.

(11) Yoga education should be a part of the curriculum led to peace of mind.

(12) Personality development programmes should also be included in a curriculum.

(13) Self evaluation of practice teaching lesson by student-teacher should be done.

(14) Values related to ICT should be included so that these students could understand about copyright or others etc.

Conclusion

As Teacher Education programme is in real crisis, so we need to empower it by different means as suggested above so that we will get a quality of teachers related to our present needs. If we empower teacher education our school education will automatically be empowered.

References

1. Shashi P. Sharma (2006); *Teacher Education*, New Delhi.
2. *Frontline vol. 25-issue* 05; March 1-14 2008.
3. *Press release, Monday*, 30 March 2009.
4. http://implementationofncf.pdf.
5. http://www.greenteacher.
6. http://ncf2005.html.

Chapter–6

Trends in Teacher Education Curriculum

Teacher Education Curriculum should be sensitive to changes in the Social, Political, Economic and Biological environments and flexible enough to accommodate implementation practices. Attempts for updating teacher education curriculum have resulted in proposing a number of curriculum frame works, Curriculum Framework 1978 adopted "task oriented" and 'skill based' approach while that of 1988 finds 'eclectic' approach more suitable. Curriculum framework for teacher education suggested in 1990 recommended restructuring of teacher education Programme in terms of content and duration. Draft curriculum framework 2006 suggested by NCERT stresses longer school attachment duration and attitudinal shift in teacher trainees and visualizes changes role to help students construct knowledge.

The present paper is limited to the curriculum of pre-service secondary school teacher education Programme and it does not relate to the duration of teacher education and various modes of its implementation. Again, this paper does relate to subject content of special/technical school teacher education Programme nor to non-formal and adult education programmes and is limited to general secondary/senior secondary teacher education programmes.

Concerns for curriculum updating had been voiced before independence, and these led to diversification of teacher education

Dr. M.S. Chhikara, Proffesor in Education at Surajmal Institute of Education and Technology, Janakpuri, New Delhi.

programmes. A number of commissions, committees and other policy documents mention and emphasize various components of teacher education programmes, while wading through the literature on teacher education programmes some major recommendations about curriculum frameworks are noted and some of them deserve mention in the present context.

National Council for Teacher Education (NCERT) observed that even after changing the nomenclature from 'Training' to 'Education' the system remained almost unchanged in terms of rigidity and scope. Teacher Education institute stood isolated from the main stream of national life in terms of political and socio-economic changes taking place in the country and this needed a functional; change in all the aspects of teacher education as objectives, curriculum, methods, modes and media, National Council for Teacher Education (NCERT) in its publication "Teacher Education Curriculum: A Framework–1978" gave recommendations on various aspects of teacher education.

Curriculum Framework–1978

The major emphasis in the framework has been on three aspects: Pedagogic theory, Working with the community, and content-cum-methodology including practice teaching and included practical work also. The Framework visualizes that a secondary stage teacher should be able to teach his subject with competence, develop skills understandings, interest and attitudes that enable him to enhance the all-round development of the children, possess theoretical and practical knowledge of health and physical education, games, recreational activities and work experience, development, individual differences and similarities and cognitive, psychomotor and attitudinal learning's, develop skills in guiding and counseling the children in solving their personal as well as academic problems, understand the role of the school in the changing society, undertake investigatory projects and action research. The teachers of Senior Secondary stage should develop competence to teach the subject of his specialization on the basis of accepted principles of learning and teaching and update knowledge of the subject by keeping in touch with the latest developments in both the subjects and the methodology of teaching, develop an understanding of the aims and objectives of education in the Indian background of promote awareness of the role of education and of the teacher in building a democratic, secular and socialist society, develop cognitive and psychomotor skills for teaching academic and vocational subjects by providing adequate learning experiences, develop skills in using educational technology in teaching academic and vocational subjects, understand the bio-psycho-social needs of the adolescents and the problems arising out of their non-fulfillment, develop skills in guiding and counseling the adolescents in solving his personal and academic problems, undertake investigatory projects, action research and experimental projects both in education and specialized subject areas, understand the role of the school and the teachers in changing the society.

The framework had a skill-based task-oriented approach; there was a consistent focus on skills and reduction of theoretical components in the entire curriculum. Working with the community with 20 per cent weight age, content-cum-methodology with 60 per cent weightage and pedagogical theory with skill based approach represented the teacher education Programme. This Programme expected the teacher to verify and validate his theoretical knowledge and also integrate different subjects by adopting an interdisciplinary approach so that methods are not only preached but are practiced meaningfully in relation to content. The aim of a teacher was visualized as a series of concrete and hierarchically graded cognitive and socio-national tasks to be accomplished by the teacher trainee.

Curriculum Framework–1988

A few significant developments had taken place after the publication of Teacher Education Curriculum- A Framework: 1978. The national Policy of Education 1986 and the Programme of Action 1986 for reorientation of content and process of school education programmes led the National Council Teacher Education (NCERT) to release the National Curriculum for Teacher Education – A Framework: 1988. This framework visualized that the future teacher will be a competent, professionally skilled teacher and will be an effective communicator, a designer and user of learning resources to facilitate learning and an active participant in community life. Framework 1988 suggested different stages of teacher education but it visualized as an inherent commonality with built in provision for horizontal and vertical mobility, running across various programmes at all stages. Three major components of teacher education were suggested for all stages:

1. Foundation courses consisting of philosophical and sociological aspects and the psychological basis of Education.
2. Specialization and professional competencies and skill in teaching relevant school subjects.
3. Field work or practicum stressing application of theory in classroom teaching and other practical activities with the involvement of the students, parents and the community.

Framework–1988 suggested modes of curriculum transaction through experimentation and innovative practices. In this sense Framework–1988 was different from Framework 1978 which was based on a singular deductive approach. Late eighties and early nineties was a period when efforts were being made to give National Council of teacher Education a statuary and these efforts culminated in the form of an Act of Parliament in 1993.

Curriculum Development Centre in Education Framework

Curriculum Development Centre was established in the Department of Education, Kerla University in 1990 by the University Grants Commission. This centre undertook another exercise towards revision of curriculum of teacher education and the recommendations were confined to secondary school teacher education. This framework includes three major components of the teacher education programme-theory, practice and internship. Knowledge component of the curriculum was more stressed and it preferred using terms like 'learner-nature and development' instead of 'educational psychology'. However, the content suggested was not much different. The Framework suggests equal weightage for theory and practice but the practice dimension includes internship as a compulsory condition for certification which can be fulfilled by increasing the duration of teacher education to two year. Another special feature of this framework is the organization of optional subjects as a part of the curriculum and two optional groups have to be studied by each student teacher depending on specialization and interest.

This Framework suggested a model of bachelor's course in Teacher Education comprising Part-A theory with three core papers i.e. the Learner-Nature and Development, Teacher and Education in India Society and Teaching Learning Process. The fourth paper is divided into two parts with first as compulsory paper on school Management and the second Part with a choice among nine elective papers, one of them being Computer Education. The second part is that of Optional Subjects with two options each consisting of two papers, one on Methodology of Teaching and the other on pedagogical Theory. In addition to the above mentioned eight papers Part-B of the course constitutes practice which includes practice teaching, practical work, camp, work experience and participation in co-curricular activities. Part C internship consists of three phases i.e. orientation in internship programme, observing school system and assisting subject teacher and working as a regular teacher.

NCERT Curriculum Framework 2006 (draft)

After going through a history curriculum concerns in Teacher Education, NCERT draft "Curriculum Framework for Teacher Education–2006" concentrated on the requirements and orientation of teacher training Programme in the light of National Curriculum Framework–2005. NCERT curriculum laid stress on removing deficiencies in the existing teacher education and meeting demands of the new challenges before it. Deficiencies are pointed out as deficiency of subject content knowledge, language non-proficiency, isolated teaching practice and ritual conduct of the practical activities. Including that the teachers do not have any role in terms of text-books and syllabi construction and they have to adjust to the existing realities the framework pointed out that teacher education programmes fail to empower the teachers as agents of change. In order to overcome theses deficiencies the draft framework suggests the need to engage teacher trainees in socio-political contexts where educators and learners are situated, engage teachers with learners in real contexts, enable teachers to reflect upon their own social position, recognize the role of teacher education to help them to adapt to the changing learning needs of children and society, help them understand psychological and developmental considerations of Learners and enable them to integrate theory and field experiences.

Stressing upon the national system of teacher education, the draft curriculum visualizes the role of a teacher as eliciting and guiding instead of informing, who can help students construct knowledge by involving them actively to develop concepts and teacher as guide in helping students construct knowledge and equip him /her with better evaluation and assessment techniques and requires teacher education programme to help develop insights, attitudes and sensitively towards socio-cultural, economic and political realities.

Framework 1978 adopts 'task oriented' and 'skill based' approach while that of 1988 finds 'eclectic' approach more suitable. Development Centre in Education framework suggests restructuring of teacher education programme in terms of content and duration. NCERT approach suggested increased duration of school attachment and places the teacher as 'guide' to help students construct knowledge. Accordingly, the teacher should use evaluation as an aid to learning rather than an indicator to learning alone.

Chapter–6

Changing Needs of Teacher Education Programme

Another policy document on education of children and teachers by the Government of India, another Seminar to assess and review the implications of this mammoth effort.

India, same as very other country, is still striving to understand the education system, how it works, whether it takes its people, in terms of "shaping their personality" to impact on the future of the country's ideals, ideologies and development in the right, desired and desirable direction.

It is no mean task while formulating a curriculum framework of such importance to take case of the entire population with varied cultures, multi-religions, ethnic variations, geographical. Climatic conditions and with varied aspirations and economic conditions of its people alongwith various intelligences and abilities of its populace. Yet this task is carried out with aplomb by our visionaries, educationists and philosophers who are at the helm of affairs to make an effort to inject the education system with their special and specific insights into human nature and specific conditions of our democratic pledges.

Without going into the details or mention of our previous efforts, I would like to plunge straight into the importance and relevance of National Curriculum Framework–2005 and Another

Dr. Sushil Dhiman, Sr. Lecture in Central Institute of Education, Delhi University, Delhi.

document which was drafted jointly by NCTE and NCERT, for discussion, namely Curriculum Framework for Teacher Education (2006).

As required and desired, the draft begins with the "Context, concerns and challenges of teacher education", highlighting its achievements and progresses made in the area of school education which has led to an increase in overall literacy, school enrolment, infrastructure and the stress laid on universalizing elementary education, which has invited significant political will to make it a success.

A significant positive change is seen in the 86th Constitutional Amendment (2002), which makes education for the children, between the edges of 6-14 years a Fundamental Right and compulsory, leading to the Right to Education Bill–2005, which makes it mandatory for each state to take pro-active action for every of 6-14 years of age.

So, now all children in this age group are expected to be in schools, which means many more schools and requirement of many more teachers. As now two children are and alike and "all abilities" children with varied ethnic, social, cultural, religious, economic backgrounds will be should be part of schools, teacher education programmes will also have to be looked at afresh and with vision and vigor, to cater to these varied groups and individuals.

The professional preparation of teachers by teacher education institutes allllso needs to be quslitatively and quantitavely invigorated. The Teacher Education Programmes need not be one-year/ two year programme, but can be four year Integrated Course for the Secondary as well as Elementary teacher. There are Regional contract Institutes offering two year teacher education programme for secondary Education and great preparations are afoot by the University of Delhi, at the Department of Education, the premier Institution of Education, for two year teacher education programme. This is not a new idea i.e. to have two year teacher education programme, it was suggested even before the Kothari Commission (1964-66).

The last twenty years have brought about a tremendous change in all the spheres of life of everyone, be it-economic, cultural, because of scientific inventions, technological advancements-nobody has been left untouched. These changes have brought the remotest areas and its inhabitants to the forefront and promised the fruits of changes to reach them as well as including opportunities to avail in the field of education.

These developments have brought significant subs but appetent changes in the relationship of teacher and the learner as well as the role of teachers IN THE LIFE OF THE LEARNER. And these changing roles and relationships have to reflect in the teacher preparation programmes.

No that the reflection is not there, but this reflection has to be more pronounced and acknowledged and in all teacher education colleges spread all over India.

The NCF–2005 has linked the ongoing debates on curriculum to the pedagogic and professional concerns for the child and the teacher. Teachers have always been very important, when the printing press had been invented and books had started being printed on mass. It was feared that now there would be no need of teachers, but actually the need for teachers became even more ardent. Similarly, when modern computers with their inbuilt programming systems had taken birth, but it was again felt that the need for teachers may reduce, but it is a fact that the exact opposite is going to happen and the requirement of teachers is going to increase even more so, albeit with slightly different roles as compared to their traditional role.

Thus, it is quite apparent that the importance and need of / for teachers is going to escalate manifold. The teachers, tasks are going to be on the escalation as well, hence the urgent need to prepare teachers for this crucial role of "mediating agents through which curriculum is transacted". That the text books on their own will be able to sensitize the students to the secular values and social norms and democratic living is not possible and can be questioned.

Hence the need for education of teachers not only as facilitators, managers, professionals, competent teachers, but also as a bridge between child and society, so as to prepare a child for his/her future role in the society as a well adjusted, modern (laced with traditions), sensitive, authentic human being.

The schools are changing, schooling has to change, society is changing, social roles and obligations have to change, contexts are changing, contextual meanings have to change, and to bring about these changes education of teachers has to change, both to understand the change and to facilitate the change in the life of the child in the right direction.

The NCTE envisages certain fundamental changes in the teacher education programme which will bring about two fold effect – (1) remove and minimize the existing deficiencies of teacher education programme, and (2) meet the demands of new challenges of the modern, technocrat world.

- Provision of qualified faculty, adequate infrastructure and learning resources using modern instructional and technological facilities.
- Frequent appraisals for quality improvement of teacher education programmes.
- To promote such values and ideals in the corporate institutional life as enshrined in the Indian Constitution amongst all stakeholders-including students, faculty and non-teaching staff.
- To promote and strengthen action research and faculty research projects.
- To encourage and promote ongoing professional development activities of teachers and provide suitable opportunities to all concerned.
- To bring about better co-ordination between teacher education programmes and school based activities for bringing about a sound and fruitful interface between school practices and theories of education.

- This is the need of the hour the importance of which can be understood if we look at the world scenario, which is fraught with conflicts and resolutions.
- The paper has addressed to the "why" and importance of the teacher education programme document, the details of "how" can be gleaned from the original document which was prepared for further discussions.

References

1. Curriculum Framework for Teacher Education (2006), NCTE in collaboration with NCERT- Draft for Discussion.
2. NCF 2005–National Curriculum Framework (2005) by NCERT.

Chapter–7

Reflection on Present Day Teacher Education Curriculum

"Education for life; Education through life; Education through out life."
– Mahatma Gandhi

Introduction

Our nation is on the march towards a bright and prosperous tomorrow. The social organ to play the most important role in this endeavour is education. Without a sound and goal oriented system of education, the dream of reconstructing nation's economic and political life cannot be realized. In order to fulfill the ideals, the quality of education imparted to the children, has to be improved considerably. In the process of making education more meaningful, or a question of improving its quality or even making it more accessible to children, one thing that always prominently matters is teacher, as teacher is the heart of the school system. The place and importance of the teacher in a society can never be over estimated. A teacher is the central figure in formal teaching learning set up.

The word "teacher" is an English word and the Sanskrit word for teacher is "Guru". Etymological meaning of the word Guru is one who removes darkness. Thus the role of teacher is important in making a nation great. If teacher is excellent the nation will have

1. Dr. (Mrs.) Nasrin, Reader, Deptt. of Education, A.M.U., Aligarh, U.P.

2. Ms. Afshan Anees, Research Scholar, Deptt. of Education, A.M.U., Aligarh, U.P.

excellent citizens. Teacher is the most important element in any educational system. It is the teacher who is mainly responsible for implementation of the educational process. No amount of investigation in improving physical and educational facilities can improve education unless there are adequate number of well qualified teachers who can willingly implement the education process in such a way that it brings about the desired educational development of students. It is, therefore, important that teacher is well prepared to do so his/her work efficiently and effectively. The quality of teacher depends, to a larger extent, on the quality of teacher education received by him/her.

India is having one of the biggest and complex education systems in the world. Out of the global population of around 60 million teachers or so, more than 5 million work in India. Most of our present teachers might have finished 10 years or more of schooling and underwent a year or two of preparatory teacher training. Immediate measures have to be taken for the improvement of education at the secondary and tertiary levels.

This paper describes the meaning of curriculum, teacher education and highlights teacher education curriculum.

Teacher Education

Teacher education is one in the midst of a dramatic and profound change. For meeting future challenges, it necessitates improved student learning, productivity, civic leadership, enhanced multicultural understanding and achieving higher levels of educational attainment. It necessitates greater integration between curricular and co-curricular experiences. After all, teachers have to give it a shape but this cannot become a reality without the guidance of the government and the willing acceptance of the society as a whole.

The Government of India realized importance of teacher education as a result of which many reforms were brought out particularly after independence. During 1947 only 51 institutions existed at the secondary stage. The number of these institutions has increased more than 50 lakh teachers and thirty five thousand teacher-educators are working in school and training institutions.

The *Education Commission (1966)* emphasized that quality of having training institute and of teacher education programme. The *University Education Commission (1948)* recommended that theory and practice of pre-service teacher education must support each other.

Teacher education is a continuous process. The National Policy on Education 1986 as up detail in 92 calls for substantial improvement in the quality of teacher education. It is well recognized that the overall quality of teacher's education depends; amongst other things on the quality of teachers and that a sound programme of profession as education of teacher is essential. Global trends prevalent in almost all countries such as improvement of Education Quality Work (EQW) in the area of curriculum; teaching and learning; and learner- centered initiatives can only be ignored at the peril of a nation losing the demand for the service among stake holders. Curriculum is one such vital area that needs substantial inputs in the form of good practices prevalent elsewhere, need not necessarily be all from the west.

Curriculum

Curriculum, according to *The Advanced Oxford Dictionary* is, "the subject that are included in a course of study of taught in a school, college, etc." In education circles the term is used in a far wider sense and it includes many things. In the curriculum of teacher education, the main purpose is to change a person who, it is assumed, knows the subject content, into a professional teacher. The professional knowledge which teachers need in their profession includes such areas as educational psychology, child and adolescent development and educational evaluation.

Two extreme views of teaching often prevailed in the past. According to the first view teaching is a charisma and so only charismatic people can teach. The followers of this view believe that teachers are born rather than they are prepared through training. The other extreme view is that any one who loves children or youths and has a command over subject matter can teach and can teach well too. Both of these views had been contested strongly in the past and the issue has been settled to a great extent (if not at a theoretical level at least at practical level). Now teaching is an activity which has enough ingredients to be considered as a profession, if not a profession like medicine or law, at least a quasi profession (Etzioni, Mahrotra etc). Therefore teachers are those professionals who have the legitimate right to practice their profession of teaching.

Curriculum is the most explicit path through which novice teachers are prepared to perform the professional role of teaching and so teacher education programme is not only a formality of therequired certification but it empowers the young people to play their role as professionals so that they can enter into a teaching profession with confidence and with required competence. Teachers as professionals require some exclusive body of knowledge and skills that provide them expertise to practice. The task of teacher education programme is to provide this very exclusive body of knowledge and skills. However teaching is not only a profession but it is a unique profession. Rich literature is available which highlights the unique nature of teaching. Teaching is in fact a complex, creative and morally laden activity. It has characteristics both of a science and that of an art. So any model for teacher preparation programme, if is only confined to technical/ mechanical approach based on apprentice model of skill development leads only towards an uninspired and lifeless teaching and so in the words of Carr such an approach can do more harm than any help to teaching and therefore in any teacher preparation programme a balance between its twin nature of science and art is to be maintained.

The time has come to forge a new implementation plan for Curriculum 2005. We need a new configuration of the steps and resources and, where necessary, a set of carefully targeted interim measures.

National Curiculum Famework (NCF) 2005

The National Policy on Education (NPE, 1986) and the Programme of Action (PoA, 1992) assigned a pivotal role to NCERT in preparing a National Curriculum Framework (NCF). Preparation of NCF, 2005 was accomplished with the help of National Steering Committee, chaired by Prof. Yash Pal and 21 National Focus Groups.

Approved by CABE on 7 September, 2005, NCF derives its objective of student learning and development from the values enshrined in the constitution and contemporary concerns for strengthening unity and national identity in a multicultural context and enabling the nation to face future challenges. The main features of the curriculum framework 2005 are:

Strengthening of a national system of education with special focus on:

1. Values enshrined in the Constitution of India;
2. Reduction of curriculum load;
3. Ensuring quality education for all (EFA).

Guiding principle of curriculum development

- Connecting knowledge to life outside school;
- Ensuring that learning is shifted away from rote methods;
- Enriching the curriculum to provide for overall development of children rather than remain textbook centric.
- Making examination more flexible and integrated with classroom life.

Learning and knowledge

- Correspondence between learner development and learning is intrinsic to curricular practice;
- Organizing learning experiences for construction of knowledge and fostering creativity.

Curricular areas

- Implication of three language formula with renewed efforts;
- Mother tongue as the best medium to built a foundation for education;
- The art and heritage crafts, and health and physical education to form critical components of school curriculum;
- Developing thinking process, decision making and reflections on social issues;
- Emphasis on teaching of mathematic, to visualize abstraction to formulate and solve problem.

National concerns

- Professional planning and significant expansion of early childhood care and education.

Systematic reform

- Teaching is a professional activity;
- Availability of minimum infrastructure and material facilities for improved teacher performance;
- Reconceptualisation of textbooks, teachers' handbooks, and other material based on new perspectives and access to interactive technologies;
- Teacher education programme to be recast to reflect professionalism in the process of training and teaching.

In the context of education last couple of years have been quite eventful at national and the global level. Making basic education as a fundamental right is considered to be a significant landmark in the history of Indian Education and its consequence will not be confined to elementary education alone. It is hoped that Universalisation of secondary education will be our national priority in near future.

Why Teacher Education Programme is Essential?

Teacher plays crucial roles in quality education and they are key forces in all educational changes. Adequate, dedicated and professionally competent teachers are a pre-condition for quality improvement in education. Worldwide there are growing demands for qualified teachers. About 15 to 35 million additional teachers are needed to achieve universal primary education and meet the Millennium Development Goals by 2015. Improving the recruitment and socio-economic status of teachers on the on hand and enhancing their professional qualifications on the other hand become high priority of all countries.

Teacher education, both pre-service and in-service, is a key factor in improving professionalism of teachers. In response to the worldwide shift of emphasis from access and inputs into quality outcomes, teacher education in many countries has been undergoing major reforms in policy, curriculum, and pedagogical approaches, networking of teacher training institutions, and the use of information, communication technology as tools, resources and level of change. A series of paradigm shifts have been emerging in varied national and regional contexts.

Role of Teacher in the Light of National Curriculum Framework–2005

The recent national curriculum framework (NCF–2005) has advocated the need for creating constructivist-learning environment in schools and for this it visualized some basic changes in the role of a teacher:

(1) In the constructivist paradigm the role of a teacher has shifted from an information provider or an instructor to a facilitator and a guide who can create such an environment where learners themselves create their knowledge. In this paradigm the concept of learning as well as its assessment has drastically changed.

(2) The role of a teacher is not now confined to that of curriculum transactor but she has to be actively involved in the process of curriculum development which includes development of the learning resources and curriculum evaluation. Since the relationship between the school education and teacher education is a synergic one so the

teacher education curriculum must be responsive to such changes that are taking place at school level that is why NCF–2005 envisages a paradigm shift in teacher education programme.

(3) The NCTE in collaboration of NCERT has brought out a draft curriculum framework for Teacher Education 2006. There is an immediate need to critically and thoroughly look into this draft curriculum too.

(4) As language teachers our main concern is with the Language, Literacy and Communication Learning Area (LA), one of eight such LAs comprising Curriculum 2005.

(5) Teachers are required to evaluate continuously how learners are performing individually against the criteria listed in each learning area.

(6) Teacher and teacher support organizations can work harder at attaching the new system's key ideas – such as learner-centered teaching methods – onto the framework of the old.

(7) Needs to lay stress on integrated teaching, in which the school subjects are combined into learning areas and taught thematically.

(8) Needs to focus on the competence demonstrated by the learners at the end of cross-curricular learning rather than expertise in individual subjects.

(9) Needs to connect the real-life experiences of a child with his school education effectively.

(10) 'Language learning is essentially a matter of acquiring the important skills of listening, speaking, reading and writing in an integrated manner, and harnessing these skills to the performance of formal as well as informal communication tasks'.

11) The learner should be able to develop sensitivity towards their culture and heritage, aspects of contemporary life and languages in and around the classroom.

Development of Resource Material Finances are required to develop educational resource materials to enhance the implementation of Curriculum 2005.

"The provisioning of these materials will significantly enhance the quality of teaching and learning in the targeted schools, and will bring great relief to teachers who, for a long time, have had to make do with the barest minimum of resources," Mr. Jeppie said:

> A project needs to the understuble to provide Grade-7 (Std. 5) teachers in disadvantaged schools in all provinces with learning support materials and teacher guides to facilitate learning. It will also enhance performance in the learning areas of Technology, Arts and Culture, Economics and Management Science, and Life Orientation, particularly in the field of human movement.

Conclusion

The growth of any nation depends on the holistic development of its various development sectors. "Education" is the key instrument in this process, and the teacher plays an active role in making the nation. A teacher is a central figure in the formal teaching learning set up. The quality of education depends upon the quality of the teacher.

In the present context, there is a need to lay stress on the quality of teachers and basically teacher educators who are to act as luminaries in the field of pre-service and in-service training to the teachers who will in turn be in the same process of luminaries for the nation builders of tomorrow. In today's rapidly growing and dynamic environment, the role of teacher educator is becoming more and complex. The teacher is being challenged with the task of increased teaching load, research responsibility and continuous improvement in skill set. The performance demand shave increased tremendously. It is upon them that the entire burden lays; the responsibility of producing quality teachers; is one of the greatest liabilities.

Teacher education is a continuous process. Curriculum is the most explicit path through which novice teachers are prepared to perform the professional role of teaching and so teacher education programme is not only a formality of a required certification but it empowers the young people to play their role as professionals so that they can enter into a teaching profession with confidence and with required competence. In the curriculum of teacher education, the main purpose is to change a person who, it is assumed, knows the subject content, into a professional teacher. Teacher preparation is an on going process. Teacher education programmes today train teachers to adjust to a system in which education is seen as the transmission of information.

References

1. Kauts. Siland, Deepa and Aggarwal. Vig, Minakshi,(2008), "*Teacher Stress: An Emerging Area of Research in Teacher Education Institution.*" *University News,* A weekly journal of higher education, Vol.46, No. 35, September 01- 07, 2008, pp. 22-28.
2. Soundararaj. Francis. (2008), "*Curricular Models, Structure and Management: Global Practice and Indian Experience,*" *University News, A weekly journal of higher education,* Vol.46, No. 2, January 14-20, 2008, pp. 1-9.
3. NCERT, (2005) "*National Curriculum Frame Work –2005*".
4. Pervez, Mohammad (2007), "*Professional development of teachers in higher education,*" *Miracle of teaching, Quarterly Journal of the Teaching Professions,* Published by the Asian Academy of education and culture, international house, vol.vii, Sept–Oct, Nov–Dec 2007, No.3, p p.121-122.
5. *The Educational Review, Vol 87, no.2,* p. 27.
6. *University News, A weekly journal of higher education,* Vol.44, No. 10, March 06-12, 2006, p. 14.
7. Siddiqui, Saima; (2006), *University News, A weekly journal of higher education, Vol. 43,* No. 52, December 26, 2005–January 01, 2006, p. 12.

8. Yadav, S. K. and Rehan Sumbul, (2006), *University News, A weekly journal of higher education,* Vol.44, No. 38, September 18-24, 2006, p. 13.

9. http://www.vcho.co.za/ondw/cur2005.htm.

10. http://www.jmi.nic.in.

11. http://www.geocetus.com.

12. http://www.nzol.org.

Chapter–8

Opportunities of Reflective Practice in Pre-Service Teacher Education Programme:

As Projected by National Curriculum Framwork–2005

Introduction

Education is a process of self-realization. It equips man to know himself and his relationship with the universe, as effectively as possible. In the process of "knowing thyself" he extends himself to the outer world and relates to its different aspects in different forms. In the process he becomes part of cultural settings, which in turn enables him to design and define his existence as a sensitive and selective human being. This capacity of being sensitive enables him to take the responsibility of understanding, modifying, refining, and transmitting the cultural heritage in such a manner that the continuity of human progress is accelerated as for as possible.

In this process of man's cultural progress, the role of education becomes very critical as it unfolds and encourages man's curiosity to know himself and the universe. The main focus of education should therefore be to understand the rhythmic relation of man and universe, his quest for its knowledge in society, its nature and pace of progress. The process of this understanding should be designed in such a manner so that it can preserve the fragrance of the past while preparing the bouquet for the future.

Dr. Arti Srivastava, Lecturer in Army Institute of Education, Delhi Cantt.

Educational opportunities should provide basis for building the bridges between past and future.

The dialogue between generations; embedded within literature, drama, oral traditions and narratives; artifacts within literature, social practices, work of art etc speak to the needs and aspirations of the people at different levels and in different ways. The beauty of education lies in facilitating and enabling connections within the impersonal world of man, and thus transforming it into an interpersonal world of informed persons engaged in critical dialogue. This effort will be reflected in the thoughts and beliefs of the people.

The responsibility, therefore for education is to encourage man to ponder over significant and meaningful experiences and evolve as a reflective individual. The experiences would be integrated and internalized, according to his unique sensitivity and rhythm. his contribution as a reflective being would thus enable him to define his responsibility as a social being. The role of education becomes very critical for providing the experiences while connecting man, to his 'Self'.

The possible connections which needs to be explored can be:

Individual Participation to allow self-experience

There is a difference in understanding of the world by different individuals because of their diverse conceptual framework. Establishing a common conceptual framework will not work for all the learners because the reference point for every understanding will be based on individual's choice. Therefore the suggestion can be to allow the learners to get involved through participatory process in the situation and gain the first hand experience of the situation.

Possibility of Intervention

Since the framework is constructed by human therefore lot of scope for the refinement, replacement and modification is there; therefore learners should be allowed to explore the ways of gaining knowledge from experience. This is essentially self-experience based process in which learner formulates his/her understanding in his/her own ways through observation and dialogue; shravan manan and reflection.

Bridging the Gap between Theory and Practice

There should be a relationship between what and how we know and those who manage and organize what how we learn (gap between theory and practice). The capabilities of learner are not fixed but dynamic and capable of development through direct experience. Therefore learner as an active participant rather than a passive recipient gets involved with the learning situations and refines his ways of experiencing, gaining and integrating knowledge with his personality, and thus perceiving an extension of his own 'SELF'.

Evolving as a Reflective Practioner

This process of learning sensitizes learner to develop capacities to understand and contribute reflectively to improve the existing situation rather than getting adjusted to it. The bonding process is enabled by an attitude of acceptance and perceiving oneself as part of the situation.

In service teacher education programme provides lot of scope for orienting trainee teachers in a manner so that they involve and evolve as reflective beings. This reflective practitioner gets involved with the process of education by addressing all the aspects of his/her being and helps him to develop the capacities of an ever evolving human being.

As a teacher educator I have tried few experiments in the Institute which echo following tenets of NCF 2005:

Learner centric and flexible,

Promotes learner autonomy,

Facilitates, supports and encourages learning,

Allows learner to participate actively,

Uses social context for promoting learning,

Helps in evolving knowledge. [NCF-2005].

The activities used for the experiments are:

1. Project on - Integrating thinking skill with different subjects

The learners were encouraged to identify and experience the practices related to philosophy of education where individual is defined as a thinking being. The pupil teachers were expected to understand the scope of thinking in their teaching subjects and experiment different ways to promote thinking skill in and through their subject in the classroom. This is done with the objective of sensitizing learners towards their capacity as a thinking being and utilizes the same to assimilate knowledge with their existing knowledge.

2. Situation based reflective topics for group work

Here the students were expected to work in group (as collaborative learning). They could open the book but were not allowed to copy from the book, their expressions after discussion with the group members are documented .The purpose was to develop confidence and make the learners responsible for their response. The observation of this activity was very encouraging as the students reported that they are using their experiences and putting them into words after analyzing and synthesizing each other's ideas.

3. Preparing a script of play on an identified *(Nukkad Natak)* on value, and stage the same

This is a creative and aesthetic activity with social responsibility. The students were told to write script of a play which could sensitize as well as provoke the thinking of the people on important social issues. Possibilities related to different issues also were worked out through participative mode. While integrating it with the different subjects made it interesting and meaningful. Thus it helps to develop a perspective on gender, environment & community.

There can be number of other ways to orient the students for the sensitivities towards the finer sensitivities of education and ultimately to sensitivities of Life.

Thus NCF–2005 provides a support to connect knowledge to life outside the school, also it acknowledges the efforts of the teacher in using the experiences of the child for creating learning situation/because process of understanding the world depends on the concepts through which experience is organized.

References

1. NCF–2005, NCERT.
2. Pring, Richard (2004): Philosophy of Education, Aims, Theory, Commonsense and Research Continuum.
3. Pollard, Andrew (2002): 'Reflective Teaching' continuum.
4. Joshi, Kireet: 'A Philosophy of the Role of the Contemporary Teacher' ICPR.

Chapter–9

A Plea for Two Year B.Ed. (Regular) Program

Introduction

Professional training of teachers is key to quality enhancement of school education. The aim of education of taking the nation into 21st century cannot be achieved unless teachers have the necessary skills and competencies. The skills and competencies can be developed through systematic approach to revitalize and modernize teacher education program. In recent years several innovations have been developed to equip teachers with requisite competencies and skills to teach effectively. However, it is a general consensus that the duration of teacher education program has a close tie up with developing requisite competencies and skills in teachers. Here, the authors pleaded for increasing the duration of B.Ed. program from one year to two year.

Existing Models of Teacher Education Program

Our country has multi model teacher education programs at secondary level. The present day secondary teacher education is having the following types of B.Ed. programme.

1. *L. C. Singh, Formerly Professor, the Department of Teacher Education, NCERT, New Delhi.*

2. *Dr. Sudarshan Mishra, Lecturer in Army Institute of Education, Kandhar Line, Delhi Cantt, New Delhi.*

- One-year B.Ed. regular face-to-face teacher education program prevailing in almost all the teacher education institutions.
- Two-year B.Ed regular face-to-face teacher education program being run by four Regional Institutes of Education of NCERT and a few other institutions, e.g., Gujrat Vidyapeeth, etc.
- Two year B.Ed. through distance mode. It is a part time course for in-service teachers.
- Integrated four-year teacher education program B.Sc., B.Ed. being run by Regional Institutes of Education (RIEs) since sixties. Few other institutions are also engaged in four-year teacher education program.
- A variety of innovative programs run by individual institutes such as, Vedchichi program of teacher education (Gujarat Vidyapeeth), Eklavya (M.P.), Anweshana (Banasthali Vidyapith, Rajasthan), Zero-Lecture program of Devi Ahilya Vishwavidyalaya (Indore), etc.

So far as Integrated four-year teacher education program is concerned, *the teachers that emerge from this program are much better than the products of the traditional one-year B.Ed. program.* (NCERT–2005). Among other things, the difference is also attributed to 'greater length of training'.

The personal observations and experiences show that:

The education and pedagogy courses comprise 30-35% of the course content of the entire integrated four-year course run by RIEs. This support the view that duration of one year teacher education program must increase.

Two year teacher education programs already exist at the secondary education levels. The program is quite demanding and has a good reputation. However, research studies are yet to be undertaken to evaluate their effectiveness.

Privatization in Teacher Education

Privatization in teacher education for the last 10 years has influenced the teacher preparation at the secondary level in many ways. Some of the features are:

- There has been mushrooming of teacher education institutions of different shades, due to lack of proper planning at the state and central level.
- B.Ed. program is being treated as one of the liberal art and science courses.
- Academic year is disturbed in several universities due to late admission and examination.
- Certain malpractices are rampant in many institutions.
- Commercialization has become common in different aspects of B.Ed. program, e.g., admissions, practical examinations, selection of teaching faculties, etc.
- The general (overall) standard of teacher education programs have gone down.
- Both of the students and the functionaries are not very serious about the training program.

However, the commercialization could be curbed out to some extent if the duration of secondary teacher education program is increased as it involves lot of curricular, financial and other implications.

Qualitative Improvement of Teacher Education

Many committees and commissions recommended for longer period of teacher education at secondary level for qualitative improvement. Kothari Commission (1964-66) did not recommend for two years B.Ed. program for financial and practical reasons. But it has recommended that there should be at least 230 working days in the one year B.Ed. program. Chattopadhyay Commission (1983-85) also recommended that if one year B.Ed. is to be continued then it should operate for at least 220 days and working hours to be increased. From practical point of view, if we exclude the vacations, holidays, examinations, admission, etc., it is almost impossible to manage 230/220 working days in a year.

Chattopadhyay Commission (1983-85) recommended for five years of secondary teacher education after 10+2. In the context of National Curriculum Framework for School Education (2005) of NCERT, the National Focus Groups on Teacher Education for Curriculum Revision was set up. The focus group also recommended, among others, that teacher education program should be ideally of five years duration after completion of 10+2 level of school education (p.28).

As a strong measure of qualitative improvement of teacher education, the NCTE published in 1998, 'Curriculum Framework for Quality Teacher Education' (p.60-61). The salient arguments are:

- The new curriculum framework included several additional components. Additional courses would develop additional competencies of prospective teachers.
- Pedagogical analysis of the teaching subjects would be made compulsory.
- Practice teaching would be done with thorough preparation, detailed supervision and adequate time.
- Internship program would provide all experiences that a teacher needs. It will provide skills for organsing co-scholastic programs.
- Fieldwork and community interaction will enable the student teacher to develop need-based pedagogy.
- Lessons to be supervised intensively and formative approach to be adopted.
- Teacher educators will devote more time in preparation and planning of their own activities.
- Professionalism will be developed which involves change in attitude and value system of the teacher.

- Teachers can earn recognition as a professional from society after acquiring new competencies and commitment.
- It will provide strong base for pursuing M.Ed. Course.

In order to fulfill the above arguments, the document recommended for enhancement of duration of conventional B.Ed program from one year to two year in order to transact the curriculum to ensure achievement of objectives of teacher education at the secondary stage. NCTE held national consultations in which a strong consensus emerged in favour of two year B.Ed. program. Subsequently, NCTE (2004) recommended that *perspective teachers will pursue a common course of study for two or three semesters and specialized studies including the practice teaching and internship for the rest of the period. These specialized courses would be in language, mathematics, environmental studies, physical education, yogic education, etc. pertaining to pre-primary, and elementary schools. Pedagogical analysis would begin from the second semester and go up to the fourth.* (p. 137)

As a follow up of the above recommendation of NCTE (1998), NCERT started 2-year B.Ed. course in its four RIEs in 2001 with satisfactory experiences. In 2004, the NCERT developed its own Curriculum Framework for Teacher Education which also recommended for running innovative and integrated four years and two year teacher education programs (p. 66). Personal observation says the program is demanding and very popular. However, there is a need to evaluate the effectiveness of two year B.Ed. program being run by RIEs.

NCTE as a regulatory body has developed norms and standards for various teacher education courses. However, in order to ensure maintenance of quality and its enhancement in teacher education, NCTE and NAAC entered in MOU in 2003. Accordingly the quality of institutions is now being assessed on six criteria. These are:

Criteria	Weight Age
1. Curriculum design and planning.	10
2. Curriculum transaction and planning	40
3. Research development and extension	05
4. Infrastructure and learning resources	20
5. Student support and profession	10
6. Organization and management	15

Realizing the significance of curriculum planning, designing and transaction as the core component of quality assurance of two year B.Ed program, the NCTE constituted a committee in 2004 on Models of Course Content, Transactional Strategies and Modes of Evaluation as per the provision if its act, 1993.

The draft course structure with detailed outline of B.Ed. (two year regular) program is now ready for approval of NCTE. The salient features of the proposed program are:

- All the theory courses, 14 in number are compulsory. Knowledge of these areas is essential for every teacher.
- Two level pedagogy courses are proposed 'A' and 'O' level with major responsibility to each one course at O and/or A level of the two school subjects. O level for secondary stage, 'A' for senior secondary.
- Post-training internship program of total six months duration.
- Guiding principle of particular course has been 'learning never guarantees performance but performance guarantees learning'. Eight intensive practical courses are recommended which will be conducted as either school based, college based, or community based. Focus is laid on teacher performance.
- Evaluation scheme aims at continuous and comprehensive evaluation assessing of both internal and external evaluation.

Areas	Marks		Internal	External
Theory	1200	(60%)	400	800
Practical	800	(40%)	400	400
Total	**2000**		**800**	**1200**

- Grading system is proposed to be finally awarded.
- Semester scheme of course design has been proposed
- Detailed syllabus of each course has been developed comprising of objective, course content having 5 units, Transactional Mode, and sessional work.

Conclusion

People may be fearing that it may be a difficult proposition to increase the duration of the program from one year to two years because of several reasons such as:

- Financial constraint as it involves recruitment of almost double of present human resources and expansion of physical resources. Most of the existing teacher education institutions don't even meet the minimum requirements of NCTE so far as human and physical resources are concerned for one-year B.Ed. regular course.
- Are we, the teacher educators utilizing whatever the available time in the existing B.Ed. course effectively for our prospective teachers? Its not how much time we are devoting for B.Ed. course but how qualitatively we are using this time is more important.

There is a tendency to resist any change be it social, or educational. Innovations are not easily accepted. Innovations take time to get institutionalized. They appeal at their face value and quality is sometimes at stake. Quality should not be compromised because of financial constraints. To minimize the financial burden, the institutions can take admission of students once in two years instead of taking admission every year. Or, the existing number of seats in B.Ed. course could be reduced in order to meet the financial constraint.

The quality of teacher education is closely related with the duration of teacher preparation. A reasonable time duration for teacher preparation that provides enough opportunity for rigorous theoretical study, self-study, cooperative learning, reflection, pedagogical skill development, involvement with the children, the school, the classroom, and the community. In the existing one-year model of B.Ed. course, the duration of practice teaching most often found to be of short duration, not more than five to six weeks and that too piece-meal in approach. There is hardly any scope to integrate the theory and practice. Due to lack of time, 'lessons' are planned with inadequate reflection on the content and subject-matter, its organization and pedagogy. Hence, there is a growing concern among the educationists and pedagogists for increasing the duration of B.Ed. programme from one academic year to two academic years.

References

1. NCTE (1998). *Curriculum Framework for Quality Teacher Education*. New Delhi.
2. NCTE (2004). *Some Specific Issues and Concerns of Teacher Education (Discussion Document)*. New Delhi.
3. NCTE (2006). *Curriculum Framework for Teacher Education (Draft for Discussion)*. New Delhi: www.ncte_in.org.
4. NCERT (2005). *National Curriculum Framework 2005*. New Delhi.
5. NCERT (2005). *National Curriculum Framework Review 2005 National Focus Groups Position Papers Volume II Systemic Reforms*. New Delhi.
6. NCERT (2006). *Curriculum Framework for Teacher Education (Draft for Discussion)*. NCTE in collaboration with NCERT. New Delhi: www.ncert.nic.in.
7. Report of the Education Commission (1964-66) Education and National Development. Ministry of Education, Government of India, New Delhi.
8. The Teacher and Society, Chattopadhyaya Committee Report (1983-85). MHRD, Government of India, New Delhi.

SECTION – II

Innovative Practices in Teacher Education

Chapter – 10

Evaluation Practices in Teacher Education in the Context of NCF–2005

Introduction

Evaluation is one of the basic forms of disciplined inquiry. *It is that form of inquiry whose focus is some evaluation (program, process, organization, person, etc.) and which results in "merit" and/or "worth" constructions (judgments) about it* (Guba and Lincoln, 1989). Merit constructions is based on the intrinsic quality of an evaluation, irrespective of the setting in which it may find applications. Worth constructions is based on the extrinsic usefulness or applicability of an evaluation in a concrete local setting.

In the Indian education system, the term evaluation is associated with examination, stress and anxiety. Examinations are given undue importance in the present education system. Examinations do not serve the needs of social justice. Examinations test mostly textbook based knowledge. The important skills and abilities, higher order thinking skills like, problem solving, reasoning, creative thinking and judgment, etc. are not tested. Several committees and commissions including NCF (2005) reported about the growing problems of psychological pressure that children and their parents feel during examination. All efforts in curriculum construction and renewal come to an end if it is not engaged with evaluation and examination. A good evaluation system should

Dr. Sudarshan Mishra, Lecturer in Education at Army Institue of Education, Delhi Cantt.

become an integral part of learning process and benefit both the learners and all stakeholders of educational system by giving credible feedback. The NCF (2005) recommends five guiding principles for curriculum construction. They are:

- connecting knowledge to life outside the school,
- ensuring that learning is shifted away from rote methods,
- enriching the curriculum to provide for overall development of children rather than remain textbook centric,
- making examinations more flexible and integrated into classroom life and,
- nurturing an over-riding identity informed by caring concerns within the democratic polity of the country.

These can also be the guiding principles for the evaluation process. The purpose of this article is to describe the conceptual underpinnings of constructivist learning along with its variations and implications for classroom evaluation.

Learning Theory and Evaluation

Constructivist evaluation is based on constructivist learning theory. Learning theories are indispensable for effective and pedagogically meaningful evaluation practices. Hence, an effective evaluation process is supposed to take into account the theoretical bases in which it is grounded. There have been several classes of theories with regard to learning that formed the basis for the evaluation process. Mayer (1992) has shown how three views of learning have emerged during the past 100 years of research on learning. They are (i) learning as response strengthening, (ii) learning as knowledge acquisition, and (iii) learning as knowledge construction.

Learning as response strengthening: According to this view, learning occurs when learner strengthens or weakens an association between a stimulus and a response. This view was developed in the first half of 20th century and was based largely on the study of animal learning in artificial laboratory settings. The role of learner is to passively receive rewards and punishments, whereas the role of instructor/teacher is to administer rewards and punishments, such as drill and practice. The teacher's role is to create environments where the learner is repeatedly cued to give a simple response, which is immediately followed by a feedback.

Learning as knowledge acquisition: Learning as knowledge acquisition is based on the idea that learning occurs when a learner places new information in long-term memory. This view was developed in 1950s, 1960s and 1970s and was based largely on the study of human learning in artificial laboratory settings. The role of the learner is to passively acquire information, and the teacher's job is to present information, such as in textbooks and lectures. According to this view, information is a commodity that can be transmitted directly from teacher to learner. The teacher's role is to create environments in which the learner is exposed to large amount of information through textbooks, lectures and computer based multimedia programmes.

Learning as knowledge construction: The third view, learning as knowledge construction, is based on the idea that learning occurs when a leaner actively constructs a knowledge representation in working memory. This view was emerged in 1980s and 1990s and was based largely on the study of human learning in increasingly realistic settings. According to this view, the learner is a sense maker, whereas the teacher is a cognitive guide or facilitator who provides guidance and modeling on authentic academic tasks. The teacher's role is to create environments in which the learner interacts meaningfully with academic material, including fostering the learner's processes of selecting, organizing and integrating information.

Constructivist Evaluation

Guba and Lincoln (1989) defined four phases of evaluation. The first phase is defined as *measurement goal-driven* to determine whether students had 'mastered' the content of the various courses or subjects to which they were exposed. The second phase is defined as *description goal-driven.* It is an evaluation approach that determines effectiveness in the attainment of program objectives with careful advance planning, student performance, or other appropriate results provide feedback for diagnosing deficiencies and improving programs. The third phase is defined as *judgment goal-driven* in which evaluation was characterized by the efforts to reach judgments, and in which the evaluator assumed the role of judge, while retaining the earlier technical and descriptive functions. The fourth phase is based on *authentic assessments and context-based evaluations.* This phase develops a constructivist approach to evaluation and assessment. Freedman (1998) described three constructs regarding constructivist evaluation and its implications for the assessment environment. They are:

- Learning is an active process,
- The learner has prior knowledge,
- The learner takes responsibility for their own learning.

Broadly, there could be two ways in which learners can be evaluated in a constructivist learning environment. They are:

Content evaluation: This involves how well students are able to function within a content domain, and whether they could use the tools and understandings of the domain to solve problems within that domain. For example, if students are involved in an authentic task, then evaluation would assess whether they successfully completed that task or not.

Process evaluation: This involves how well students reflect on the processes whereby they came to their conclusions and document this process. According to Jonassen (1991), evaluating how learners go about constructing their knowledge is more important than the resulting product, suggesting that evaluative procedures must become an integral part of the instructional process. Jonassen also feels that goal free evaluation could be an important part of constructivist evaluation, since that would allow the evaluator to be unbiased by the goals of instruction.

Constructivist Assessment Environment

In the constructivist assessment environment teachers takes the role of facilitator. According to Freedman (1998), the assessment environment has two major subdivisions. They are:

- What defines the assessment environment, and
- What influences the assessment environment.

Defining assessment environment: The defining elements of assessment environment are:

- Teacher beliefs,
- Teacher practices, and
- Student engagement.

Teacher beliefs: Three beliefs are found that guide the teacher in a constructivist assessment environment. They are:

1. Teachers need to change in order to assess students to meet the changing needs of students. They have to change their perspectives. They have to do this by exploring new avenues in order to incorporate a wide variety of assessment strategies. In order for change to occur teacher needs to accept it.
2. Doing and thinking is more important than being able to recite facts. It creates interests and brings motivation. Teachers should believe that developing skills and attitude is more important than mere assessing memorization of facts.
3. Students can be responsible for their own assessment and learning. They have to be offered an opportunity and environment where they will feel safe and comfort to take on responsibilities.

Teacher practices: In addition to beliefs, teachers follow a number of practices that add breath to the assessment environment. They are:

1. Teachers should not feel restricted to text-embedded assessments. They should change and modify existing assessment based on perceived students' needs and abilities, personal goals and government policies.
2. Teachers should use students input to design and modify assessments. When student inputs are accepted, they feel responsibility of presenting their opinions, designing their own assessments and selecting the criteria for assessment including judgment.
3. Teachers should use variety of questioning strategies to assess students' prior knowledge. Response to questions can reveal what students already know and what their beliefs are.
4. Teachers should use a variety of inquiries. It increases understanding and reasoning abilities. Inquiries include observation, accommodation, validation and reflection.

Student engagement: Students have an active role in constructivist assessment environment because their minds are engaged. They are not empty vessels. They question themselves, with their peers, their teachers on the new knowledge and try to incorporate them into their existing mental structure. Teachers can encourage students to involve in the assessment environment in various ways. They are:

1. Teachers should encourage students in directing their own assessment and learning.
2. Teachers should involve students in decision making process of judgment and grading. Sometimes their involvement could be direct and sometimes it is indirect.
3. The process of learning does not shut down during assessment (Brooks and Brooks, 1993). So, teachers should engage students in learning in constructivist assessment environment. Teachers can use relevant local issues to draw students into the learning process.
4. Students should be intrinsically motivated by different kinds of assessment. These are (a) goal-oriented (b) student

self-directed or (c) entertaining. The one that motivates students is performance-based assessment.

All of the assessment in constructivist environment involves group work. Students interact with each other in all circumstances including during assessments (Zahorik, 1995). So, assessment is not an after thought but an integral component of classroom environment. NCF (2005) argued to integrate examination with classroom life. Assessment environment is one where there is active learning in a social context.

Influences on the assessment environment: Influences on the assessment environment are both internal and external. Internal influences include the daily interactions of the students and teachers within the context of classroom instruction. Internal influence on the assessment environment is the constant curiosity of the teachers to find out a better solution to a given problem of assessment. Networking with student community, peer teachers and professionals is a source of generating new ideas to solve assessment problems. They should seek information from various sources such as, interviews with students, peer teachers, professionals, attending workshops, reviewing literature, etc. External influences come from higher authorities such as district education authorities, SCERTs, CBSE, NCERT and other examination bodies. Pressure is applied from a variety of sources regarding coverage issue. They are parents, communities, examination bodies such as district boards, state boards, CBSE, etc. Externally constructed national standardized tests are not usually relevant to student's everyday learning. Consequently, their use is often forced (Freedman, 1998). Teacher is compelled to cover the courses limiting the scope of developing higher order thinking skills (HOTS).

Variety of Assessment Environment: Teachers use a variety of assessments to make students grading. Students are given multiple opportunities to show their competencies. Variety may be in terms of visuals, performing, writing, talking, designing, and presenting knowledge as individuals and in groups. Variety also means that grades are a profile of many areas of competence which may include: concepts, inquiry, application, creativity, attitude and world view. Variety also includes demonstration, explanation, writing a script, drawing cartoons, inquiry, observation, using a rubric, making a checklist, drawings, skits, concept mapping, role play, projects, collage, logbook, explorations, experiments, etc.

Assessment of students' knowledge should be application oriented. It should include higher order thinking skills (HOTS) and problem-solving. Going beyond recall such as, comparison, analysis and evaluation is essential if students are going to accommodate information into new mental structures. Variety should also include social configuration of assessment. Students like to work in group. They enjoy interaction. This can be possible through peer assessment and collaborative assessment. Collaborative assessment through project work, presentation and performances allows students to exercise their strength and receive support for their weaknesses. The knowledge gained through collaborative assessment is more than that expected from an individual. While working in group they should come to a consensus of how they could interpret, look or observe an event, a problem or a phenomenon.

Constructivist Evaluation Process

An instructional environment needs to be assessment-centered, and teaching and assessment need to be "constructively aligned" with the curriculum objectives. What is already known influences what can be learnt next. A teacher needs to pay attention to what learners bring to the learning environment, including cultural knowledge and preferred ways of learning. Teacher as facilitator of knowledge construction should plan activities that will provide appropriate cognitive challenges to the learners so that their existing knowledge can actually be revealed. Some of the methodologies of evaluation in a constructivist environment are described below.

Formative evaluation: Most often, summative assessment has been the only assessment provided in a programme. Students complete a unit of study, submit their assignments, and move on to a new and different unit with the feedback from the assignment which is becoming redundant in terms of their learning. So far active learning is concerned; the challenge for teacher is to find ways to provide continuous assessment throughout the programme. For this, formative assessment should be undertaken during the programme. The learner can use the formative feedback to revise and correct learning gaps and misconceptions. The teacher will be able to use the results of formative assessment to adjust content and activities to better meet the learning needs of the learners.

Self-evaluation : According to Glasersfeld (1995), each individual constructs meaning, knowledge and conceptual structures differently. So the teachers should be cognizant that students may view curricula, textbooks differently than they do. Accordingly, teachers should not attempt to transfer conceptual knowledge to students through words. Instead, they should be concerned with how learners understand the process of knowing and how they justify their beliefs. If the constructivism provides the learners with lots of opportunities to make meaning, the evaluation also should be made by the learners themselves. Through self-evaluation, each learner can evaluate his or her process of meaning making. Teacher should be a facilitator and should ask thought provoking and challenging questions to refine and fix the students' position.

Since the learning is individualistic in constructivism, self-evaluation provides a strong element both for teachers and students. Each and every learner constructs knowledge based on their previous knowledge. Writing the reflective statements will increase the authenticity of self-evaluation because teachers can verify it. Students develop greater understanding of their particular learning style when they self-evaluate and reflect on the evidence they have selected to demonstrate their competence. Ability to self-assess will provide a constructive feedback to learners and this is not only an assessment process but also a learning process.

Peer Evaluation: Here, students work in pairs, threes, or more formal learning-sets to read each other's work and to give feedback against the marking criteria. They also explain what feedback they have received and discuss how they will apply it in their next activity. Peers can use checklists, rubrics or give a written response to peer work.

Collaborative evaluation: Collaborative assessment is an effective way to help students take more responsibility for judging the quality of their own learning efforts. Students like to work in group. They enjoy interaction. Collaborative assessment through project work, presentation and performances allows students to exercise their strength and receive support for their weaknesses. The group should take joint responsibility for providing feedback on the quality of the work. Learners can share ideas which will be helpful to their peers and work on improving their assignments before final submission. The knowledge gained through collaborative assessment is more than that expected from an individual. While working in group they come to a consensus of how they could interpret, look or observe an event, a problem or a phenomenon. It also improves their communication and planning skills.

Portfolio evaluation: In a constructivist classroom, teachers can effectively use portfolio assessment. Ongoing assessment could document a learner's progress through the portfolio mode (NCF–2005). Portfolio assessment can be explained as a purposeful, multifaceted process of collecting documentation of children's growth, progress, and effort over time. It is a reflective document rather than a simple list of student's teaching and learning experiences. It will reflect the competencies that the student is required to demonstrate in the course or module.

There are several criteria that should keep in mind while using portfolio assessment. The portfolio must:

- be *clearly linked with instructional objectives*. If the two are not connected, the portfolio is just an accumulation of work with little assessment value or future instructional value.

- be *an ongoing assessment system* that allows teachers to observe the continuous, dynamic movement of children's growth. Teachers must avoid discontinuous or static methods of assessing children's skills and abilities.
- avoid becoming a teacher-made document. To analyze growth and development, both *children and their families must have a voice in inclusion of items*.
- be *performance based*; emphasize purposeful learning; be ongoing in all cultural contexts of school, home, and community; and celebrate, support, and encourage a child's development and learning.

Effective learning requires meaningful, open-ended, and challenging problems for the learner to solve. In portfolio assessment teachers' role is vital as a facilitator. Teacher should assess, evaluate, manage, organize, and use information for problem-solving, decision making, and critical thinking.

All knowledge is socially constructed and social interaction plays a pivotal role in learning. Hence, parents and community members need to understand portfolio assessment. It provides a new perspective on learning for both teachers and students. Students, principals, teachers, and parents should work together to make portfolio assessment much more successful. If the parents are provided with an opportunity to see students' challenging and engaging work, they will get information about how their children are developing.

Conclusion

Indian school board exams are largely inappropriate for the 'knowledge society' of the 21st century and its need for innovative problem-solvers (NCERT, 2008). If learning takes place through interactions with the environment around, then evaluation should be carried out in a meaningful context that is relevant to the students and the society. A good evaluation system should be an integral part of the learning process. It should be beneficial for students, teachers and the society. There is a growing need to understand philosophy, pedagogy and teacher practices in order to implement constructivist evaluation process.

Teacher education institutions have several obstacles to overcome before accomplishing the goal of constructivist evaluation practices including administrative apathy, centralised curriculum, inadequate literature; a lack of consensus on methods of evaluation; conditions that require classroom management at the expense of academic instruction, ètc. National bodies like NCERT, NCTE, etc. must make a long-term commitment to provide inservice training; involve experienced teachers in the selection of instructional materials and testing programs and appoint a committee to guide curriculum development. Teacher education institutions assign mentors to new teachers; allot time for teachers to share effective strategies for evaluation. Inservice training that helps teachers to remodel their lesson plans and integrate the elements of evaluation, should be provided on a contionous basis. Adequate literature should be developed on the construcivist evaluation practices for teacher preparation both through face-to-face and distance mode.

References

1. Brooks, J.G. and Brooks, M.G. (1993). *In search of understanding: The case for Constructivist classrooms*. Alexandria, C.A.: Association for Supervision and Curriculum Development.
2. Elbow, P. (1994). *Will the virtues of portfolios blind us to their potential dangers?* In P. Stillman (Ed.). *New direction in portfolio assessment*. Portsmouth, NH: Boyton/Cook Publishers.
3. Freedman, R.L.H. (1998). *Constructivist assessment practices*. Website: http://www.eric.ed.gov/ERICDocs/data/ericdocs2sql/content_storage_01/0000019b/80/15/1e/98.pdf Retrieved on 30th March 2009.
4. Glasersfeld, E.V. (1995*). A Constructivist Approach to Teaching*. In L.P. Steffe and J. Gale (Ed.). *Constructivism in Education.* Hillsdale, N.J.: Lawrence Erlbaum Associates.
5. Lincoln, Y.S. and Guba, E.G. (1981). *Effective evaluation.* San Francisco: Jossey-Bass.

6. Guba, E.G. and Lincoln, Y.S. (1989). *Fourth Generation Evaluation.* Newbury Park, CA: Sage Publications.

7. Jonassen, D.H. (1991). Objectivism versus constructivism: Do we need a new philosophical paradigm? *Educational Technology Research & Development*, 39(3), 5–14.

8. Mayer, R.E. (1992): Cognition and Instruction: On their historic meeting within Educational Psychology. *Journal of Educational Psychology*, 84, 405–412.

9. Matthews, M.R. (2000). Appraising Constructivism in Science and Mathematics. In D. Phillips (Ed.) *Constructivism in Education*, 161–192. Chicago: University of Chicago Press.

10. NCERT (2005). *National Curriculum Framework 2005.* New Delhi: NCERT.

11. NCERT (2008). *Position paper: National Focus Group on Examination Reforms.* New Delhi: NCERT.

12. Pelech, J.R. (2006). *Benedictine pedagogy through a constructivist lens: curricular theorizing of a high school math teacher turned college professor.* National-Louis University. Website: http://www.eric.ed.gov/ERICDocs/data/ericdocs2sql/content_storage_01/0000019b/80/1b/d2/8d.pdf Retrieved on 30th March, 2009.

13. Popham, W. J. (1995). *Classroom assessment: What teachers need to know.* Needham Heights, MA: Allyn and Bacon.

14. Richardson, V. (1997) (Ed). *Constructivist Teacher Education: Building a World of New Understandings.* Bristol, Pa.: Falmer Press.

15. Senapaty, H.K. and Pradhan, N. (2005). Designing Instruction for Constructivist Learning. *Staff and Educational Developmental International.* 9 (2&3), 93-102.

16. Zahorik, J.A. (1995). *Constructivist Teaching.* Bloomington: Phi Delta Kappa Educational Foundation.

Chapter–11

Innovations in Teacher Education

Teacher education is said to be very significant investment for bringing qualitative improvement in education. If a revolution in education has to be initiated, it is the teacher-education on which the start can be ignited. Any program of qualitative change in education, pre-requisite the improvement of teachers. The teacher has the critical role in the development of country. In the field of teacher-education many new trends and innovations have emerged in our country and abroad. These are few practices, procedures, policies in the area of teacher- education. The only need is to absorb them in teaching – learning process.

The whole world is passing through the process of globalization, privatization and liberalization requiring economic, political, social and educational changes in developing and developed countries. If changes are not made to suit the changing needs, the stagnation will set in. Therefore, a climate, which can promote innovation, is absolutely essential for any system for its growth and development.

The International Dictionary of Education describes "Innovation" as promotion of new ideas or practices. But National

---

1. Aashim, Lecturer in Army Institute of Higher Education, Pathankot.

2. Bhawna Sharma, Lecturer in Vaishno College of Education, Himachal Pradesh.

Council of Educational Research and Training (2007) states that innovation is more that having new ideas, it includes the process of successfully introducing them or making things happen in a new way.

The NCERT organized a national seminar on 'Innovation in School Teacher Education' in 1997. It focused on important characteristics of innovations. Such as:

1. New to the system of environment as perceived by individuals.
2. Better than what is already in existence.
3. A deliberately planned.
4. Suitable for achieving predetermined goals.
5. Something which results in the improvement of a system.

Need for Innovative Teacher Education

The very law of nature is 'change'. As per the nature, socio-cultural aspects also change. 'Education' is no exception to this law. The role of a teacher is no longer confined to teaching alone. They need to be thorough professionals, which means, they should be fully equipped with high academic standard, ethical and moral values. The purpose of teacher education is to produce teachers who have professional competencies. As teacher education is meant for preparing future teachers who will lead society and nation, hence, the responsibility of teacher educators increases manifold.

Delors Commission in its report, "Learning: The Treasure Within" (UNESCO, 1996) highlights challenges that are to be responded by teacher educators and teacher preparation system. The teacher Education must, therefore, create necessary awareness among teacher educators about their new roles and responsibilities. Unfortunately, however, the programs of teacher educations are alleged to be static and stagnant and not fulfilling the needs and requirements of the present society.

It appears that, the quality of teacher education is deteriorating day by day and there is a need for drastic change in all aspects of teacher education program so as to enable teacher educators to face the challenges of the dynamic world. One way to improve the situation is to absorb the innovations in the field of teacher education. The situation in India is little different. Studies on innovation are very limited in number.

Rai (1972) studied the factors affecting diffusion of innovations in secondary schools. Similarly Joshi (1972) made a comprehensive study on Innovation and change. He tried to find out what types of innovations have been adopted by training colleges in India. Gupta studied the effectiveness of innovative methods in the colleges of education. He made a conclusion that method like discussion, workshop etc. was more effective than the lecture method.

It is very necessary to bring awareness for the adoption of an innovation to its consumers. If the adopters are well aware of the innovation it is likely to be accepted.

Chaliha (2003) stated that the awareness creates interest in the innovation and the attitude for its adoption and co-operation to other members in their educational ventures. He also pointed out that the attitude and support from the institutions are contributory factors for the spread of innovation in teacher education institutions.

Recent Trends in Teacher Education

Best practices evolved and put into action if remain dormant at the birthplaces without crossing the borders, are of no use. They should be disseminated for meaningful reflections and under adoptions in various institutions with slight modification wherever necessary. Few of them are mentioned under:

Seminar Method: It is a subject centered method. It provides more interaction among students. A problem of common interest is specified. Participation in seminar helps in development of higher cognitive powers, formulation of hypothesis, analysis, synthesis and evaluation skills.

Tutorial Method: It is also a student centered method. The teacher initiates discussion. It may consist of assignments to be done in the class or at home. The assignments are evaluated on the spot and the outcomes are discussed with individual students. It gives stress on individual development which is neglected in normal classroom lecture. The individual differences are taken care of. While the slow learners get compensatory treatment, the gifted ones get enrichment treatment.

Laboratory Method: Laboratory is used for teaching strategies involving experiments, demonstrations, computer assisted instruction etc. It is useful for development of manual skills and process of scientific inquiry. The steps of this method are- sensing a problem, collecting data, formulating hypothesis, arriving at solution and generalizing and applying. This is an age of technology. Even in the field of education no. of advancements using technology have taken place. No. of instructions have been based on technology. Such as;

Individualised Instruction: There have been many individualized instruction strategies, some of which are– computer assisted instruction, programmed instruction, etc. Computer assisted instruction has been proved effective in case of students who have gained certain hold over the subject. Programmed instruction is a revolutionary device in the science of learning, now-a- days, its use in the field of teacher education has also attained importance. Now-a-days , there is a new trend in teacher education to use the technique of programmed instruction for such areas as an expedient. The Education Commission (1964-1966) has also realized the importance of teaching various subjects with the help of programmed instruction.

Suggestions

To keep proper consonance with the nation's vision of education proper attention must be paid to the implementation of some suggestions:

1. The teacher-educators should be made mobile so that they get the opportunity to see their professional world outside

the institution and are able to know more about recent trends of their professional world.

2. The practicing schools, administrators, student teachers, guardians and community should provide proper service and support and encourage the teacher educators.
3. Though every teacher education institution are fulfilling N.C.T.E. norms and providing infrastructure but teacher educators fail to utilize them properly and to train the teacher trainees in proper directions. They should utilize the facilities available properly.
4. The fresh teacher educators have no experience of organizing the training program due to that the quality is affected. They should be given 2-3 months training as internship in teacher education program.
5. Inspiring leadership from head of the institutions would serve as a key to the spread of innovation.
6. Freedom and autonomy to teacher educators can go a long way in promoting innovative ideas in the training institutions.
7. For their professional growth, proper incentives shall be given to the teacher educators.
8. Well qualified staff and organization of in-service and extension program are other facilitative factors for spread of innovations.

Nothing is constant in this world but change ...

In conclusion, it can be said that by providing / enhancing the quality services in teacher education, we can provide a quality nation in this competitive world. Time has come when Teachers education should not only teach and teach better the areas that make a nation advanced but also be innovative enough and technologies that keep nations great.

Chapter–12

Preparation of Science Teachers in View of NCF–2005

Introduction

Development of scientific attitude in our learners has always been valued aim of teaching science. With the development of technology and overtake by globalization this aim is becoming more valuable to those who recognize the importance of human consciousness not being overshadowed by the "myths" which accompany this "development". We are burdening our learners with so many expectations that the endeavored aim of all round development of individual is being lost in all the stages of education. Science as a subject is seen as a source to gain entry in prestigious engineering and medical institutes, but for even those who "achieve" this aim, we can not say surely that they would have developed basic scientific attitude expected. There may be lots of reasons behind it but one of the basic reasons is the way we teach science in classroom. As pointed out nicely by the NCF–2005: there is a deep disquiet about several aspects of our educational practice: (a) the school system is characterized by an inflexibility that makes it resistant to change; (b) learning has become an isolated activity, which does not encourage children to link knowledge with their lives in any organic or vital way; (c) schools promote a regime of thought that discourages creative thinking and insights; (d) what

Subhash Chandra, Lecturer in Lady Irwin College, University of Delhi

is presented and transmitted in the name of learning in schools bypasses vital dimensions of the human capacity to create new knowledge; (e) the " future " of the child has taken centre stage to the near exclusion of the child's "present ", which is detrimental to the well-being of the child as well as the society and the nation. We need to plan and pay attention to systemic matters that will enable us to implement many of the good ideas that have already been articulated in the past. Paramount among these are;

- connecting knowledge to life out-side the school,
- ensuring that learning is shifted away from rote methods,
- enriching the curriculum to provide for overall development of children rather than remain textbook centric,
- making examinations more flexible and integrated into classroom life and,
- nurturing an over-riding identity informed by caring concerns within the democratic polity of the country.

Science education in schools needs to be reviewed thoroughly by everyone concerned with the education of children. There has been many efforts in past attempting to make science more activity based in schools which has certainly helped the cause by still there is lot to be done in terms of all related aspects including attitude of those who are concerned. Works like project 2061 and Houshangabad experimental science teaching have emphasized on the participation of the learners in the understanding of the scientific concepts. Learning by doing has actually being practiced in varied situations. Making science interesting for students so that they enjoy while doing science should be the aim of teaching science at all level. If they will enjoy doing science they will definitely develop interest for science in future also.

In this view the whole paradigm of teaching science pedagogy course in teacher education needs to be reviewed. Preparation of teachers at teacher education institutions is considered to be a platform from which the future teachers take a leap towards their teaching careers. In view of changes in the whole orientation to the curriculum framework for science teaching at all the levels, it is important that changes take place at the preparation stage also. The whole vision of a classroom where students construct their own knowledge and apply it in their daily life will be impossible if the teachers are not prepared to deal with the challenges a constructivist classroom brings. For teachers to be innovative with the methodology and going beyond examination focused approach will be difficult if they are not prepared well at the time of their respective teacher education course. Although at present, institutes do encourage innovative methodology and activity based teaching in pedagogy courses there is need to re look at the methodology used with teacher trainees. A theoretical approach to teacher preparation in science pedagogy courses would not encourage trainees to use constructivist approach in their future classes. Thus it is important for the teacher educators to make changes in their pedagogy classes. There is a need to seriously consider following points for science pedagogy teachers at teacher education institutions:

1. Changes in methodology
2. Reorienting practical classes
3. Use of local recourses:
4. Use of ICT
5. Collaborative learning

Methodology

If one wants his/her students to do something different, he/ she has to be a role model for them. It's an old saying but is relevant in present time also, thus a teacher educator need to present a good example in front of their learners by using constructivist approach in their own class. Teachers trainees come prepared (assumed to be well prepared) with their teaching subjects but the main problem is with using this preparation in their subject in schools at different level. Lot of the trainees faces difficulty in relating with the constructivist approach, which is expected to be used in their science classroom. It may be because they are "taught" differently at their secondary and tertiary level. Thus the whole orientation related to methodology in pedagogy class becomes very important. In view of the NCF, teacher's role in a school has changed specially in classroom. It can be said that NCF has again emphasized on issues which were emphasized earlier by people who wanted more activity based, experience based learning in science classroom. Thus use of a methodology which encourages self exploration and group learning needs to be paid attention to pedagogy classes. Teachers need to give more demonstrations and encourage students to come up with alternative methodology to teach at school level. Group teaching in institutions becomes important here. Where the teacher educator can work with the trainees and let the students explore their strengths and utilization of them in constructivist classroom practices. Problem solving methods are important in developing student's ability to learn and construct knowledge, thus teachers should make a deliberate effort in making trainees solve problems in pedagogy class and develop a problem solving attitude themselves so that they can translate it in their own classes. Brainstorming is another activity which can explore the student's ideas and abilities. Students can be given tasks which give them opportunity to work in small groups and come up with solution to specific problems and issues related to science teaching. Projects should be given to trainees which can be self identified or teacher given. Activities using materials from immediate environment helps in understanding and applying concepts better. Thus teacher trainees should be equipped with skills to develop learning material on their own. Practical classes of science should be thus given more importance for hands on experience in institutions.

Reorienting Practical Classes

Practical classes should be given much more time if trainees are expected to develop positive attitude towards exploring learner centered teaching methods. At present trainees generally perform secondary school practical in their practical classes at institutes where practical are given some importance. Alternative methods of teaching and utilizing students ideas can be critical for achievement of aims kept by NCF–2005, and these methods should not only be learnt theoretically in classroom but also execute them in practical classes.

Use of Local Recourses

Developing kits using waste materials is one of the most important tasks which every trainee should take up. If the teachers are made to use such material in their school life experience (generally called practice teaching) more often with other learner centered methods then it will lead to a better classroom in coherence with constructivist approach later also. Things which are easily available in environment are best for classroom utilization thus trainees should be able to relate the concepts of science with them. For example using waste CD to show reflection or other concept. Multiple uses of things can help in developing student's creative thinking ability also.

Use of ICT

In recent years there has been lot of progress in use of ICT (Information and Communication Technology) in education. Use of recent technology in classroom can be very effective for a constructivist classroom. From authoring techniques to using technology in classroom processes, ICT can be helpful in many views. Use of LAN and internet can be a useful tool for sharing information from different sources. Lot of software is available which can be used by the teacher in classroom to develop different abilities of a learner. These software will not only be very interesting for students but also have lot of potential to develop problem solving attitude in students. Teachers should be trained to use them effectively in class as well as develop them on their own. Mobile phones are used extensively and are available easily in present time. Teachers can use them in their classrooms for multiple teaching purposes. One of them could be recording some clip of event which can be relevant in teaching in classroom. Lot of information is available on internet which can be used by students in different ways, thus trainees should be prepared well with utilization of information effectively.

Collaborative Learning

Collaborative learning or teaching is not just restricted to classroom but also outside in activities which can lead to learning experiences. It is important that teachers in school do collaborative teaching in view of recommendations made by NCF, thus for this they need to trained in the same way. To reach a common goal people work together, it means we need to encourage intra subject collaborative work but also inter disciplinary approach in teaching. Research based collaborative tasks can give lot of positive influence to development of constructivist ethos in the teachers in school as well as at teacher education institutions. Focusing on pertinent issues and finding possible solution can be taken up.

Issues like global warming, water safety, biodiversity etc. have taken front seat in view of concerns of society. Thus these issues have gain lot of importance in school education, especially in science teaching. Thus teachers should be given exposure at preparation stage for better handling of these critical issues with their learners. Organizing short workshops for in-service teachers is taken up by various institutions in view of NCF but if science teaching needs to be improved in present situation, teachers need to be prepared in their teacher education institutions before they go to school. Thus there is an immediate need to reorient teacher education in terms of curriculum and methodology.

Chapter–13

Innovative Practices and Ideas in Teacher Education: In the Light of National Curriculum Framework–2005

Introduction

The quality of education depends to a great extent on the quality of teachers. Unless we bring quality in teachers we can not expect quality in education. Teacher education is considered as an integral part of the educational system and improvement in the quality of teacher education is one of its major objectives.

Though teacher education is defined in several ways in professional literature, the definition and meaning given in the National Council for Teacher Education (NCTE 1993) Act is worth mentioning. Teacher education means programme of education, research or training of persons for equipping them to teach at pre-primary, primary, secondary, senior secondary stage in schools and non-formal education, adult education and correspondence education through distance mode.

The number of teachers and teacher education institutions in the country have grown manifold during the last few decades. NCTE, established in 1995 to grant permission to these institutions to run Teacher Training Colleges as per the provisions of the NCTE Act. As on 31 January 2006, 5854 Teacher Training Institutes offering 6647 courses have been recognized by NCTE with an

Talat Jamil, Research Scholar in IASE, Faculty of Education, Jamia Millia Islamia, New Delhi.

approved intake of 5.22 lakh teacher trainees. Teacher preparation programmes have not changed during the recent past and are, therefore, under severe criticism for being static, unresponsive to the emerging challenges of the present time. The contemporary model of teacher education have failed to reflect the changes taking place in other spheres of our national life.

Teacher education has to be responsive to the challenges of expansion, Universalization of Elementary Education and overall quality of school education. Changes in policies, practices, curriculum, research areas and priorities in teacher education need to be continuously examined. The education of teacher, utilizing new technology and techniques can be a great contributing factor. It has to respond to various changes in its social, political, economic as well as cultural context. These changes can be done through innovation in teacher education.

Meaning and Definition of Innovation

The word 'innovation' means the introduction of novelties, something newly introduced, (*Oxford English Dictionary*, 1970). The Dictionary of Education (1977) has also defined innovation as promotion of new ideas and practices.

Change is another term used to describe innovation. The Oxford English Dictionary gives 'a change made' as one of the meanings of innovation. In the context of education, the term change is used with a qualifier as 'educational change'. Ordinarily speaking, change is of two types. One, of the incidental and the other, a deliberate or planned change which is for the better. Of the two, innovation refers to the planned or deliberate type of change. In other words, an innovation is something better than what it replaces (Per Dalin, 1978). This view is shared by Munro (1977) when he states that innovation is a deliberate attempt to improve educational practice.

Another definition given by Havelock, innovation is a deliberate effort directed towards the significant improvement of the system. Since our concern here is teacher education, innovation in teacher education can be defined as a 'deliberate effort directed towards the significant improvement of teacher education'.

National Curriculum Framework

The National Policy of Education (NPE, 1986) and its Programme of Action (PoA, 1992) made a strong case for improving the quality of teacher education because it was the pre-requisite to improve the quality of school education. NPE proposed a national framework for curriculum as a means of evolving a national system of education capable of responding to India's diversity of geographical and cultural milieus while ensuring a common core of values along with academic components. "The NPE – PoA envisaged a child-centred approach to promote universal enrolment and universal retention upto14 years of age and substantial improvement in the quality of education in the school" (PoA, p. 77). The PoA further elaborated on this vision of NPE by emphasizing relevance, flexibility and quality as characteristics of the National Curriculum Framework. Thus both these documents envisioned the National Curriculum Framework as a means of modernizing the system of education. This paper attempts to highlight the innovative practices and ideas in teacher education in the light of National Curriculum Framework–2005.

National Curriculum Framework–2005

The National Policy on Education (NPE,1986) and the Programme of Action (POA,1992) assigned a pivotal role to NCERT in preparing a National Curriculum Framework (NCF). Preparation of NCF, 2005 was accomplished with the help of a National Steering Committee, chaired by Prof. Yash Pal, approved by CABE on 7th September 2005. The National Curriculum Framework for school education (2000) and that of (2005) have certain expectations from teacher education.

Innovative Ideas and Practices as mentioned in National Curriculum Framework–2005

Multiple/Plurality of Textbooks

Textbook writings should be decentralized so as to increase teacher's involvement in these tasks. Teachers should understand the children's developmental levels, effective skills of communication and design etc. While SCERT, which has been given the task of textbook writing at present, the actual envisioning of the process, selection and writing of content must be done in collaborative manner by teams rather than individual subject experts.

Lessons are often written without relating them to the time assigned for the subject taught. It maybe a good idea for the identical lesson to be piloted i.e. to be taught on a trial basis with the textbook writer observing its transaction in the class while also receiving feedback from both teachers and students. This is also important when innovating with textbook content in order to understand and place them within the realities of the classroom and teacher preparation. The availability of multiple textbooks for schools as they widen teachers choices and also provide for the incorporation of diversity in relation to children's needs and interests. The availability of multiple textbooks would increase teacher's autonomy and choice. Alternatively, they can also provide opportunities to encourage children to explore diverse sources and understand how the same content may be presented in different ways. This will encourage library work. The sharing of libraries between schools must also be consciously planned for, and this can be built into partnerships between private and government schools. The setting up of community libraries can also be explored.

Encouraging the production of multiple textbooks that are officially prescribed by schools will increasingly bring the private sector into the area of textbook production. In this context, it is important to equip state institutions for research and training in education to complete with private publishers and capacities built for this purpose. NGO'S have also produced excellent textbooks and supplementary materials that can be used in schools. Discussion of textbooks by parents, teachers and citizen's group must be encouraged, and they must be made available in the public domain for discussion, feedback, critique etc.

Encouraging Innovations

Individual teachers often explore new ways of transacting the curriculum in addressing the needs of the students within their specific classroom context (including constraints of space, large numbers, absence of teaching aids, diversity in the student body, the compulsions of examination, and so on). The sharing of teaching experiences and diverse classroom practices can provide opportunities for an academic discourse to develop within schools as teachers interact with and learn them from each other. This will also encourage new ideas and facilitate innovation and experimentation. There is a need to create structured spaces within schools, and at the level of cluster and block where teachers are encouraged to share and discuss classroom practices and experiences. It is also important to bring together groups of teachers within and across schools and provide support to them in terms of resources as well as time to work together. This is also, a need for documentation and research of identified 'good practices'. At present, there are funds for this purpose with DIETs and SSA also has funds for school-based research. Some of this could be used to document the diverse practices that teachers used in different classroom context. In addition to providing funds the creation of such environment that provides support to such initiatives is also important. Efforts should be made for mainstreaming the innovative processes and practices. The main objective of creating resource centres at the cluster level was to break the isolation of schools and bring teachers together for sharing their ideas and innovations with their peers. This is important if teachers are to develop their own professional identities and sense of belonging to a larger teaching community.

The Use of Technology

The intelligent and judicious use of technology can facilitate the educational programmes, management of the system, as well as help address specific learning needs and requirements. For instance, mass media can be used to support teacher training, facilitate classroom learning and can be used for advocacy. The use of ICT will help in self learning, teaching–learning at varied paces, dual modes of study etc. Technological innovations are also necessary for meeting the learning requirements of children's with special needs. Technology could be integrated with the larger goals and process of educational programmes instead of viewing in isolation. In this context, technological use that turns teachers and children into mere consumers and technology operators needs to be reviewed and discouraged. Interaction and intimacy are key to quality education, and this cannot be compromised as a principle in any curricular intervention.

Suggestions

In the light of these innovative ideas, the author has given certain suggestions:

- Teacher's autonomy should be increased so that the teacher can use diverse textbooks according to the ability/ needs of the child.
- Teacher educators should be encouraged to conduct researches on the textbooks in schools so that necessary changes can be done according to the changing needs of the society.
- Counseling of the students can be done by the teachers. Teacher can personally listen the problems of the students and guide them accordingly.
- In teacher education programmes, community surveys, work experience and N.S.S camps should be encouraged so that the community interaction can be increased.
- Financial aid should be given to the teachers so that they can use that fund for the purchase of new machines, teaching aids, etc.

- Teachers can develop their own websites, through which they can give their ideas to the students and students can use the sites according to their need and availability of time.
- Teachers should be aware of the student needs and abilities in order to use new technologies and techniques.
- In teacher education programmes projects and assignments on innovative ideas should be made compulsory.
- During the teaching practice student-teachers are encouraged to use their new ideas.
- Teachers can use Mind Maps to explain concepts in an innovative way. (Mind Maps were developed in the late 60's by Tony Buzan as a way of helping students make notes that used only key words and images).They are much quicker to make and much easier to remember and review because of their visual quality.

References

1. Government of India, (1986), *National Policy on Education,* 1986, GOI, New Delhi.
2. Government of India, (1992), *Programme of Action,* 1992, GOI, New Delhi.
3. Kohli, V.K., (1993), *Indian Education and its Problems,* Vivek Publishers, Ambala.
4. *National Curriculum Framework, (2005),* NCERT, New Delhi.
5. Singh, L.C. (ed), (1990), *Teacher Education in India*: Source Book, NCERT, New Delhi.
6. http://india.gov.in/sectors/education/national_council.php
7. http://www.vedamsbook.com/no23961.htm
8. http://math.arizona.edu/~atp~

Chapter–14

Role of Constructivist Pedagogy in Teacher Education Programme

Introduction

Constructivism is philosophical framework or a learning theory which argues humans construct meaning from current knowledge structure (Jean Piaget,1967). The basic values of constructivism emphasized on appropriate facilitator–supported learning that is initiated and directed by the learner. The idea of constructivism is that the learner must construct knowledge; the teacher cannot supply it (Bringuier,1980). The constructivist paradigm as advocated by Piaget (1981) and Bruner (1990), stress that whatever gets into the mind by the individual through knowledge discovery.

Russian psychologist, Lev Vygotsky's (1978) theory of Social Constructivism emphasizes the critical role of language and culture in human development. According to his ideas, knowledge exists in a social context and is, at least initially, shared by others rather than represented solely in the mind of the individual.

The recent National Curriculum Frame work of NCERT–2005, highlighted that there is an urgent need to bring Pedagogical reforms in teacher education programme in the light of constructivist learning theory. Further in the forwarding note of NCF–2005 by Prof Yash Pal, reiterates that the mother tongue is a conduit, that social, economic and ethical backgrounds are important for enabling

---

Dr. S.K. Mohanty, Sr. Lecture in RCIT, Najafgarh.

children to construct their own knowledge. He categorically emphasized on the role of constructivist pedagogy in school education and need to be incorporated in teacher education programme in India.

Basic Postulates of this learning Theory

The theory of constructivism is basically attributed to Jean Piaget (1967), who articulated mechanisms by which knowledge is internalized by the learner self. He advocated that through the process of accommodation and assimilation, individual constructs new knowledge from their experiences. In the process of assimilation, the learner incorporates the new experience into an already existing framework without changing that framework. In contrast (accommodation), when learners' experiences contradict their internal representations, they may change their perceptions of the experiences to fit their internal representations.

Lev Vygotsky's (1978) theory of social constructivism stresses on critical role of language and culture in human learning. It has significant implications for peer collaboration is that of zone of proximal development; language and social interaction; and the role play in helping the students acquiring and understand the culture in which they live.

Bruner (1967) on the theory of cognitive development of children, proposed three modes of representation (i.e Enactive – action based, Iconic-image based and Symbolic-language based) which help the successive mastery of any concept. He defines mental representation is a set of rules in term of which one's conserves encounters with events. Further suggests that a learner is capable of learning any subject so long a s instruction is organized appropriately. In his theory of learning, he emphasizes the role of language and culture in the development and construction of thoughts and knowledge.

- Learning is an active and social process.
- The learner as a unique individual.

- The importance of backgrounds and culture of the learner.
- Motivation for learning (fast hand experience, Glaserfeld, 1989).
- Support collaborative learning.
- Emphasizes Learning rather than instruction; opportunity for the creation of ideas and concept.
- Encourage the spirit of enquiry.
- Knowledge should be discovered as integrated whole.
- Features of Learner– centre curriculum

  The learner centered school curriculum has the following salient features:
  - How to learn is more important than what to learn.
  - Importance is given to the process of learning rather than to the product. The contents of text book are open ended type.
  - Learner– center approach in the classroom; activity-based classroom where the teacher is facilitator, and peer group learning in class.
  - Importance on learner's own space of learning and individual differences.
  - Multiple intelligence (EQ) theory instead of traditional intelligence quotient (IQ).
  - Continuous and comprehensive based evaluation.
  - Use of ICT in learning process.

Methods of Teaching: Constructivist approach basically emphasizes on learning rather than instruction and provides opportunities for the creation of ideas and concept. It stresses on the method of teaching such as laboratory work, field trips, peer discussions, collaborative, seminars, projects, debate, simulation would involve the learners as active participants in the process of learning; make their learning more challenging, enjoyable and adventure. Social constructivist pedagogy emphasised on discovery method, problem based method, enquiry based learning and learning by doing method.

Constructivist Teaching Sequence Given by Rosalind Driver–1989

A constructivist learning is an intervention where contextualized activities (task based) are used to provide learners with opportunity to discover and collaboratively construct meaning as the intervention unfolds. Learners are respected as a unique individual, and instructors act as facilitators rather than as teachers.

Teaching Sequence. Driver, 1989	
PHASE	**Overview**
Orientation	Teacher introduce the topic
Elicitation of ideas	Opportunities are provided for students to explore and explain their ideas.
Restructuring of Ideas -Clarification and exchange -Exposure to conflict situation	Students are given a chance to recognize scientific ideas and examine their own ideas.
Construction of new ideas. Evaluation	Students are provided with situation in which to test limitations of these ideas. Opportunities to test the validity of newly constructed ideas.
Application of ideas	Students are provided with opportunities to apply their ides in new situations, in order to reinforce their ideas.
Review change in ideas	Students are provided with opportunities to reflect upon how and why their ideas have changed.

Procedure of learning assessment: as a continuous and interactive process that measures the achievement of the learner.

Role of teacher in classroom and school: The teacher acts as a facilitator, co-learner, democratic leader, and as a diagnostician (Brooks and Brooks,1993).

Conclusion

The philosophical ideas of constructivism helps to the third generation teacher to apply Piaget's and Vygotsky's principles to classroom learning and development. It suggest that teacher must provide experiences, guide discussions and assume a supportive role in assisting students attempts at developing understanding. Social constructivism theory of Vygotsky stress on language and social interaction and the role play in helping the students acquiring and understand the culture in which they live.

References

1. Simon, B (1996). *Why no Pedagogy in England*: In Teaching and Learning in Secondary School , Bob Moon and Ann Shelton Mayyes, London: Macmillan.
2. John, Sagy (2008). *Constructivism and Child Centered*, Journal Edutrack, vol.6.
2. Kalara, R.M. (2005). *Pedagogy of Science in third World*: In Towards Quality Secondary Education (CBSE), Delhi: Vikas Publishing. pp. 218-223.
3. NCERT (2005): *National Curriculum Framework–2005*, New Delhi.
4. NCERT (2005): *National Focus Group Position Paper–2005,* Vol. II, New Delhi.
5. Siddiqi and Siddiqi (2005): *Teaching of Science: Today and Tomorrow*, New Delhi: Doaba House.
6. www.wikipedia.org: *constructivist intervention.*

Chapter–15

Role of Educational Technology Towards the Management of Learning Disabilities in the Classroom

Introduction

Teachers are expected to reach unattainable goals with inadequate tools. The miracle is that at times they achieve this impossible task. Schools, however, cannot survive on miracles. Every teacher deserves effective tools and skills. The question is; Can psychology provide them? Can therapeutic concepts be translated into specific educational practices?

The simple answer is "Yes".

On the basis of techniques developed in child therapy and tested in the classroom, concrete suggestions and practical solutions are offered in this paper for dealing with daily situation and psychological problems faced by all teachers with all the students and more so with the management of *special children.*

Teachers create environments. So do zoologists at the zoo and botanists at the arboretum. Learning is a common factor in all the artificial environments. Zoologists and botanists have a purpose to maintain the life of the creatures with which they work.

The learning is incidental to maintain healthy live organisms. Teachers maintain the life of their pupils but that is incidental to

1. *Dr. Amita Puri, Lecture in Education, Army Insititue of Education, Delhi Cantt.*

2. *Dr. Mahabir Yadav, Principal at Army Insititue of Education, Delhi Cantt.*

the main goal of learning. Brains operate differently. Learning occurs in different manners. The teacher must be able to determine if a pupil is exhibiting an alternate learning pattern or if the pupils has a learning problem. If the teacher suspects there are learning problems than it is necessary to seek assistance from the experts.

Problems Faced by the Teachers

In the beginning of their professional career, the reality that most teachers face, is the arrival of a variety of students having mild to severe disabilities.

Viewed by many administrators as a cost-cutting measure, inclusive education has been implemented with no increase in support personnel, specialized instructional materials, or adaptive technology to help the mainstream teacher meet the instructional needs of the exception students.

The debate over inclusion continues, and schools are left to develop their own models and schemes for implementing full inclusion. Little research is available to offer guidelines, and infusion of funding has not materialized to provide the kinds of support systems needed to address the move from a continuum of services to a one-size-fits-all paradigm.

Although returning exceptional children to the mainstream has always been a goal of special education, the need for more than one method of service delivery has been viewed as critical to rendering adequate service to students whose disabilities are varied and range from *mild profound.*

Many schools have embraced the inclusion philosophy with the assumption that good, regular education teachers can instruct all students appropriately. Although this assumption sounds flattering to the general education teacher, it overlooks the realities inherent in moving a variety of students with learning and behavior disorders into the typical classroom.

Regular classroom teachers are experts at teaching approaches for the vast majority of pupils.

Special Education teachers are experts at learning styles and alternate approaches to pupils who have a learning disability. Special education teachers provide an important resource for the classroom teacher.

Practical Management of the Child with Learning Problems

Special education teachers have a magic bag of alternate interventions that they might share. The first thing most protocols require is paperwork. The paperwork expected will include one or more of the following.

- **Basis record:** birth date, address, phone number, grade level, recent test scores etc.
- **Reasons for referral**: specific behaviors test scores or other relevant facts should be identified.
- **Intervention strategies**: data used, description, result.
- **Attendance record**: types of absences, tardiness, parent notes.
- **Teachers' log**: Dates, Observed behavior, etc.
- **Contact with parents**: dates and results.

The teacher pays many roles in the classroom. An important role is the recognition of pupils with learning difficulties. The teacher must be able to appraise the situation and decide on a course of action. Understanding the process and protocc of identifying a learning disabled child may help the teacher in understanding this important role. With 4 to 6 percent of all students classified as having specific learning disabilities (SLD) in our nation's public schools every teacher can expect to find students with learning disabilities in the classroom.

The pediatrician or family physician is often the first professional , parents contact when they become concerned that their child may have a learning problem. The physician thus has the opportunity to play a critical role in guiding parents toward appropriate evaluation and intervention.

Types of Learning Disorders and Diagnostic and Management Strategies

There are many types of learning disorders, and the diagnostic categories can be confusing for a number of reasons:

- First, the symptoms of most learning disorders overlap, making differential diagnosis difficult.
- Second, there is a high incidence of co-morbidity amount learning and behavioral disorders.
- Third, may of the symptoms are subjective, leading professionals and the general public to feel that these diagnoses are "in the eye of the beholder".
- Fourth, the many children, the manifestations of their learning disorders change over time. Although this can aid the clinician in diagnosis if he or she follows the child for several years, it makes initial diagnosis more difficult.

The most common learning disorders are described below, with hallmark characteristics, types of evaluations, and most appropriate intervention approaches discussed.

Speech/Language Disorder

This occurs in perhaps 10-15% of preschool and school-aged children and thus is very common. Language disorders can be broadly classified as either a language comprehensive (receptive) disorder or language expression (expressive) disorder, although may children with developmental language disorder have both.

Learning Disabilities

A learning disability (LD) is defined as a significant, persistent deficit in one or more academic achievement areas, including reading, writing, and mathematics. Specific deficits in language and reasoning skills also may be considered a learning disability. A conservative estimate is that about 5% to 10% of children have LD. Tremendous progress has been made in understanding and treating the most common learning disability dyslexia.

Dyslexia refers to reading and spelling disability and is usually associated with deficits in specialized language skills that enable us to perceive and mentally manipulate individual letter sounds within words. These skills are collectively referred to as phonological processing skills, which have been shown to comprise the core deficit for most individuals with dyslexia. In most cases, dyslexia is a language-based disorder.

Some of the more prevalent learning disabilities are:

(a) Reading disabilities (dyslexia)

(b) Disability to comprehend or speak-Dysphasia

(c) Writing disabilities – Dysgraphia

(d) Arithmetic disabilities (dysgraphia)

(e) Disability to express orally – aphasia

(f) Disability to read or write printed matter – Alexia

Early identification of children at risk for dyslexia is now possible due to the widespread availability of brief phonological processing tests. To diagnose LD, a child needs comprehensive psychological and educational testing to identify patterns of learning strengths and deficits. Such assessment can also identify co-morbid conditions, such as language disorder, attention-deficit/hyperactivity disorder (ADHD), anxiety or depression that need to be treated concomitantly with the LD.

Although dyslexia presents itself somewhat differently in each person, it has some common characteristics that can be determined through evaluation techniques. It is important to address reading problems early so that the child can get appropriate help.

- There are several things one can do to help the child remain interested in learning her letters. A multi-sensory approach can be tried. The child may be a tactile learner instead of an auditory or visual learner, or she may just need a variety of sensory input to learn best. Help her to identify how each sound feels on her mouth. Use a mirror to help. For example your lips come together for/m/.

- One may also want to try coming up with a rhyme or song about each letter.
- Use alphabet magnets or alphabet coolie cutters with clay in lieu of flash cards. These activities may be more fun and engaging than flashcards and help the child develop her communication.
- Use pictures. Give your child a picture (e.g. a cat) and have her sound out the name while placing marbles, drawing marks, or tapping her fingers for each of the individual sounds in the word (e.g., /c/.../a/.../t/ is composed of 3 sounds, thus the child would use 3 marbles, marks, or taps.) Stick with short words with a consonant-vowel-consonant pattern, like bat, top, pen, dad, etc. you can also clap or tap out the number of syllables in a word.
- Sometimes online products claim to cure dyslexia. One must remember that dyslexia is a neurological difference in the way language is processed by the brain. It is not a disease that can be cured or a habit that cane broken, but there are effective educational strategies that can be used to help people with dyslexia become successful readers. These strategies take time and effort. There is not a magic, quick or easy solution. Any product or program claiming to "cure" it is misleading.
- Several excellent teaching programs designed to improve phonological processing skills, reading, and spellings are available and can be used in either individual or group instruction.
- Explicit training in phonological processing and phonics has been shown to result in the best gains long-term for most children with dyslexia. Although it is rare to completely "cure" dyslexia, the long-term prognosis is better when appropriate intervention is initiated early in elementary school.
- Family consultation with a psychologist who is knowledgeable about LD diagnosis, teaching approaches, and educational options is often beneficial, as it may save

families time and money in finding the best services for their child's needs.

- Remedial techniques that explicitly address critical language units, including letter sounds, syllables and words are likely to be most successful long-term.

Mental Retardation

(a) Slow learners – (IQ 75 to 89 IQ)

(b) Mild mentally retarded (IQ 60-65 to 70-75 IQ)

(c) Moderate Mentally Retarded (IQ 35-40 to 60-65 IQ)

(d) Severely retarded (IQ 20-25 to 30-35 IQ)

(e) Profoundly retarded (IQ 20-25 and below).

Mental retardation occurs in approximately 3% of the population and is defined as having intelligence and adaptive functioning two or more standard deviations below normal. Its is diagnosed using psychological and educational tests similar to those used for an LD evaluation.

Most mentally retarded youngsters require long-term special education. Some main streaming into the regular curriculum may be appropriate for those with mild mental retardation.

Pervasive Developmental Disorder/Autism

Pervasive developmental disorder (PDD) is a broad class of disorders for which autism is the most well known subtype. Current incidence estimates indicate that approximately one child per 1,000 has autism, although recent studies suggest a higher incidence rate (1:500), which may reflect a growing awareness of milder cases with normal intelligence.

Attention-Deficit/Hyperactivity Disorder

Attention-Deficit/Hyperactivity Disorder (ADHD) is characterized by poor sustained attention, impulsive and distractible behavior, and sometimes hyperactivity. It is one of the most controversial diagnoses in existence. Approximately 3% to 5% of school-age minor education accommodations in the regular classroom. For those with severe AD/HD or concomitant LD, special education may be necessary.

Gifted Children with Learning Disabilities

These are the students with an outstanding gift or talent and are capable of high performance, but who also have a learning disability that makes some aspect of academic achievement difficult. Some of these students are identified and their needs are met. This happens only rarely, however, unless a school specifically decides to identify and then serve these students. The majority of students who are gifted with learning disabilities "fall through the cracks" in the system.

Other Behavioral and Emotional Disorders

Many childhood behavioral and emotional disorders manifest themselves as school performance problems, inattention, and hyperactivity, which may be the symptoms that a parent first discusses with a physician.

Some of the more common disorders in this category include anxiety, depression, oppositional-defiant disorder, conduct disorder, and obsessive-compulsive disorder. Thus, we see that various disabilities hamper classroom performance, play upon the patience of the regular classroom teacher who has to keep on devising and designing new techniques to deal with learning disabled children.

Using Technology in the Classroom

Technology can open doors and break down barriers for children, youth, and adults with disabilities. Whether in the classroom or workplace, assistive technology (including devices, software, recordings, and much more) can increase, maintain, or improve the capabilities of individuals with disabilities. Also, technology that is used by everyone, such as spell check, can be particularly helpful to people with learning disabilities. Here we explore new developments in technology that can accommodate people with learning disabilities.

For example, in the management of AD/HD, social skills training is given, using various techniques.

Social Skills Training

Many children with AD/HD have difficulty with social relationships because of impulsiveness, lack of attention to social feedback, or behaviors that are perceived by others as immature, aggressive, or defiant.

Although most children develop social skills by observing and interacting with others, the child with AD/HD may not as readily profit from these interactions or may have diminished opportunity to learn because of social rejection. A number of **social skills training programs** are now becoming available for use by teachers (Walker & Fabre, 1991; Walker et. al., 1983), which address a variety of social skill deficits that occur in school settings.

Some of these social skills curricula are designed to systematically cover a variety of topics such as basic manners, asking for help and permission to do things, beginning and carrying on a conversation, initiating a play activity, sharing belongings, recognizing and expressing feelings, dealing with aggression, developing friendships, responding to group pressure, demonstrating sportsmanship, and a variety of other essential social skills.

User of Computer for Management of Di:ability

As computers and networks become indispensable in the information age, access to these tools is important for all students. Computer technologies have the potential to help children with disabilities who then become more fully participating and contributing members of society. They can be used as tools for communicating, accessing information, writing, learning, and performing other tasks. For individuals with disabilities they can help assure equal opportunities in education and facilitate the transition to work and community living.

Compensatory Tool

Participation in school activities can be difficult for individuals who cannot write, see, speak, or hear. Besides using computers for the same purposes as non-disabled student, children with disabilities can use them as compensatory tools to overcome functional limitations imposed by their disabilities. Technology can be used to increase sensory input, enhance mobility, perform as a prosthesis, and facilitate receptive and expressive communication. For example, a portable computer equipped with speech output can be used as a "voice" in class discussions for a child who cannot speak.

A computer with adaptive technology can be used as a writing or drawing instrument by someone who cannot use his/her hands. In short, computers make it possible for students with disabilities to perform tasks for themselves that they otherwise would be dependent on others to perform. Once satisfactory methods are found to operate computers, new activities are open to disabled students and the amount of time that it takes to complete their work can be reduced. Application of appropriate technology early in life is useful because it enables children to control their environment, may even help prevent learned helplessness.

Computer Assisted Instruction

Computers allow students with disabilities to more independently participate in learning activities and thereby reduce the impact of their disabilities on acquisition and use of skills and concepts. Drill and practice, tutorial, simulation, word processing, problem-solving, and other software programs give these students learning opportunities that would not be available in other ways. For example, word processing and tutorial software may help students with hearing, learning, and language disabilities develop language and writing skills. Educational software where the computer provides multi-sensory experiences, interaction, positive reinforcement, individualized instruction, and repetition can be useful in skill building for children with specific learning disabilities.

Special software can even teach children who are severely and multiply disabled the concept of cause-effect by demonstrating that their actions (e.g., hitting a switch) have an impact on their environment (e.g., a picture is created, music is played, or a toy is activated). Computers offer infinite patience, learner control, immediate feedback, branching capabilities, multi-sensory interaction, and a non-threatening learning environment. Some of their qualities that teachers of exceptional children have found to be particularly powerful include their ability to hold attention, increase motivation, and enhance self-concept.

Access to Information

Computers and networks provide new options for accessing information through on-line library catalogs, encyclopedias, dictionaries, journals, books, newspapers, databases, and other resources. For those with disabilities that make it difficult to visit libraries and/or turn pages of publications, information sources on networks, CD-ROM, and other media provide opportunities to independently read publications on their computer screens. Computer technology can also assist in the process of media conversion. For example, a blind student who has the technology to access newspapers and journals on-line can use adaptive software and hardware to read the materials aloud or print them in Braille. The expansion of networking service around the world gives disable students equipped with appropriate technology access to a wealth of resources without assistance and reduces the necessity to move about.

Electronic Communication

Telecommunications is a powerful mode of communication. Those with hearing and speech impairments who have personal computer, modem and appropriate software can communicate with others on electronic networks. When teachers use computer-mediated communications for classroom discussions, they allow deaf and speech-impaired students to communicate on an equal level with other students. By stimulating and enhancing interactions with peers, electronic communication can also facilitate social and language development.

Adaptive Technology that Provides Computer Access

Some students with disabilities face barriers to providing computer input, interpreting output, and reading documentation. Thousands of commercially available adaptive hardware and software products have been developed to provide functional alternatives to standard operations. Some computer devices assist individuals with a variety of disabilities. For example, equipment which provides flexibility in the positioning of monitors, keyboards, and table tops is useful for many disabled users. Adjustable copy holders can also ease accessibility. Similarly, the availability of portable computers can assist students with note taking and communication in classes. Some other approaches to removing input, output, and documentation barriers for children with specific disabilities are described below:

Input

Software that aids in efficient and accurate input can assist some learning disabled students. Children can compensate for high rates of input errors by using spell checkers, thesauruses, and grammar checkers. In addition, word prediction programs (software that predicts whole words from fragments) have been used successfully by students with learning disabilities. Macro software which expands. Abbreviations can reduce the necessity to memorize keyboard commands and can ease the entry of commonly-used text.

Output

Some learning disabled children find adaptive devices designed for individuals with visual impairments useful. In particular, large print displays, alternative colors on the computer screen, and voice output can compensate for some visual and reading problems. People who have difficulty interpreting visual material can improve comprehension and the ability to identify and correct errors when words are printed in large fonts or spoken.

Documentation

Computer documentation provided in electronic forms can be used by enlarged character and voice synthesis devices to make it accessible to those with reading difficulties.

To Sum Up

Students with disabilities face barriers to educational opportunities and careers. However, computers are helping to remove some of these barriers. As word processors replace typewriters, electronic spreadsheets replace typewriters, electronic spreadsheets replace handwritten books, and on-line services replace telephone and written communication, disabled students who have computer access become capable of handling a wider rang of activities independently.

Thus, despite technology and with technology, it is the teacher who is the decisive element in the classroom. He has the power to humiliate or humour, hurt or heal. In all situations, it is his response that decides whether a crisis will be escalated or de-escalated and a child humanize or dehumanized. Teachers are actually the experts in effective and affective education. In today's scientific milieu, it is still the human knowledge that precedes technological development.

References

1. St. Clair, K.l. (1989). Counseling gifted students: a historical review. *Roeper Review*, 12 (2), 98-102.
2. Hickey, G. (1988). Goals of gifted programs: Perceptions of interested groups. *Gifted Child Quarterly*, 32 (1), 231-235.
3. Gunderson, C.W., et. al. (1987). The gifted/learning disabled student. *Gifted Child Quarterly*, 31(4), 158-160.
4. Chalfant, J.C. (1989). Learning disabilities: Policy issues and promising approaches. *American Psychologist*, 44 (2), 392-398.

5. Hammil, D. D. (1990). On defining learning disabilities: An emerging consensus. *Journal of Learning Disabilities*, 23, 74-94.

6. Silverman, L. K. (1989). Invisible gifts, invisible handicaps, *Roeper Review,* 12, 37-42.

7. Aaron, P.G., Phillips, S. & Larsen, S. (1988). Specific reading disability in historically famous persons. *Journal of Learning Disabilities*, 21, 523-538.

8. Adelman, H.S. (1992). LD: The next 25 years. *Journal of Learning Disabilities*, 25, 17-22.

9. Association for Children with Learning Disabilities (1985). Definition of the condition of specific learning disabilities. *ACLD News briefs*, 158, 1-3.

10. Biederman, J. et. al. (1997). Correspondence between DSM-III-R and DSM-IV attention-deficit/hyperactivity disorder. *Journal of the American Academy of Child and Adolescent Psychiatry*, 36, 1682-1687.

11. Jordan NC, Goldsmith-Phillips J. (1994). *Learning Disabilities: New Directions for Assessment and Intervention.* Boston: Allyn and Bacon.

12. *American Psychiatric Association. Diagnostic and Statistical manual of Mental Disorders. 4th ed.* Washington, D.C.: American Psychiatric Association; 1994: 78-85.

13. MacArthor, C.A, et. al. (2001). Technology applications for students with literacy problems: a critical review. *The Elementary School,* 101, 273-301.

14. Mastropieri, M.A., et. al. (1996). Reading comprehension: A synthesis of research in learning disabilities. *Invention Research.* 10 (Part-B), 201-227. Greenwich, CT: JAI Press.

15. Meyes, Laura. (1994). Access and Meaning: The Keys to Effective Computer Use by Children with language Disabilities. *Journal of Special Education Technology.* 12(3), 256-75.

16. Rosegrant, Teresa 1985. using the Microcomputer as a Tool for Learning to Read and Write. *Journal of Learning Disabilities*. 18 (2), 113-15.

Chapter–16

Somatic Inkblot Series (SIS): An Introduction

The Somatic Inkblot Series (SIS) developed in 1984 is a structured, projective, diagnostic procedure and is an adjunct to psychotherapy and counseling. The SIS is structured by a sequential presentation of intentionally designed and field tested inkblot like image. These images demonstrate typical and atypical response potentials. The SIS procedure is projective because it is based on spontaneous, individually generated responses to semi-ambiguous figures which elicit intra-psychic associations specific to the person presented with them.

Existing Inkblot Tests

There are three major standardized tests based on inkblots. The pioneer amongst them was the *Rorschach* Inkblot test published in 1921. It's a test of measuring the subject's psychopathology and personality. A research publication by Reynolds and Sundberg (1976) ranked the Rorschach as number one. They based their findings on Buros Mental Measurement Year Book. A survey conducted on the members of The American Psychological Association Division–12 and the Indian Association of Clinical psychologists showed concerns from respondents about

1. *Dr. Amita Puri, Lecture in Education, Army Insititue of Education, Delhi Cantt.*

2. *Dr. Mahabir Yadav, Principal at Army Insititue of Education, Delhi Cantt.*

the limitations of the test (Wade et. al., 1978, Dubey 1982). Seven major failures were enumerated;

1. Failure to provide an objective system, free of arbitrary conventions and showing high inter scorer agreement.
2. Lack of satisfactory internal consistency or test retest reliability.
3. Failure to provide cogent evidence for clinical validity.
4. Failure to provide cogent evidence for clinical validity.
5. Lack of prognostic or predictive validity with respect to the outcome of treatment of later behavior.
6. Individual differences between groups of normal subjects.
7. Failure to find any significant relationships between Rorschach scores and intelligence or creative ability.

Holtzman (1956) pointed out that much of the controversy over the Rorschach arises from the failure to distinguish between the Rorschach as a projective technique in the hands of a skilled clinician and Rorschach as a psychometric device that yields scores having relevance for personality assessment. The advantage which Holtzman introduced in his test was to offer an alternate series of the inkblot stimuli test for reassessing the personality after some type of intervention. Holtzman provided 45 cards in each series. The subject is required to give one response per card. Holtzman categorically selected only 22 variable such as: reaction time, location, form appropriateness, colour, shading, movements, pathogonomic verbalization, integration, human, animal, anatomy, anxiety, hostility etc. the Holtzman test has wide application and is popular. However, the research output is not as prolific as the of Rorschach test.

The **Somatic Inkblot Service** (SIS) is a recent extension of the traditional inkblot projective techniques. The test was developed specifically to understand the manifestation of problems through Summarization and to hear the suffering individual's "inner cry". The test images are viewed on a television using a video cassette recorder (VCR). The subject's responses are recorded on a separate response sheet.

The SIS originally conceived in 1959, after years of research and field testing on SIS–1, the SIS–II (62–image Booklet Form) was developed in 1980. As a result of tremendous success of the success of the booklet form, the SIS-Video (Video version of 62 images Booklet Form) was launched in 1984. It provides diagnostic and therapeutic aid. This SIS-Video is a self administered test consisting of five segments.

1. A series of beautiful flowers to reduce test anxiety.
2. An instructional section in which a "subject" illustrates how to give free associations to a video inkblot.
3. An induction period in which semi hypnotic relaxation suggestions are given.
4. A test section in which 62 specifically designed images having colour, structured from and at times, movements are presented.
5. A recovery portion in which a series of non threatening nature scenes, combined with upbeat music, bring the viewer back to the time and space reality of the test situation.

The viewer writes responses on an answer sheet. Viewing the SIS has both diagnostic an therapeutic applications that are far reaching.

The SIS Video is highly innovative and may be termed as a "time machine". It takes the viewers away from the present reality.

Need for Development of SIS

Projective techniques, particularly inkblot tests are especially helpful in evaluating patients with limited language and verbal skills such as children, foreign born or new immigrants, native people, the learning disabled or mentally subnormal. There is enough structure in many of the inkblots to provide a sense of security and a measure of self confidence. Those with limited language and verbal skills usually rely more on verbalization and adapt better to projective technique than verbal interviews or testing the requires reading or language skills. Such images use the language of dreams, visual imagery and symbolic thought, the most basic forms of thinking and expression. It is also the language of repression and brings whatever is buried in the mind closer the consciousness, accessible for processing.

With such strong notions in mind, cassell stared developing the Somatic Inkblot Series.

Somatic Inkblot Series–I: 20 Cards

SIS–I consists of 20 inkblot images printed on white cares, each measuring 16.5 x 20.5 cms. The images are printed in black, red and grey (Screened black). Eight of them are black and red (serial no. l, 2, 3, 4, 5, 6, 7, 8), three are exclusively red (serial nos. 10, 11, 12) and nine are achromatic (serial nos. 9, 13, 14, 15, 16, 17, 18, 19, 20).

Apart from using it as a diagnostic tool, SIS can be used to help design a treatment program which might include body awareness exercises, such as physical therapy. It also may be used in many other therapies such a sensory feedback training, behaviour therapy etc. (Cassell, 1977).

Somatic Inkblot Series–II: Booklet (62 images)

It consist of A series and B series, each with 31 images for a combined series total of 62 images. There is also a sample image in the beginning. The stimulus images are printed in rectangles measuring about 5 x 6 cm., each with a space provided below the image for writing the response. All the images are contained in an eight page booklet. The first seven pages consist of the stimulus images and the space for responses. The last page is printed with instructions for self administration, and a place for a brief health history and personal data. Unlike SIS–1, it consists of images printed with blue ink on grey paper.

As there is no time limit, "anxiety" is reduced, and the individual is free to react in his time, often exhibiting significant verbal an non verbal clues to each of the inkblots. Since there is not test to read, the Somatic Inkblot Series does not require a high reading level, therefore, it is applicable to all age groups and a wide variety of cultures.

In SIS–II, the subject is asked to rate the three inkblot images that he "most liked" and the three images that he "least liked". This inquiry invites positive or negative charge. The subjects emotional investment provides valuable diagnostic clues to his/her psychological function.

Administration of the SIS

The administration of the SIS is designed to maximize the pulling power of inkblot projection. The subject is given an answer booklet. The first section includes a health questionnaire. The process of filling out the health questionnaire create an immediate perceptual set to project images related to medical and psychiatric problems for themselves or for loved ones. The space/time dimensions of the viewing situation are subtly altered by the video presentation of mesmerizing flowers. These are electronically transformed so that viewers experience a magical feeling of traveling through a mental garden of beautiful flowers. Following this sequence, a photograph of a beautiful mountain, followed by an artist's rendition of the same scene, heightens the hypnotic effect.

By writing responses, rather than verbalizing them just like in hypnotic writing, the subject may more readily access and release painful material. In addition to the cathartic therapeutic responses, the person may gain some insight and sense of mastery of the traumatic material by the act of drawing and labeling the images.

In many instances, there is a sufficient richness of material elicited by interviewing the subject concerning the "threatening" images that little more needs to be delved into. Occasionally, an insightful subject may after having completed the procedure or having experienced previously repressed post traumatic dreams, opens the interview with a statement about how helpful it was.

Application of SIS

In clinical settings, the Somatic Inkblot Series (SIS) has both diagnostic and therapeutic applications. In regard to the former, it has been used extensively as a structured, projective, diagnostic procedure. Through the power of projection, it can reveal material from the inner self (Cassell 2002, Dosajh 1999, Dubdy 2000, Verma 2000). The 62 image series ranges from those that are relatively unstructured, to the semi structured, to the highly structured. This affords the trained examiner a wide range of opportunities for the comprehensive examination of the subjects cognitive and emotional processes.

Research data obtained from a variety of clinical setting internationally indicates that the clinical investigations using the SIS technology can distinguish different diagnostic categories with acceptable levels of statistical confidence. (Dubey et. al. 1995, Verma, et. al. 2002). SIS has been proven to provide a useful aide to therapy by a number of innovative clinicians. (Mishra et. al. 2001, Verma et. al. 2001).

In addition, industrial psychologists have found the SIS particularly useful as a technique for the assessment of personality and vocational ability in industrial settings. (Dubey 1993, 1996, 2002).

Apart from the above, the SIS may be used as a guide to develop personalized usual imagery for meditation and enhanced spiritual awareness. Many images can be used in innovative ways to take the subject through the various stages of biological metamorphism. Image B19 can symbolize of conception and the origin of the individuals' body. Image A 26 deicts can intrauterine phase of existence. Viewing this can lead to philosophical speculation about the down of the viewer's psychological and spiritual energies. Image B27 suggests a live d\fetus on the right and a dead one on the left. Here, the projective discussion can explore the precarious nature of life as well as the unfairness of suffering holding a child. This can serve to stimulate discussion on early childhood experiences with parental figures and other past caregivers.

The Cry for Help

Clinicians worldwide have heard the cry for help in a variety of ways. These ranges form abused children who escape stress through dissociagive disorders to victims of catastrophe of war, who suffer from post-traumatic stress disorders.

The Somatic Inkblot Series can help therapists more sensitively "hear" a suffering individuals cry for help the "inner cry" that is not only hidden from others, but often hidden from one's own conscious awareness as well. This is the "magic", the unique and distinguishing feature of projective testing.

While the SIS uses Somatic Inkblots that involve body and organ imagery, a variety of personal problems and mental disorders have been identified by them also. SIS have been successfully used in alleviating examination anxiety (Cassell, 2002). This test sees to have great future in the hands of innovative educationists too, apart from clinicians and therapists.

References

1. Cassell, W. (2003). Conceptualization of SIS procedure. *Journal of Projective Psychology & Mental Health* 10 (1), 9-11.
2. Cassel, W.A. (2002). Symbolism in Violent Hallucinations, SIS *Journal of Projective Psychology & Mental Health* 9:81-92.
3. Dozajh (1999). A case of Family Therapy. SIS *Journal of Projective Psychology & Mental Health* 6:2, 4-6.
4. Dubey, (1982). *A Pragmatic view of Rorschach Inkblot Technique*. National Psychological Corporation. Agra, India.
5. Dubey, B.L. (1992). *Diagnostic utility of Somatic Inkblot Video.* Proceedings of 50th International Council of Psychologists, Amsterdam, July 1992.

6. Dubey, B.L. (2002). SIS Technology in Millennium Year SIS *Journal of Projective Psychology & Mental Health* 7: 91-92.

7. Holtzman, (1956). *Inkblot Perception and Personality*. University of Texas Press, Texas, U.S.A.

8. Mishra, M. (2001). Therapeutic utility of SIS–II, SIS *Journal of Projective Psychology & Mental Health* 8: 51-52.

9. Reynolds and Sundberg, (1996). A survey of Rorschach Teaching in APA approved Clinical Graduated Programs. *Journal of Personality Assessment*. 40: 228-233.

10. Significance of SIS–II. *Journal of Projective Psychology & Mental Health* 2: 72-76.

11. Verma, (2000). Distortions of Body Image on SIS–II and DAP Test. SIS *Journal of Projective Psychology & Mental Health* 7: 39-43.

12. Verma, (2002). SIS as an instrument of Change. SIS *Journal of Projective Psychology & Mental Health* 8: 1-2.

13. Wade et. al., (1978). The Status of Psychological Testing in Clinical Psychology: Relationship between Test use and Professional activities and orientations. *Journal of Personality Assessment*. 42: 3-10.

Chapter–17

Implementing the NCF-2005: Vision of Teacher Education

Introduction

"Teacher Education for Curriculum Renewal" is taken up in chapter-5: "Systemic Reforms" of the NCF–2005. Section 5.2 and its 3 subsection 5.2.1 through 5.2.3 deal with teacher education. While Teacher Education sections 5.2.1 and 5.2.3 describe Vision for Teacher Education and 'Major Shifts in Teacher Education Programme'. The Vision for Teacher Education starts with the two macro roles of the teacher envisaged in the NCF viz. encouraging supportive and humane facilitator in teaching learning situations to enable learners (students) to discover their talents, realize their physical and intellectual potentialities to the fullest, and to develop character and desirable social and human values to function as responsible citizens; and active member of a group of persons who makes a conscious effort for curricular renewal so that it is relevant to changing social needs and the personal needs of learners.

The document recommends that to be able to realize this vision, teacher education must comprise the following features to enable student teachers to:

- Understand the way learning occurs and to create plausible situations conducive to learning.View knowledge as personal experiences constructed in the shared context of

Dr. Vandana Ghai, Lecture in Army Insititue of Education, Delhi Cantt.

teaching learning rather than embedded in the external reality of textbooks.

- Be sensitive to the social professional and administrative contexts in which they need to operate.
- Develop appropriate competencies to be able to not only seek the above-mentioned understanding in actual situations, but also be able to create them.
- Attain a sound knowledge base and proficiency in language.
- Identify their own personal expectations, perceptions of self, capacities and inclinations.
- Consciously attempt to formulate one's own professional orientation as a teacher in situation specific contexts.
- View appraisal as a continuous educative process.
- Develop an artistic and aesthetic sense in children through art education.
- Address the learning needs of all children, including those who are marginalized and disabled.
- In the context of change perspective, it is imperative to pursue an integrated model of teacher education for strengthening the professionalization of teachers.
- Develop the needed counseling skills and competencies to be a 'facilitator' for and 'helper' of children needing specific kinds of help in finding solution for day to day problems related to educational, personal and social situations.
- Learn how to make productive work a pedagogic medium for acquiring knowledge in various subjects, developing values and training multiple skills.

NCF–2005 also presents an eight point version which states that 'teachers need to be prepared to:

- Case for children, and should love to be with them.
- understand children within social, cultural and political contexts.

- be receptive and be constantly learning.
- view learning as a search for meaning out of personal experience, and knowledge generation as a continuously evolving process of reflective learning.
- view knowledge not as an external reality embedded in textbooks, but as constructed in the shared context of teaching learning and personal experience.
- own responsibility towards society and work to build a better world.
- Appreciate the potential of productive work and hands on experience as a pedagogic medium both inside and outside the classroom.
- Analyze the curricular framework, policy implications and texts.

The NCF–2005 envisages major shifts in teacher education so that teachers may be abled to perform their expected roles. These shifts would necessitate abandoning the status quo and embracing and institutionalizing recommended emphases. These can be briefly expressed as under:

Expected Major Shifts

From	To
Teacher centric, stable designs	Learner centric, flexible process
Teacher direction & decisions	Learner autonomy
Teacher guidance & monitoring	Facilitates, supports & encourages learning
Passive reception in learning	Active participation in learning
Learning within the four walls of the classroom	Learning in the wider social context
Knowledge as 'given' and fixed	Knowledge as it evolves and is created
Disciplinary focus	Multi-disciplinary, educational focus
Linear exposure	Multiple & divergent exposure
Appraisal, Short, Few	Multifarious, continuous.

Critical Comments

While the objectives delineating the 'Vision for teacher education' have been well stated and are comprehensive, the road-map to achieve these has not been described anywhere in the NCF–2005. However, 'The New T E P describes the Needed Action in the Position Paper on 'Teacher Education for Curriculum' offers seven suggestions. Considered vis a vis the objectives, these are too few and it would have helped teacher educators a lot more if these were made more situation specific and action oriented.

There is absolutely no doubt that the prevailing system of teacher education, the pre-service as well as the in service needs to be thoroughly reformed. Teacher Educators by and large need a blue print on how to get away from the existing one and to replace it with the one suggested in the NCF–2005.

The NCF was published in December 2005. More than three years have passed and the Indian universities have hardly prepared any plan of action for the suggested nine major shifts in teacher education programmes.

Initiating action for the suggested changes would be possible only if the UGC and the Universities take the NCF vision for teacher education seriously and promote the NCF vision among the universities and formulate a plan of action with annual targets that are to be attained by each university.

If bottom up approach has to be the means for attaining the NCF vision then faculty members of a cluster of local teacher education institutions would need to come together and discuss how best the necessary changes can be initiated, sustained and achieved.

In order to make the bottom up approach successful, the management of non-aided teacher education institutions would also need to promote the NCF vision. How best this can be done needs to be considered by the Universities, the UGC, the NCTE and possibly the MHRD.

Positive attitude to children and their training is essential to realizing the NCF vision for teacher education. However, bringing about any meaningful change in adults is not an easy task. It takes a relatively longer duration and sustained effort to about somewhat stable change in an adult. Teacher Education Programmes of one year duration are totally unsuitable for promoting a significant and stable change in student teachers.

At present the two year B.Ed. programme is offered by the Regional Institute of Education of the NCERT. The University of Delhi plans to offer the two year B.Ed. programme instead of its one year programme. The four year B.Ed. programme is now available in a number of colleges of the University of Delhi. But hardly any study has been conducted on how duration of a teacher education programme impacts student teacher's attitude towards children especially the differently-abled and supporting and caring for their learning. It is time that such research is conducted on teacher education programmes of different duration.

Conclusion

Judged by its objectives and promise of caring and supporting and humane teacher education, the NCF–2005 vision of the teacher education is refreshingly path breaking. One would also say that in its present form it is incomplete. This is so because its details in terms of curriculum components are yet to be worked out. It has unmistakable reflection of Constructivism. And it is this feature that makes it so promising. Once implemented, it would surely transform the teacher education system and the school education system in our country. All the more reason that it be given a fair trail and its effects in terms of the change in the mindsets of teachers and learners be researched and documented.

Chapter–18

Constructivist Classroom Activities for Biology Learning

Let us compare the biology teaching of two of my student teachers.

Classroom–A: Biology Teacher – Padamaja

Padamaja was teaching 'Ecosystem' in her biology classroom. Padamaja considered science to be a body of knowledge to be learned. Her job was to "give out" what she (and the textbook) knew about science to her students. Thus the learning environment Padamaja tried to maintain in her classroom facilitated this transfer of knowledge; the desks were neatly in rows facing the teacher and the blackboard. Lecture notes and assignments from the text were given to students. Padamaja tried to keep students quiet and working all during the class period to ensure that all students could "absorb" the science knowledge efficiently. Another consequence of Padamaja's notion of teaching and learning was her belief that she had to cover so much that she had no time for laboratory activities.

Let's look at an example that typifies Padamaja's teaching style. Padamaja's students were to complete a worksheet that "covered" the concept of ecosystem. In this worksheet students were given certain exercises on food-chains like to fill the names of organisms at certain trophic levels. Some questions like what will happen if grass is missing in the grass–deer–lion food chain

Dr Bharti Dogra, Lecturer in Army Institute of Education, Delhi Cantt

were also included in the worksheet. After the students completed the worksheet, Padamaja went over the answers so the students could have the correct answers for the test later in the week. From a constructivist perspective, what opportunities did Padamaja's students have to relate the concept of ecosystem to their own experiences? Were these opportunities in Padamaja's lesson plan were provided to negotiate meanings and build a consensus of understanding? Padamaja spent one class period covering the concept of ecosystem; is that sufficient time for students to learn a concept with understanding?

Classroom – B: Biology Teacher – Alka Basu

Alka Basu is another student teacher whose classes, in contrast, were inspired by constructivism. This student teacher was given four topics by her school biology teacher:

(1) Organization of the living world,

(2) Nutrition,

(3) Respiration, and;

(4) Blood Circulation.

Her classes were always student-centered and activity-based. At secondary level, she introduced students to above mentioned biology topics with short lectures, textbook readings, and confirmatory laboratories. After the introduction she would ask students what interested them about the topic and encouraged them to pursue and test these ideas. Students usually divided themselves into groups and then, conducted a library research, formulated questions/problems, and procedures to test the questions/problems. In other words, the students were acting as scientists in the classroom. In one class she was teaching students about ecosystem. Included in Alka's lessons were activities to get the students involved. Students were shown the 'Aquarium' in the biology laboratory. They discussed:

- different food-chains in this man-made ecosystem,
- how different living organisms depend on each other in an ecosystem,

- use of dissolved oxygen in water by aquatic plants and animals,
- what happens if any particular trophic level is missing in the food-chain?

Students were also involved in role-play activity where they played the roles of different plants and animals in different food-chains. They used certain props and few dialogues in the role-play activity. Few cases were also discussed where when the rain forest was cut then many of the animals became extinct due to destruction of their habitat. Then a few animal sanctuaries were discussed to highlight the importance of habitat for wild animals. Alka spent two weeks teaching this topic on *ecosystem*. Were Alka's students given opportunities to make sense of the concept of ecosystem? Were they able to use personal experiences? Whose students do you think had a deeper understanding of ecosystem?

A close understanding of the two classrooms has revealed the following points of difference between them.

	Classroom – A	**Classroom – B**
Materials	Primarily textbook	Includes Primary sources and other resources
Learning	Based on repetition, explanation by the teacher.	Interactive and build on what the student already knows.
Knowledge	Seen as inert, to be passed on from teacher to taught	Seen as dynamic, ever changing, to be constituted by the learner.
Teacher's Role	Giver of information, rooted in authority	Creative collaborator, facilitator, mentor, guide who moderates, suggests, coaches.
Student's Role	Passive recipients of knowledge	Interactive, construct their own knowledge based on previous experiences, ask questions, explore, experiment, reflect, discuss.

	Classroom – A	Classroom – B
Transaction Strategies	Teaching facing class	Group Work and Pair Work, using peers as Resources
Approach	Lecture method, teacher asking questions as well as answering them.	Construction of meaning by learner by formulating their own questions-inquiry allowing multiple interpretations and expressions of learning – multiple intelligence encouraging collaborating learning.
Learning Process	Teacher led class. Students' are not used as a resource for learning.	Students' full participation in learning activities such as projects and hands-on experiments. Collaboration among students, peer teaching helps them to review and reflect on their learning processes and pick up strategies and methods from one another.

As a teacher educator in Army Institute of Education, I got the privilege of supervising the biology classes of a number of students. Here I have mentioned the biology classroom teaching of only two students – Padamaja and Alka Basu.

For many years the conventional wisdom of teachers has been similar to Padamaja's teaching style: to control student behavior so that the class is quiet. Most of the time there was an oral-expositive teacher participation Teachers in many cases is not aware of the practices or strategies to help students in *constructing knowledge*. Alka Basu believed in child-centered methods. Alka Basu in her classes never forced students to stay quiet but rather she managed the classroom in such a way that they must get ample opportunities to talk with one another and utilize collaborative learning strategies. Alka Basu encouraged students to visit school library for referring books and other self-learning materials. She encouraged students to create a small library corner in the classroom. A list of selected websites related to each topic was also given to the students before hand to provide them an idea about the content. Certain advanced organizers were also given to the students to set the pace for teaching. Students were encouraged to reflect and question their own understanding. The central point of Alka Basu's teaching was to elaborate original concepts, in an enjoyable and enthusiastic way.

What is Constructivism?

Constructivism is a learning theory based on scientific observation and research and explains how people learn. They construct their own knowledge of the world around them through reflection on their experiences. When we are faced with new knowledge, we tend to relate it to our previous experiences and either modify our ideas or discard the new information. In the process we tend to create new knowledge by asking questions, explaining and assessing what we already know

Constructivism as applied to education is a more recent development derived from the work of development psychologist *Jean Piaget* (1973) and Russian psychologist *Lev Vigotsky* (1978). Its underlying principles are also influenced by the developmentalistideas of the French philosphaer *Jacques Rousseau* and later the theories of *John Dewey, G Stanley Hall* and *Arnold Gessell.*

National Curriculum Framework (2005)

In this path breaking document by NCERT, the constructivist approach and its implications for practice have been brought out in great detail. Some of the key principles are summarized below:

- In the constructivist perspective, learning is a process of construction of knowledge.

- Learners actively construct their own knowledge by connecting new ideas to existing ideas on the basis of materials/ activities presented to them (experience).
- The structuring and restructuring of ideas are essential features as the learners' progress in learning.
- The engagement of learners, through relevant activities, can further facilitate in the construction of mental images of the relationships (cause-effect).
- Collaborative learning provides room for negotiation of meaning, sharing multiple views and changing the internal representative of external reality.

Constructivism in Biology Education

From a constructivist perspective, biology is not the search for truth. It is a process that assists us to make sense of our world. Using a constructivist perspective, teaching biology becomes more like the biology that biologists do; it is an active, social process of making sense of experiences, as opposed to what we now call "school biology." Indeed, actively engaging students in science (we have all heard the call for "hands-on, minds-on science") is the *goal of most science education reform.* It is an admirable goal, and using constructivism as a referent can possibly assist in reaching that goal in a constructivist epistemology:

- tools available to a knower are the *senses*. It is only through seeing, hearing, touching, smelling and tasting that an individual interacts with the environment. With these messages from the senses the individual builds a picture of the world.
- Experience involves an interaction of an individual with events, objects, or phenomenon in the universe; an interaction of the senses with things, a personal construction which fits some of the external reality but does not provide a match.
- A cooperative learning strategy allows individuals to test the fit of their experiential world with a community of others. Others help to constrain our thinking. The

interactions with others cause perturbations, and by resolving the perturbations individuals make adaptations to fit their new experiential world.

- The process of learning should not stop at what has been learned in the negotiation of a class consensus. This process can involve accessing other learning resources such as books, videotapes, and practicing scientists.

Constructivist Classroom activities in Biology Learning

Knowledge is constructed by the learner, not received. How does knowledge construction (i.e. learning) take place? Learners come to biology learning with existing ideas about many natural phenomena? What ideas do learners' bring to biology classes?, and what is the nature of these ideas? Each individual has a unique set of ideas. How much commonality is there between learner's ideas in biology? The learners' existing ideas have consequences for the learning of biology. How do learners' ideas interact with teaching? It is possible to teach biology more effectively if account is taken of the learner's existing ideas. How should 'constructivist' teachers teach biology? There are a number of ways by which teachers can come to know about the previous knowledge of students. Some exercises are mentioned in this section:

1. ***Concept maps*** - In the study of Biology, the ability to build interrelationships among concepts and related topics, and to relate newly acquired knowledge to prior knowledge, is crucial to the understanding of biological concepts and how the systems work together to bring about a coordinated response. Concept maps, diagrams and other graphic organisers are useful tools to illustrate the links between concepts and topics. Once a teacher has explained ecosystem, ask students to connect the following terms: *ecosystem, biotic components, abiotic* components, soil, water, air, decomposed organic matter, C02, N2, O2, water, climatic conditions, temperature, producers, consumers, decomposer, food-chain, *energy flow, recycling of nutrients and biogeochemical cycles.*

Every term should be connected with arrows labeled with a word that describes the link between the processes – example: change, causes, provides, directs, etc.

When students are able to discover the links between concepts themselves, they move away from rote or surface learning, and replace it with deep and meaningful learning, thus increasing the level of understanding and an appreciation for the subject. This encourages cooperative learning also.

2. ***Use of newspaper articles in making T-charts*** –Tell students to bring newspaper articles about science. List the topics of the articles on the board as the students give a 30 second summary of their article. From this list choose 5-6 topics which are relevant for them. Make 5-6 groups of students and allocate one topic to each group.ton. Give each group instructions to make a T-chart on a large piece of chart paper. Tell them that a T-chart is a large T drawn on the paper…with the topic written at the top of the T. On one side of the T bar students will write what have you heard about the topic? On the other side they will write what questions do you have about the topic?

Now you can discuss these T-charts either in the construction of the concept maps or can understand their previous knowledge to initiate discussions in the class.

3. ***Scenarios*** - You are discussing homeostasis in living organisms. The students are now part of a multi-disciplinary team put together to design the perfect animal that can survive and reproduce successfully under the following conditions: an environment that is very hot and dry during the day, but turns cold and windy at night, and that has many fast and aggressive predators. In their design of this animal, they should consider integument, body support, reproductive strategy, excretion and mode of locomotion.

In this exercise students need to think, work in a group, discuss and apply already covered/taught topics like adaptations, thermoregulation, morphological features, lifeprocesses, defense mechanism etc. This requires structuring and restructuring of concepts which is possible only with good understanding of concepts. Learning benefits from multiple views of a subject area.

4. ***Graphs*** - After studying human growth, ask students to draw a graph of average growth after birth showing the relationship between heights (in cm.) and age (years). Once they have made this graph then tell them to plot a graph of male and female comparative growth rates showing the relationship etween change in height (cm/ year) and age (years).

This graphical representation helps in better understanding and interpretation.

5. ***Brainstorming*** - When reviewing thermoregulation, ask students to come up with five ways in which snakes can prevent overheating on a hot summer day.

This exercise helps in developing thinking skills, structuring and restructuring of conceptual knowledge.

6. ***Observations/Predictions*** - When you are about to explain the hormonal control of female reproductive system, show an illustration of hormonal control of female reproductive system and ask students to make a list of six observations. When you discuss the positive and negative feedback systems controlling the production of estrogen and progesterone by the ovary with the students, they have already spent time studying the names of different glands involved and hormones produced by them and will be more receptive to learn more about the role of hormones in ovulation and menstruation. Then, ask students to predict what would happen to the endometrium if progesterone level does not fall during the last days of the menstrual cycle?

This exercise will help students in observation, comprehension, analysis, interpretation and prediction.

7. ***Problems*** - This problem is designed to help students understand the functioning of the circulatory system in the human body. Suppose you are staying on the second floor of the building and due to low pressure of the water, the water reaching your taps is not sufficient. Then you are advised to install water pump at your house. Predict:

- What will happen?
- What if there is any blockage in the water pipes supplying water to your house taps?
- What will happen if you now shift to the ground floor flat?

This activity provides an analogy to understand circulatory system in human beings. This helps in better understanding of the organ system (circulatory system) as well as its functioning.

8. ***Use of Cartoons*** – Use of cartoons in classroom teaching can make learning joyful. One page cartoons can be shown to the students like a cartoon showing a small boy holding his stomach with both hands and his face is looking very painful. On one side of the boy is shown the inner view of his stomach. Inside the stomach a lot of bacteria are jumping and releasing a lot of gas. Now teacher can ask questions like:

- what is happening in the stomach of this boy?
- name that part of the digestive system in which these bacteria are present.
- name the foods which are likely to produce more gas.
- how can we avoid flatulence/stomach discomfort?

This exercise helps in making learning an enjoyable experience. The engagement of learners, through relevant activities, can further facilitate in the construction of mental images of the relationships (cause-effect).

9. ***Songs for teaching biology*** – There are many songs which can be used for promoting learning in a joyful manner. One such song is given ahead:

Ecosystems

Science Maniacs

(Chorus)

I've got a big pond in my backyard
It's my own little ecosystem working hard
All the organisms are part of the food web
They play specific roles to make sure that they all get fed
The grasses growing on the edge and the algae in the water
The producers photosynthesize with light, CO_2 and water
CO_2 is in the air, the light comes from the sun
They produce the oxygen and the food needed by everyone

(Chorus)

Some snails eat the algae and some snails eat the grass
They're the primary consumers'cause they eat only plants
And even when the grass has died there's still some energy left
For the decomposers, dead things are what they like best

(Chorus)

The fish eat the snails and the turtles eat the fish
And every time that one of them eats it only gets 10%
So every gram of turtle needs 10 grams of fish
A gram of fish needs 10 grams of snails to fulfill its energy requirements

(Chorus)

An ecosystem relies upon this energy pyramid
It takes an awful lot of plants to let 1 turtle live
1000 plants, 100 snails, 10 fish would be just right
To keep 1 turtle well fed and it all starts out with light

(Retrieved from http://www.songsforteaching.com/biologyecology/ecosystems.htm)

Let us Sum Up

Constructivists claim that we have no access to an objective truth and that all knowledge is subjective and dependent on the learner. From a constructivist perspective, science is not the search for truth. It is a process that assists us to make sense of our world. Using a constructivist perspective, teaching biology becomes more like the biology that biologists do - it is an a*ctive, social process of making sense of experiences*. It is an enjoyable activity and the role of the teacher is very challenging.

Learning in classrooms is facilitated by well designed activities. These activities offer the opportunity to examine the problem from a variety of perspectives and also to collaborate. Listening to the multiple views on the subject makes the understanding better. Through different classroom activities, students get an opportunity to reflect and build on and consolidate existing knowledge. Students get an opportunity to construct knowledge. Just as teachers have to learn how to teach from a constructivist point of view, so too must students learn how to learn. Educating students to be effective learners is an important priority in establishing environments conducive to effective learning of biology.

References

1. Kramer, I. (n.d.). *Constructivist Teaching and Biology*. Retrieved on Feb.2, 2009 from http://www.cellbiol.eu/docs/Constructive_teachingKramer.pdf

2. NCERT (2005). National Curriculum Framework 2005 Retrieved on 24 Jan. 2009 from http://www.ncert.nic.in/html/pdf/schoolcurriculum/framework05/prelims.pdf.

3. NCERT (2005). *National Focus Group on Teaching of Science*. New Delhi : NCERT

4. Saul (2002). Intestinal Gas. Retrieved on Feb. 20, 2009 from http:/www.biologyinmotion.com/minilec/gas.html

5. Science Maniacs (2002). Ecosystems song Retrieved on Feb. 22, 2009 from http://www.songsforteaching.com/biologyecology/ecosystems.htm.

6. Sharma, S. (2006). *Constructivist Approaches to Teaching and Learning (Ed.)*. New Delhi : NCERT. teaching. Synthese 80 (1): 121-140.

7. Tobi, K. (1990). Conceptualizing teaching roles in terms of metaphors and beliefs sets. Paper presented at the annual meeting of the American Educational Research Association, Boston.

8. Von Glasersfeld, E. (1989). Cognition, construction of knowledge, and teaching. Synthese 80 (1): 121-140.

SECTION – III

Curriculum Transaction

Chapter–19

Integration of ICT in Pre-Service Secondary Teacher Education Curriculum

Introduction

Teacher education programmes today train teachers to adjust to a system in which education is seen as the transmission of Information. Attempts at curricular reform have not adequately supported by teacher education. Large scale recruitment of para-teachers has diluted the identity of a teacher as a professional. Major initiatives of the mid-nineties were focused on in-service training of teachers. This has accentuated the division between pre-service and in-service teacher education. Pre-primary, Primary and secondary teachers continue to be isolated from the centres of higher learning and their needs for professional development remain unadressed. Existing teacher education programmes neither accommodate the emerging ideas in context and pedagogy nor address the issue the issue of linkages between school and society. Use of ICT can minimize this problem to some extent.

Objectives of Research

1. To identify the types of Integration of ICT in PSTE Curriculum of Universities.
2. To analyze the extent of integration of ICT in PSTE Curriculum of Universities with respect to: (a) courses of TEP, (b) components of TEP, (c) different states.

Susanta Kumar Pathy, Lecture in Lingaya's College of Education, Old Faridabad (Haryana).

Research Methodology

In the present research qualitative and descriptive approaches has been used. The contents of syllabus of different Universities are analyzed through content analysis, Frequency and Percentages analysis.

Sample

The study includes Pre-Service Secondary Teacher Education programmes of twenty-four Universities of India mainly from three states.

Universities (Sample)

State	Universities
Orissa	(6 Universities)
Uttar Pradesh	(8 Universities)
Haryana	(4 Universities)
Others	(6 Universities)

The Analysis Process and Findings

Through preliminary content analysis, total six Types of Integration of ICT had been identified.

Types of ICT Integration Level Code:

There is no description of integration of ICT	Nil	0
A general description of audio-visual technique	Lowest	1
Computer is described as a means of mass communication	Low	2
There is a description of functions of general tools of ICT	Moderate	3
Conceptual description of using ICT for professional processes.	High	4
The integration of ICT has been described at application level	Highest	5

Data Analysis Process

- Exhaustive list of Courses and Components has been obtained through content analysis.
- The list of components again classified under five categories:
  1. Theoretical Compulsory Foundation Courses.
  2. Compulsory Courses related to Professional functions of schools.
  3. Optional Specialization Courses.
  4. Teaching Method Courses.
  5. Practice of Teaching Findings.

Findings

- No description of integration of ICT found in three **Theoretical compulsory foundation courses** like Philosophical, Sociological, Psychological Foundations of Education. Except in Psychological Foundation course in one University of Orissa, where a computer is described as a means of mass communication.
- With reference to four **compulsory courses related to professional functions of schools,** only Computer Education has highest application level of integration (code 5) which is found in 8 out of total 10 Universities. In only 2 Universities it is found at conceptual level (code 4). In other courses only Educational **Technology and Classroom Management** course has conceptual level of integration. But in other courses like **Measurement and Evaluation in Education** and **Educational Administration and School Management** no such integration has been found. Exceptionally, but remarkably 2-3 Universities have adopted some kind of integration.
- Out of the twelve optional specialization courses, only the **computer based teaching** has highest application level of integration (code 5). In the other courses, only **Educational Technology** has conceptual level (code 4)

of integration which is found in four Universities. Integration of ICT in the **Population Education** course is found almost in all the Universities but at low level. In other courses only few Universities have moderate or low level of integration.

- Out of the nineteen Teaching Method courses only the **English Teaching** has highest application level (code 5) of integration in 5 Universities. In science courses like Chemistry, Physics and Biology has high to moderate level of integration which is found in four-five Universities. In other courses most of the Universities have lowest or low level of Integration in their Teaching Method Courses.
- In general, it can be concluded that in teaching methods the integration level varies from course to course and also from University to University.
- There are no directions or descriptions found regarding the integration of ICT in Practice Teaching courses. It may be possible that some of the University Departments and Colleges use ICT in Practice Teaching, but these practices have not been described in the syllabi.
- The state wise analysis shows that the integration of ICT in compulsory courses related to professional functions of schools is found less in syllabus of Universities of U.P. (out of four state categories) and more in Haryana than others.
- The state wise analysis shows that the integration of ICT in teaching methods courses is found less in syllabi of Universities of Uttar Pradesh (out of four state categories) and more in Orissa than others.

Suggestions/Recommendations flowing from this research

- It is recommended that all the Universities should update their PSTE syllabus with reference to integration of ICT.
- Some of the Universities have adopted integration in some of their courses at highest level which indicates that other Universities can also adopt it .

- State wise differences gives ground for further research (to know the causes) and policy reformation.

References

1 Dikshit, J., Garg, S. and Panda, S. (2007): *Pedagogic Effectiveness of face-to-face Instruction, Interactive CD-ROM Self-study, and On-line Learning,* The AAOU Journal, (submitted)

2. Dikshit, J., Gaba, A., Bhushan, S., Garg, S. and Panda, S.(2005): Learning Attitude, Motivation and Preferences of On-line Learners, *Indian Journal of Open Learning*, 12 (3), 149-167.

3. Panda, S. (2007): *Media and Technology in Distance Education (Handbook 7),* New Delhi: IGNOU. (Forthcoming).

4. Panda, S. (2007): Teacher Education through Distance Learning, *Asia-Pacific Journal of Teacher Education & Development*, 6 (1), 65-81.

5. Panda, S. and Chaudhary, S (2003): 'Tele teaching for open and distance education', In S. Panda (ed*): Open and Distance Education: Policies, Practices and Quality Concerns*, New Delhi: ABI.

6. Pandey, S. (2004): In-service Training of DIET Faculty through Distance Mode: *An Experience, Staff & Educational Development International,* 3 (2), 211-222.

Chapter–20

Curriculum Framework for Quality Teacher Education in Indian Scenario

Introduction

Education is as a lifelong and complex process. The pattern of education and its transaction process is changing very fast. It has been observed that the development of any society depends upon the dynamic nature of its education systems. If the education system were dynamic, futuristic and challenging, it would lead to the development of the society and *vice-versa*. The development of one's education system depends on its planners, administrators, educationists and the teachers. Keeping all the other things constant, one thing i.e. teachers can be manipulated to make an education system developed. That's why it is said that a good mass of teachers can change the fate of a society. It has also been reflected in the report of Education Commission (1964-66) as the commission begins its report with this statement "the destiny of India is now being shaped in her classrooms". Transformation in the classroom can be brought by effective and efficient teachers. To prepare effective and efficient teachers those can manage the society at the speed of change; there is a need of dynamic, contingent and pragmatic teacher education system. This can be called as quality teacher education system that can tolerate the change and can adjust itself to face the frontline demands of the

Rekha Rani, Research Scholar in Aligarh Muslim University, Aligarh.

society. Education Commission (1964-66), in its report, emphasized the importance of the quality, competence, and character of teachers and their professional preparation for qualitative improvement of education. "Investment in teacher education can yield very rich dividends because the financial resources required are small when measured against the resulting improvements in the education of millions. The essence of a teacher education program is its 'quality' without which, it becomes, not only a financial waste, but also a source of overall deterioration in educational standards", the Commission added.

Subsequently, the National Policy on Education (1986) and its Programme of Action (1986, 1992) proposed several specific steps for revamping of teacher education programmes at different levels in the country to bring about qualitative improvements in school education. "An educational system can only be as good as its teachers. Researches show that a good teacher in every classroom is the most effective way of improving student performance. Teacher training, both pre-service and in-service, must be reformed so that teachers have the competence and motivation to interact with students and to facilitate their development. It is felt that pre-service training focuses almost exclusively on knowledge acquisition, with little attention to pedagogy instructional practices and classroom management skills, is not preparing teacher for the 21st century." (NCTE 1997) In this context, our teacher education system requires substantial systematic reforms and reconceptualization of curricular areas and resources to improve the quality and efficiency of teachers.

Curriculum Framework for Teacher Education

The National Council for Teacher Education (NCTE) was established as a statutory body in 1995. The curriculum framework developed by the NCTE was released in 1998 as a publication. The NCTE has chosen a pragmatic approach for influencing the teacher education system. It has developed a curriculum framework instead of fixing curricula for different categories of teacher education programmes. The expectation of the NCTE is that by offering flexible suggestions the organizations and institutions responsible for deciding teacher education curriculum may be able to select from the curriculum framework what would meet their specific needs within the constraints of their resources. Accordingly, the NCTE has prepared the curriculum framework keeping in mind the diversity of the school system and those of the teacher education institutions that train teachers for it. It has evolved a curriculum framework through the process of intensive national level consultations with teachers, teacher educators and thinkers in education, so that the teacher education may become futuristic and dynamic. The new type of teacher, who would be forward-looking, who would be able to adapt appropriate pedagogy, who would be able to prepare suitable instructional materials to suit the needs of the teaching-learning and who would be able to carry out the other tasks envisaged for him/her , the NCTE hopes, will be produced when courses of theory, practice teaching and practical work in the teacher education programmes are restructured as per the framework. Realizing the aforesaid situation the National Curriculum Framework (NCF–2005) identified certain broad aims of education. These include independence of thought and action, sensitivity to others' well being and feelings, learning to respond to new situations in a flexible and creative manner, predisposition towards participation in democratic process, and the ability to work towards and contribute to economic processes and social change, To overcome the burden and stress on children and their parents, the NCF–2005 proposes five guiding principles for curricular development:

- connecting knowledge to life outside the school;
- ensuring that learning shifts away from rote methods;
- enriching the curriculum so that it goes beyond textbooks;
- making examinations more flexible and integrating them with classroom life; and
- nurturing an overriding identity informed by caring concerns within the setup of the country.

NCF–2005 feels that teacher education must become more sensitive to the emerging demands from the school system. For this it must prepare the teachers for the roles of being an:

- encouraging, supportive and humane facilitator in teaching-learning situations to enable learners (students) to discover their talents, realize their physical and intellectual potentialities to the fullest, and to develop character and desirable social and human values to function as responsible citizens; and
- active member of a group of persons who makes a conscious effort for curricular renewal so that it is relevant to changing societal needs and the personal needs of learners.

Teacher Education Curriculum Needs Reforms

The Principals of some public schools hold the view that there is hardly any difference between the performance of trained and untrained teachers because of outdated teacher education curricula. Teacher education programmes today train teachers to adjust to a system in which education is seen as the transmission of information. Attempts at curricular reform have not been adequately supported by the teacher education. Existing teacher education programmes neither accommodate the emerging ideas in context and pedagogy nor address the issue of linkages between school and society. There is little space for engagement with innovative educational experiments. Experiences in the practice of teacher education indicate that knowledge is treated as 'given', embedded in the curriculum and accepted without question. A key problem associated with the content of teacher education courses is that teachers are both perceived as and trained to be transmitters of information from textbooks, rather than as professionals who can teach students to think, find answers and understand concepts on their own. Most teacher education programmes provide little scope for student-teachers to reflect on their experiences and thus fail to empower teachers as agents of change. NCF–2005 has already been implemented in most of the states but a National

Curriculum Framework for Teacher Education is yet to be developed based on NCF–2005.

Thus teacher education curriculum needs to be constantly defined and redefined based on the changing contents and emerging areas need to be integrated. There is a need for proper cooperation between different agencies to implement it for all types of teacher education programmes. Therefore, substantial attention to the content and process of teacher education is required. Existing teacher education programmes do not encourage students to reflect on their own experiences and assumptions, which otherwise would be a way for teachers to set aside their own biases and beliefs. Instead, assuming that the latter can be easily set aside, these programmes 'fail to empower the teacher as an agent of change.

The Shifting Role of Teacher Educators

The teacher education programmes that are followed throughout the length and breadth of the country have remained static both in form and content for over 100 years. The pedagogy which was introduced in the later part of the 19th century, relevant to the society then, has continued in its unchanged form not only throughout the 20th century but even today teacher educators follow the same nineteenth century teacher education curriculum, which obviously is no longer relevant. Our student teachers themselves have to be helped in becoming life long learners, and are to be enabled with the ability of learning how to learn. Only such teachers as who know learning how to learn when they will enter teaching profession will be able to recognize diversity of learning needs of children and provide them an environment for their own growth as autonomous learners.

There is a need for the teacher educators to shift their role to improve the quality of the process of teacher education for preparing dynamic teachers, seeing teacher educators as bearers of knowledge to be communicated to seeing themselves as stimulators of knowledge to be constructed and developed by pupils through the learning experiences. Teacher educators' role will be shifted from teacher to knowledge workers, consultants and counselor. Teacher educators should internalize their changing role and to make themselves ready for this change. Even in accepting the changing role of the teacher educators, there is a need to be cautious to adopt according to the changing world, hence teacher educators have to empower themselves to do justice with the future students and to try hard to increase the quality of their teaching learning.

Role of Apex Bodies

For the sake of quality teacher education institutions, the quality evaluation is must. A list of parameters have been developed by NCTE, UGC and NAAC like, Curriculum Design and Planning; Curriculum Transaction and Evaluation; Research, Development and Extension; Infrastructure and Learning Resources; Student Support and Progression; Organization and Management; workload allocation, and many more criterion for accredit and assessment of the teacher education institutions. While assessing the quality of teacher education institutions, more emphasis should be given on the adoptability of the curriculum according to the changing need in the school education, adaptation of contingent and pragmatic approach and the process of curriculum transaction according to the changing curriculum. Curriculum design mechanism, it's planning and implementation should be emphasized in the process of evaluation and accreditation of teacher education institutions. Inbuilt mechanism of flexibility need to be incorporated in the criteria of assessment, and it should be easily defined and interpreted according to the need and change of a specific geographical locality, accessibility to facilities, economic status of the funding agencies like, state government and the management bodies.

Conclusion and Suggestions

As the Yash Pal Committee Report points out, existing programmes of teacher education are inadequate to deal with the (poor) quality of teaching and learning, implying that programme content should be revised, keeping in view the changing requirements of school education. A key problem associated with the content of teacher education courses is that teachers are both perceived as and trained to be transmitters of information from textbooks, rather than as professionals who can teach students to think, find answers and understand concepts on their own – a conceptualization which provides continued impetus to poor quality schooling. Changing the latter, therefore, demands substantial attention to the content and process of teacher education. Existing teacher education programmes do not encourage students to reflect on their own experiences and assumptions, which otherwise would be a way for teachers to set aside their own biases and beliefs. Instead, assuming that the latter can be easily set aside, these programmes 'fail to empower the teacher as an agent of change'. Warning against such thinking, as a UNESCO report on EFA notes, 'both in developing and developed countries, there is a temptation to lower teacher training standards'. This experience highlights the need for teacher education courses and institutions to recognize the profile of persons who become teachers and structure content accordingly. The content of teacher education programme should be restructured to ensure its relevance to the changing needs of school education.... The emphasis in these programmes should be on enabling the trainees to acquire the ability for self-learning and independent thinking. Following suggestions are given to reform curriculum of teacher education programme:

- There is a need to revamp our teacher education system to tune with the changing need of the society particularly the changing need of the school education.
- Teacher Education programme should be redesigned keeping in view the National Curriculum Framework (NCF–2005) and should be based on the changing contents and emerging areas. As teacher education is a continuous process, teacher educators too need to update their knowledge, sharpen their pedagogical skills and enhance

their research aptitude. In this era of Globalization, Liberalization and Privatization and with the new opportunities offered by ICT, it is essential that teacher educators be suitably empowered in terms of handling content and process of teacher education in new ways.

- There is a need to design, develop and implement a similar type of frontline curriculum for all types of teacher education programmes in the line of contingent and pragmatic outlook.
- There is a need for keeping space in the existing curriculum of pre-service teacher education programmes in the subjects like, education in emerging Indian society, educational psychology, classroom management, information and communication technology, measurement and evaluation, methods of teaching subjects of Science, Mathematics, social sciences and special field areas like, guidance and counseling, computer education, educational technology, health education and educational management. It can help teacher education programmes to accommodate new researches, innovations, skills, methods and approaches to prepare dynamic and efficient teacher trainees to handle the frontline curriculum of school education.
- There is a need to prepare tomorrow's curriculum today. There is a need to create a super industrial and rational educational system. The curriculum of teacher education should be so contingent and dynamic that it can prepare teachers to face the changes in the school curriculum keeping themselves ready for random change.
- Apart from the theoretical components, there is a need to strengthen the practical aspects of teachers' education programmes to empower future teachers with appropriate skills, techniques, values and attitudes to implement the change in a most rational and scientific way which can help to create dynamic and efficient teachers for future.

References

1. Biswal, A. (2007): Quality Process Norms for Frontline Teacher Education: Need of the Changing World. *University News,* 45 (7), 1-8.
2. Ministry of Education, *Report of the Education Commission (1964-66),* Government of India, New Delhi.
3. Ministry of Human Resource Development (1986,1992) *Programme of Action, National Policy on Education,* Government of India, New Delhi.
4. Mohanty, S.B. (2008): *Ensuring Quality in Teacher Education.* University News, 46 (08), 18-25.
5. NCTE (1998): *Curriculum Framework for quality Teacher Education.* New Delhi: NCTE.
6. NCTE (1998): *Quality concerns in secondary Teacher Education,* National Council for Teacher Education, New Delhi.
7. Maheshwari, A.N. (1998): *Curriculum Framework for Quality Teacher Education,* 137, NCTE, New Delhi.
8. Chauhan, C.P.S. (2004): *Modern Indian Education Policies, Progress and Problems.* Kanishka Publishers, Distributors, New Delhi.
9. Goel, D.R. and Biswal, A. (1996): *TQM in Education-Reality, Desirability and Feasibility.* University News, 34, 44.
10. www.*theindiapost*.com.
11. www.aacte.org.
12. http://www.ncert.nic.in/sites/publication/schoolcurriculum/curiindex.htm.
13. http://www.thesouthasian.org/archives/2005/comments_on_national_curriculum.html.

Chapter–21

Dynamic Assessment of the Evolving Cognitive Functions in Children

Introduction

Parents and teachers have frequently observed that with the appropriate help and in collaboration with a more experienced partner, a child is capable of more advanced performance than when functioning independently. It was Vygotsky, however, who elevated this otherwise trivial observation to the rank of the scientific paradigm known as zone of proximal development.

Generally considered as a "space" where the evolving psychological functions of a child emerge during the process of joint or shared activities with a more competent partner and where "everyday" concepts shift to "scientific" concepts, ZPD has practical implications in the two educational domains of assessment and instruction. In this article, ZPD is considered as the conceptualization of the approach to evaluation of students in educational and remedial contexts known as Dynamic Assessment (DA).

DA is a theory driven approach. The following notions provide the core of its theoretical base:

---

1. *Dr Amita Puri, Lecture in Education, Army Institute of Education, Delhi Cantt.*
2. *Dr Mahabir Yadav, Principal at Army Insititue of Education, Delhi Cantt.*

1. Cognitive, language and social functioning in educational settings are not innate abilities or disabilities but are socio-cultural formations resulting from the interactions of a child with culture. What is to be measured therefore, is a child's evolving individual ability to master psychological tools that are in the process of development.

2. Assessment is not an isolated activity that is merely linked to intervention. Assessment, instruction and remediation can be based on the same universal explanatory conceptualization of a child's development (typical and atypical) and within this model are therefore inseparable. A true diagnosis must provide an explanation, prediction and scientific basis for practical prescription.

Moreover, the means of assessment and the means of instruction need to be age specific, always attuned to the characteristics of development.

3. The size of ZPD is determined by the child's ability to benefit from collaboration with an expert in order to advance the child's performance beyond what is already achieved by non-assisted performance.

Thus, DA should be able to describe the child's ever changing ability to learn with assistance or guidance as well as to assess the individual length of ZPD.

4. Vygotsky insisted that assessment of the child's ability to learn through the method of collaborative activity was a better predictor of future cognitive functioning than a measure of independent performance through such measures as traditional tests of intelligence.

5. An essential feature of learning is that it creates the zone of proximal development, that is, learning awakens a variety of developmental processes that are able to operate only when the child is interacting with people in his environment and in collaboration with his peers.

6 Collaborative or assisted performance is viewed as an indicator of the status of the learner's maturing psychological functions, i.e. we ask the child to solve

problems that are beyond his mental age with some kind of cooperation and determine how far the potential for intellectual cooperation can be stretched for the given child and how far it goes beyond his mental age.

7. Vygotsky turned to the psychological concept of imitation as a way of identifying maturing psychological functions that were still inadequate for independent performance. Imitation is possible because there are maturing psychological functions that are insufficient to support independent performance, yet are developed sufficiently to take advantage of collaborative actions.

Vygotsky also offered one of the most original and insightful critiques of standardized tests. His major objections to standardized tests were that they confused latent capacities with developed abilities; they mixed lower (natural) capability with higher (socially learned) expertise and they were only marginally relevant to educational processes. He suggested as an alternative, the approach based on the notion of ZPD that is now called DA. He never suggested the total abandonment of standardized tests; rather he postulated the possibility of using both models of teaching.

The traditional testing paradigm includes the notions that;

1. The manifest level of functioning reveals the child's inner abilities more or less accurately.
2. Unaided performance is the best format for assessment.
3. The primary goals of testing are to predict future functioning and to classify the child according to the level of abilities.

DA includes the assumptions that:

1. Cognitive processes are modifiable and an important task of assessment is to ascertain their degree of modifiability, rather than to remain limited to the estimation of the child's manifest level of functioning.
2. Interactive assessment that includes a learning phase provides better insight into the child's learning capacities than unaided performance.

3. the primary goal of assessment is to suggest psycho-educational interventions aimed at the enhancement and realization of the child's latent abilities to learn.

Thus, it can be said that traditional standardized assessment follows the child's cognitive performance to the point of "failure" in independent functioning, whereas DA leads the child to the point of achievement of success in joint or shared activity.

DA begins where standardized testing begins.

Types and formats of Dynamic Assessment

As of now, there is a wide variety of procedures under the general umbrella of DA. DA itself is not limited to any single domain, content, activity or age. It is a family of different procedures that share a set of principles and formats.

Sternberg and Grigorenko (2002) describe the two most common formats of dynamic assessment as 'Sandwich design' and 'cake design'.

In the sandwich format of dynamic testing, the instruction is given all at once between the pretest and posttest.

In the cake format of dynamic testing, the instruction is given in graded layers after each test item in response to the examinee's solution of each test item.

In Vygotsky's works, both types of formats are described tersely, "We assist each child through demonstration, leading questions and by introducing elements of the task's solution". And describes the actions of the examiner, "We show the child how such a problem must be solved and watch to see if he can do the problem by imitating the demonstration. Or we begin to solve the problem and ask the child to finish it. Or we propose that the child solve the problem that is beyond his mental age by cooperating with another, more developed child or, finally we explain to the child the principle of solving the problem, ask leading questions, analyze the problem for him etc."

Concerns about the issue of how to provide assistance is far from idle. Because of the centrality of Vygotsky's assumption of the social origin of development of higher mental functions, it would be important to discriminate between those interactions that promote such development and those that do not, assuming that all interactions are not equal. Vygotsky emphasized the importance of language as a (if not the primary) mechanism of internalization of experiences.

Development of Dynamic Assessment

On the basis of Vygotsky's general conceptualization, different approaches to DA that reflect the diverse cultural contexts of application may be developed.

Application of Cognitive Functions Scale

The Application of Cognitive Functions Scale (ACFS) (Lidz & Jepsen, 2000) is a dynamic assessment procedure developed for use with children functioning between the ages of 3 and 5 years. The six scales were designed to represent typical tasks tapping basic cognitive processes that represent foundations of learning and that characterize most preschool curricula in preschool programs throughout the United States.

As it is a dynamic assessment procedure, each task is first administered without intervention, then followed immediately by intervention, and finally followed immediately by repetition of (or variation of) the pretest without intervention. The interventions provide mediation for the child through exposure to basic strategies and principles of task solutions on materials that differ from the pretests and posttests.

The ACFS provides curriculum based and descriptive information that responds to questions concerning the child's degree of mastery of each task, the child's approach to task solutions, the child's interactions with the examiner as mediator and the child's responsiveness to intervention.

The six tasks of the ACFS include 4 core scales and 2 supplementary scales.

Core Scales

1. Classification: The child sorts multi-attributed blocks into groups.
2. Auditory memory: The child retells a short story.
3. Visual memory: The child recalls a series of 8 pictures and shares thoughts about how she or he will help herself or himself to remember the pictures.
4. Sequential pattern completion: The child completes a series of incomplete sequential patterns and justifies correct solutions with the reason for selection of the correct pattern piece.

Supplement Scales

5. Verbal planning: The child verbalizes a plan for a familiar cooking task.
6. Perspective taking: The child teaches the assessor how to draw a picture from a model.

Provided

The interventions for each of these scales tap the component known as mediated learning experience. The assessor offers intentional intervention, assuming a leading and guiding role that is sensitive and responsive to the child's responses and abilities and supplies scripted interventions that offer strategies and principles of task solution intended for generalization to the pretest posttest tasks.

A Behaviour Observation Scale accompanies each task and is completed after each pretest and intervention phase of the subtests. This scale captures the affective – motivational and meta-cognitive aspects of the child as learner. The 7 dimensions rated on this scale are self regulation, persistence, frustration tolerance, flexibility, motivation, interactivity and responsibility.

The ACFS yields scores to document the degree to which the child has mastered each of the tasks, summary scores for pretests and posttests as well as change or gain scores between pretests and posttests, and the behaviour scale ratings. These scores are useful for research and monitoring, however, the more significant value of the ACFS is the possibility of writing descriptive observations of the child in the process of performing each of the tasks independently and in interaction with a mediator.

Case Study

Lidz (2003) cites case studies of the use of the ACFS with some children who were adopted from overseas orphanage and who currently live with their new families in the USA. In all cases, the children were administered standardized tests as well as dynamic assessment.

One of the cases was that of a child Raymond, a 5 year 4 months old boy who was adopted from Russia at the age of 2 years 9 months and had been diagnosed with Pervasive Developmental Disability (PDD).

The ACFS revealed two distinct characteristics of Raymond's current cognitive –language functioning and learning ability. First, Raymond presently possesses the cognitive skills needed to perform all of the tasks of this procedure. In fact, the examiner had to modify the Perspective Taking subtest and terminate the administration of the Short Term Visual Memory subtest after the pretest because Raymond had reached the ceiling even before the teaching phase had been introduced.

In two other activities (classification and sequential pattern completion). Raymond quickly attained a high level of performance on his own and his functioning therefore did not show much improvement after the teaching intervention because of his high performance on the pretest.

The testing demonstrated that Raymond had no difficulty with cognitive functioning *per se*.

However, the dynamic assessment did reveal the extent and nature of Raymond's difficulties with the social behavioral aspects of learning as well as with his self regulation while engaged in mental activities. His responsiveness (the ability to be socially engaged) was inconsistent, and his interaction with the adult in a teaching role appeared defensive and resistant. His autistic like behaviour pattern blocked cooperation with a teaching authority and reduced his ability to benefit from scaffolding of the cognitive activity. In fact, he performed less effectively in the context of social collaboration with the examiner in a teaching learning situation (dynamic assessment) than he did independently in the pretest phase of the ACFS or during standardized testing. This suggests that in order for learning to occur, Raymond would require considerable more time and intensity from a collaboratively adult led learning experience than expected for his typically developed peers.

Concluding Remarks

Dynamic assessment procedures are in a stage of rapid development and research documenting their utility has been rapidly accumulating as well. Perhaps Luria's conviction that "the time has come when the high value given to psychometrics will come to an end" was premature but a high value ascribed to the dynamic approach to the assessment seems on the horizon. However, the utility of dynamic assessment procedures does not require the demise of more traditional psychometric approaches. The full and meaningful diagnostic exploration of learners and the means of linking assessment with intervention require a full repertory of assessment approaches. Dynamic assessment is unique in providing a basis for creating and exploring what Vygotsky has passed on as the ZPD.

References

1. Gauvain, M (2001): *The Social Context of Cognitive Development,* New York : Guilford.
2. Kozulin et al (2003): Vygotsky's *Educational Theory in the Cultural Context,* Cambridge University Press.
3. Lidz & Jepsen (2000): *The Application of Cognitive Function Scale.* Unpublished manuscript. (Author: zdilsc@aol.com).

3. Luria (1961): An objective approach to the study of normal child. *Journal of the American Orthopsychiatric Association.* 31, 1-16.

4. Sternberg and Grigorenko (2002): *Dynamic Testing : The Nature and the Potential of the Learning Child.* New York : Cambridge University Press.

Chapter–22

Gender Issues in Education

NCERT

Educational discourses in the nineties and twenties have accorded a pivotal place to *Gender Issues in Education*. Changes ushered by Globalization, liberalization and by the techno savvy revolution have eroded the human face of development. "Learning to live together" is gradually becoming a distant dream and a target that all countries world over including India are struggling to achieve. Ethnic conflicts, racial and caste discriminations compounded by gender based violence emotionally and physically are impacting delicate human relations between genders in the family, workplace and in the community. Compared to men women are more at the receiving end. Trafficking of girls and women in South Asia is also emerging as a major societal issue that has now questioned the human face of development. According, debates in the academia has now increasingly focused on the paradox that development has ushered, that is technological advancement is seen as a binary opposition to issues related to equity and equality in education.

Gouri Srivastava, Professor in the Department of Women's Studies at NCERT, New Delhi.

Discussions centered around the removal of all kinds of contradictions in education have accorded a special place to gender issues in education. It is envisioned that a gender sensitive educational process would be a harbinger of the much desired social change that would help in addressing all kinds of disparities in education cutting across caste, class and region. It would help in informing gender in all disciplinary areas as a cross cutting edge and become a critical marker of transformation in the content and process of education. It is also felt that integrating voices of both genders in textual materials and contextual situations would help in achieving the cherished goals of gender justice, harmony and peace.

This would entail a conscious effort made by policy makers, educationalist and administrators of undoing gender bias and stereotypes and prevalent myths that on the one hand marginalizes the contributions of women and on the other hand perpetuates tailored made masculine ad feminine roles ascribed to boys and girls by primary agents of socialization.

A landmark step in the context of addressing gender issues in education was the enactment of the National Policy on Education, 1986. The policy assigns a crucial role that education can play in bringing about a change in the status of women by playing a positive intervention list role in the empowerment of women through redesigning of curricula, syllabus textual materials and in the training and orientation of teachers, decision makers and administrators.

The Programme of Action (PoA) 1992, reinforces the significant role of education in addressing issues related to gender bias and gender stereotyping in empowering girls.

By promoting all activities that would help in instilling confidence building skills among girls so that it raises self confidence and self esteem, enable them to think critically, foster in them decision making capacities so that they can make informed choices in the area of education, employment and health.

While policy parameters have tried to address gender issues in education Studies conducted in the context of gender issues in education have highlighted that in textual materials very often in the selection of themes, visual depiction and in the content portrayal in school text books particularly in the domain of Sciences and Social Science have neglected the contributions of the half of the humanity in the evolution of societies world over (for details see Srivastava, Jaireth, Raj Rani, 1996-97), Srivastava (2005-06). The above research studies have depicted that gender bias is visibly reflected in school text books of India as well as neighboring countries. The other phenomena that is normally found in text books is related to gender stereotyping. Boys and girls are shown in masculine and feminine roles in text books.

Since text books are important teaching aids for children in developing countries including India, the knowledge constructed from available text books do not help them in demystifying biases and stereotypes. Further, textual materials do not promote in instilling critical and a questioning perspective among children to question the existing power structures.

The contextual situations i.e. the school and classroom process also reinforce masculine and feminine traits that are reinforce knowledge embedded in text books. Classroom management which includes – designing of classes, sitting arrangement, display of children works, assignment of roles and responsibilities, try to transmit ascribed roles that boys and girls imbibe through primary agents of socialization. The pedagogical processes are also colored with approaches that do not give spaces to voices of girls, especially from the marginalized groups. Classroom talk, subject talk and outside classroom voices are dominated by boys. Girls represent the silence bunches. Studies in the context of classroom processes have highlighted that the hidden curriculum adversely impacts the retention and overall personality development of the girl child. Teacher's body languages, eye contact, language of addressing both sexes are often visibly discriminatory towards girls. Very often motivational words that are used by the teachers – such as good, excellent, you can do it, is directed more for boys than girls. Stigmatizing girl child and even boys belonging to lower caste have been observed in few classroom observations (Nayar, et.al. 1996-97).

Thus, classroom management pedagogical processes and outside classroom activities do not address gender discriminations and social barriers in education that cumulatively impact access, enrolment, retention and achievement of girls at different stages of education. Educational indicators depicts that despite, conscious effort made by the government since Independence such as formulation of schemes and programmes for addressing gender disparities in education have not been able to successfully address gender issues. The agenda of providing education to all children continues to remains a distant dream.

According to 2005-2006 the enrolment of boys and girls at Primary level was 70.5 for Boys, 61.6 for Girls, at the Upper Primary level it was 28.9 for Boys and 23.3 for Girls, at the Sr. Secondary stage it was 22.3 and 16.1 (Selected Educational Statistics 2005-06, Figures given are in million). These figures reinforce gender disparities at all level of education. The literacy rates are also indicative of this phenomenon. According to literacy rate in 2001 it was 75% for males and 54% for girls. (Census: 2001).

Therefore, to remove social, economic and educational barriers in the context of textual and contextual situation a very significant effort has been made by NCF–2005 and the position papers on Gender Issues in Education. For the first time both the documents treat gender issue as an integral part informing all disciplines. Further, the position paper very rightly states that gender is not a women's issue, but a people's issue, a human issue. The approach in the context of gender is to treat it not as an add on approach but one that weaves into the content and process of education. Text books based on NCF–2005 are gender inclusive as they capture the voices of both genders, particularly girls and women from marginalized group in visuals and in the content. Effort is also made to situate concepts such as equality, discrimination and various forms of diversities in real life situations. This approach would make children understand various concepts and its actual operationalization.

In the context of pedagogy the position paper has very rightly mentioned that curricular changes cannot be realized without the teacher who is at the forefront of the teaching learning process. Gender issues integrated in pedagogical processes would give an opportunity to the teacher's to reflect on their own socialization processes and would enable them to integrate their own experiences with the content of different disciplines. It is expected that gender sensitive teaching learning process would promote self-esteem and self-confidence, stimulate critical thinking and develop in the learners the abilities to question power relations, enable them to access resources, especially to an expanding framework of information and knowledge, ability to analyze options available in making informed choice, challenge relations of power and enable girls to take control of their lives and assert their rights as independent human.

In the present paper an attempt has been made to suggest to the teacher educators and teachers some suggestive ways of managing classroom and pedagogical processes from a gender lens.

Classroom Processes

Gender inclusive classroom reforms necessarily demand that teachers try out different instructional materials and methods and equipment to bring about qualitative changes in the physical and social environment of the classroom to make it gender friendly. Given the present reality, teachers can initiate a change in the existing status – quo by reflecting on processes that would help in cultivating among boys and girls to value each other, promote qualities that would strengthen values like caring and sharing and skills for negotiation, consensus and critical thinking. Being at the center of the educational processes, the teachers in their performance of their multifaceted roles can bring about changes in structures, attitudes and the direction in which changes are needed. A teacher who is gender sensitive can pioneer the needed change, first by being convinced that changes are needed and their by as a facilitator can initiated through several activities that help in bringing about attitudinal changes in both sexes. Even though teachers have very little say in deciding policy issues in school, their perceptions are crucial variables in reframing classroom instructional practices. Several research studies have shown on how classroom environment can facilitate students learning and help in removing gender bias and stereotyping and create an environment that would help in inculcating a spirit of equality and harmony between girls and boys in their early years and prepare them for equal partnership and shared roles for a common future. A gender sensitive teacher can plays a crucial role in creating such an atmosphere in the classrooms. As a manager of gender friendly classroom environment the following activities/interventions can be thought off :

- Ensuring that physical and social environment in classrooms promotes healthy relationship among sexes.
- Creating conducive conditions that help in equal participation of both sexes in teaching and learning process by giving attention to those boys and girls who have no voices in discussions, clarification of doubts and in questioning and answering sessions.
- Adopting different participatory method such as role play, problem solving, quiz, innovative games etc., in the teaching of languages, social-science, science and math's.
- Organizing of classroom activities that insure participation of both sexes in few activity such as– cleaning the blackboard, putting up charts, newspaper clippings, poems, short stories etc. on bulletin boards etc.
- Strengthening shared responsibility in organizing multifaceted activities such as reading, recitation, discussions, debates, dramatics that would develop effective communications skills among boys and girls.

- Identifying slow learners and organizing remedial classes for them.
- Highlighting examples of women achievers who have contributed in making meaningful contributions in different fields.
- Using different teaching aids for motivating students such as audio-visuals, pictures including print and videos, puppets, depicting women working in fields, in the production of different crafts and women's and in the service sectors of the economy for demystifying gender bias and stereotype related to profession taken up by both sexes.
- Transacting curriculum in mathematics, environmental studies, sciences and languages emphasizing on examples that depicts the contributions of boys and girls, men and women from different walks of life.
- Encouraging children to speak about their lived experiences by giving opportunity to both genders.

Organization of the above mentioned activities that can go a long way in bringing about the much needed attitudinal changes in boys and girls. This would help them grow up in a caring and sharing mode. The National Policy of Education 1986 and the National Curriculum Framework for School Education 2005, also stresses the crucial role the teachers can play as an agent of social change.

Classroom Organization and Management

Broadly speaking the classroom consists of two sets of environment the physical and the social. The physical environment consists of classroom size, ventilation and light and the usual furniture and equipments which are necessary pre-conditions for assisting in a meaningful teaching and learning situation. The behavioral aspects that determine relationship between the teacher and the taught and among peers represents the social environment of a classroom. A combination of physical and social environment determines classroom dynamics. In the context of gender, physical organization of classroom and its management are very crucial. Studies in classroom management have indicated that physical conditions of classrooms are not always gender friendly. In the selection and in the arrangement of furniture and in determining seating arrangements there is a bias. In co-educational schools boys and girls especially in upper primary levels are seated in a segregated way. In this connection, some of the studies have supported this fact and have also stated that the furniture's that are available to children are not according to their height. It is more visible in case of girls who due to nutrition deficiency are not able to attain the required height according to their age. Generally in some urban and rural setting in co-educational schools boys and girls are made to sit separately, spacing between rows is not kept uniformly. Very often girls trend to sit in front rows and hardly move. Further, in over crowded classes faulty arrangements of furniture leads to jostling and pushing. This affects both boys and girls, perhaps more in case of girls, resulting in discipline problems.

The arrangements of bulletin boards in the class are located in a gender insensitive manner. The placements of reading materials are located at a height that normally becomes difficult for the girl child to read and reach. In such circumstances only boys get access to using the board for displaying items made by students. Studies also show that teachers do not show interest in the management of extra space in the classrooms. Often the space is left unutilized and in some cases where the space is utilized tables and chairs are arranged in such a manner that it promotes segregation among sexes.

Normally schools established by the government in rural areas, municipality in urban areas have poor ventilation and lightening (see Srivastava, 2001) such conditions affect the health and overall physical development of children. In case of girls the impact is more visible as their health status is generally poor, particularly in cases of those who come from poor households or families where preferential treatment between boys and girls exists. With restricted on freedom of movement, girl's physical condition leave much to be desired. In order to make the physical environment of the classroom gender friendly the following activities/steps can be initiated.

Classroom Organization and Management

- Encouraging mixed seating arrangement seating can be based on alphabetical list in the class attendance register. Ensuring adequate space in selection and in the arrangement of furniture's to encourage free movement of children.
- Seating in a circle could be explored to ensure maximum, face to face interactions among children for sharing of experiences between boys and girls and between sexes.
- Planning and identifying specific classroom spaces that could be designed for various activities.
- Placing the bulletin board at a height that can be easily accessible to both boys and girls. This will encourage boys and girls to display their creativities in the form of short stories, poems, plays and other forms of literary expositions.
- Teaching aids in classroom should be properly placed so that they are visible to all children.
- Ensuring that items displayed in the class are not gender biased and stereotyped in their content, illustration and presentation.
- Creating opportunities for girls and boys to work co-operatively, promoting sharing in mixed sex grouping.
- Organizing classroom activities without having pre-conceived notion about innate ability of any sex.

Roles and Responsibilities

Studies in connection with classroom practices have generally shown that teacher show biased attitudes towards boys and girls (Srivastava, Gouri, 1997 Valerie. E.Lee, 1995). The above studies have highlighted these stereotyped attitudes prevalent among teachers especially in assigning roles and responsibilities that strengthening the extended roles of house hold chores. Nurturing and caring qualities are encouraged for girls and this is visibilized in assigning roles such as cleaning, dusting and looking after sick peers to girls and boys are given responsibilities duties such as monitors of the class, leaders in debates dramatics and all outdoor activities. Also, as far as occupational aspirations are concerned the former studies depict that teachers want boys to go into unconventional professions such as Engineering, Aeronautical Engineering, Computer Sciences etc. and girls to take up professions such as teaching, and taking up courses such as Home Sciences etc. Thus, the general expectation from the teachers as well as the parents is that a boys needs a career whereas girls need husband. In other words this expectation stems from the traditional perceptions of a male being the bread earner of the family and girls as home maker. Parents and later teachers normally trend to be dismissive and discouraging towards girls and give more attention to boys, who are usually more demanding. Even when girls are encouraged to peruse a career, they are expected to opt for 'caring and soft' professions such as teaching and nursing. As stated earlier, the hidden curriculum of school practices reinforces messages about girls' inferior status on a daily basis and provides them with a negative learning experience, that create a culture of low self-esteem and low aspiration levels among them. In a way school and classroom processes attempt to reinforce the socialization processes of the family and the communities that perpetuate gender stereotypical attitudes and values. A reflective teachers need to be aware of this aspect.

Pedagogical processes also strengthening. It is normally found in a classroom situation that in the distribution of questions discussions on various themes, in, the reading of passages from books, recitation of poems, girls are generally given less chance. Also, girls' contribution in class discussions are disregarded or undervalued. There is a general feeling that boys fare better in schools than girls in all activities.

Therefore, to encourage greater participation of girls especially from marginalized groups in all classroom activities and make the pedagogical processes participatory for all children the following activities can be thought of:

Participation of Girls

- Distribute questions equally among boys and girls.
- Discourage the dominance of particular group of children or individual who dominate classroom discussion.
- Locate children (boys and girls) who are shy and do not participate in classroom activity and encourage them to ask question.
- Girls as well as boys should be encouraged to speak, voice their opinion, answer question and generally verbalize their thoughts in a constructive way.
- Boys and girls should be taught to respect each other's opinion consensus and skills of negotiation should be developed in both the sexes.
- Reward good performance of boys and girls.
- Encourage healthy competition between boys and girls.
- Stigmatizing boys and girls for failure of performing any kind of activities should be consciously avoided.

Some Suggestive Steps for Curriculum transaction in Few Subject Areas:

Languages

Language is a means of communication among different individuals. It is the major medium through which different content areas are taught to students. Language has the largest potential to encompass all human interactions, ideas, values, philosophies. In the context of languages, it usage should not be a marker of discrimination between sexes. Conscious efforts should be made for avoiding words that are derogatory for girls and women. In the teaching of languages the following steps can be taken:

- Avoid use of sexist language that is derogatory, especially for the girls.
- Constant use of he, himself, man, mankind should be avoided. Instead they, themselves, people, human beings etc. should be used depending upon the content and the context.
- Language should be used to develop a sense of mutual respect and dignity.
- Create situation where girls and boys can express themselves freely and develop self confidence and mutual trust.
- Highlight examples of women who have contributed in different fields.

Mathematics

Mathematics has the possibility of leading the child from concrete to the abstract. It is therefore possible to show the equal contribution which men and women make in different walks of like such as sharing labor and resources. In the teaching of mathematics some suggestive steps can be taken for making the subject gender inclusive:

- Dignity of work in all walks of life should be reflected through exercises projecting computation of time, labor and energy devoted to each task.
- Growing participatory role of women in all walks of life must be reflected in mathematical problems.
- Gender disaggregated data on literacy, enrolment and work force participation in different sectors of the economy can be used as examples in mathematics.

Social Sciences

The subject matter of social studies deals with interaction of human beings with physical and social environment around himself/ herself in the context of time, space and institutions. Therefore, the contribution of men and women at different points of time needs to be woven in different disciplinary areas in a conscious manner. This can be done if the following is addressed:

- Substantiate Social-Science lessons with women's contributions particularly from the marginalized sections of the society. In the chapter on freedom struggle examples of women like Sarojini Naidu, Madam Bhikaji Cama, Annie Besant, Ramabai Ranade and many more can be given who contributed effectively in the attainment of *Swaraj*.
- Films, pictures, slides of men and women performing occupation jointly in primary, tertiary and service sector can be substituted with the lesson taught based on the context and requirement.
- Fundamental rights and duties should be explained with concrete examples from personal experience of children from diverse social origins.
- Emphasis should be placed on examples that highlight– Equality and Equal abilities of men and women in performing various functions in different fields.
- Thoughts and sayings of eminent persons both men and women should be told to the children wherever it is required.
- Encourage students to identify women who have made significant contribution to the society such as Sudha Murty, Ela Bhatt, Radha Phadkar and many more from deprived groups in different fields.

In addition to make the pedagogical processes gender inclusive, an important site that needs to be tapped in the schooling processes and which needs to be nurtured and strengthened is the voices of children that are very perceptible in peer group interactions.

Peer Group Interactions

Studies have shown that for analyzing behaviors and attitudes of students, observations of peer group interactions in classroom situations and outside classroom activities are very important. They give first hand information about students perceptions about their notions about various issues concerning them. Normally, there is no guiding principle regarding peer group formation. Such groups are formed on the basis of mutual liking, interests etc. Sometimes peer groups are also based on socio-economic backgrounds and at times sex is a determining factor in formation of groups. Peer groups are not always well adjusted, sometimes behavioral problem keep erupting e.g. intra-group rivalry. This phenomenon is sometime visible in situations when boys tease girls and when jostling, pushing and fighting also occur between groups and within groups. Peer groups also display different treatment towards their teachers and seniors. Sometimes teachers face behavioral problems from certain students belonging to a group. In such cases teachers have to try out steps to handle children with behavioral problems. In order to promote harmonious and healthy peer group interactions among sexes some suggestive steps can be undertaken:

Guidelines for Group Interaction

- Encourage formation of mixed peer group.
- Mixed group formation including children who conform to school and classroom rules and those who adopt a deviant attitude.
- Encourage sharing and caring between peers.
- Promote healthy competitions between group.
- Identify tasks for accomplishment through group activity.
- Form mixed groups to carry out multifaceted tasks in keeping the school environment emotionally and physically free of biases and stereotypes.
- Form groups which includes boys and girls to explore the nature of events, for instance survey of social practices.

Thus, gender issues in education entails a very conscious effort made on the part of teacher educators and teachers, who as change agents can attempt to translate the textual materials, make pedagogical processes and classroom management gender sensitive. Such an effort on the part of the teachers in the long run would help in undoing gender bias and gender stereotypes perpetuated by primary and secondary agents of socialization.

References

1. *National Policy on Education,* 1986, MHRD, New Delhi.
2. *Programme of Action* 1992, MHRD, New Delhi.
3. *National Curriculum Framework 2005*, NCERT, New Delhi.
4. *Position paper National Focus Group on Gender Issues in Education*, 2006, NCERT, New Delhi.
5. Srivastava, G. Jaireth, S. Raj Rani, Evaluation of NCERT *primary and upper primary text books from the view point of gender bias and gender stereotyping*, Department of Women's Studies, 1996-97.
6. Srivastava, Gouri, *The Study of Impact of Incentive Schemes on the Progress of Education of Girls.*
7. Form disadvantaged groups SC, ST, OBC in Rajgarh and Dhar districts of Madhaya Pradesh.
8. Department of Women's Studies, NCERT, 2000.
9. Srivastava, Gouri, *Gender concern in the Social studies text books of Pakistan and Bangladesh*, International Textbook Research, July, 2005, Braunswigh, Germany.
10. Nayar, Usha, et. al, *Identification of factors related to Difficulties* in the Recruitment and Posting of Women Teachers in Rural Areas, 1995-96, Department of Women's Studies , NCERT.
11. Cuff, E.C., Cassidy A. Hustler D (eds.): *Action Research in Classroom and Schools*, 1986, London, Allen and Unwin, Sydney.
12. Denscombe, Martyn, Classroom Control: *A Sociological Perspective*, Allen and Unwin Publishers, 1985, U.K.
13. Govinda, R. (Ed.), *Indian Education Report : A Profile of Basic Education*, NIEPA, Oxford University Press, 2002.
14. Husen, Torsten, and Boalt, Gunna, *Educations Research and Educational Change*, John Wiley and Sons, Inc, Sydney, 1968.

15. Jerome, H., Freiberg and Driscoll, Amy, Scoll, *Universal Teaching Strategies*, Allyan and Bacon, London, 1992.

16. *"Teacher Education in a Changing Society",* Commonwealth Conference on Teacher Education, held in Nairobi, Kenya, 26 April – May 1973, Commonwealth Secretariat, 1974.

17. Nayar, Usha, From Girl Child to Person: *Resource materials for Teachers and Head Teachers of Primary Schools in India,* UNESCO, 1995, New Delhi Office.

18. Steere. F. Bob, Becoming on Effective Classroom Manage: A Resource Book for Teachers, 1988, State University of New York Press. Walker, Rob, A Guide to Classroom Observation, 1975, London, Methuen and Co. Ltd.

19. Wheldall, Kevin and Glym, Ted, Effective Classroom Learning, 1989, Basil Blackwell, Oxford.

Chapter–23

Construction and Standardization of Pupil Classroom Learning Behaviour Observation Schedule

Introduction

Proper Education of the future citizen of the country is important, it goes without saying. For this one has to look both formal training in and beyond school i.e. at home, in the neighborhood and in the other social institutions through various customs, festivals, bringing up techniques, etc. which goes on all the time. Formal training in the school require healthy atmosphere there for proper growth of the students, one of the methods for assessing it is through observation of classroom behavior of pupils. For objective assessment of classroom behavior little research work has been done, particularly in our country. There is dearth of such objective tools. The development of Pupil Classroom Leaning Behavior Schedule (PCLBOS) is one such attempt in this direction. This should be seen in this light and needs further studies to enlarge the scope and applicability of this tool.

Aim of the Schedule

There are number of observation schedules available which have been cataloged in Simon and Boyer (1967). These tools were not found to be relevant as classroom learning behavior of Pupils did not receive the emphasis, which was envisaged in the study (Yadav 1993). So, Pupil classroom learning observation schedule

Dr. Mahabir Yadav, Principal at Army Insititue of Education, Delhi Cantt.

(PCLBOS) was designed and constructed by the author, keeping in view of the specific need for use in India. This observation is an instrument to observe and record not only pupil learning behavior but also envisages observation and recording of teacher behavior as additional to pupil classroom learning behavior.

Development of the Tool

For identifying categories of pupil classroom behavior, the observational system available in Simon the Boyer (1967) and Cohen (1976) were studied. Besides, four science lesson of class X were observed at four different point of time during the academic session – two lesson in the beginning and two toward the end of the session. Descriptive notes were taken regarding the classroom learning behavior of pupil and teacher behavior either initiator stimuli or responses to pupil behaviors. The observational notes and their contents were analysis was listed. They relevance and logical inter-relationships notes and logical inter-relationships. From this exercise, seven areas emerged *viz.*:

i. Attention
ii. Response
iii. Seatwork
iv. Soliciting Teacher Help
v. Peer Interaction
vi. Helping Teacher
vii. Managerial Activities

Similar exercises were carried out in respect of teacher behaviors. The teacher behavior categories emerging out of the analysis were:

a) Explanation
b) Questioning
c) Helping
d) Supervising.
e) Management according to the function of the behavior sets.

The present tool has twenty-five specific pupil classroom learning behavior categories selected on the basis of their occurrence during the classroom transactions. Some categories were added on the basis of the analysis of the process of instruction.

The teacher behavior were categorized in five areas: these five areas of teacher behavior have 13 specific behavior categories. The tool provides specific pupils classroom-learning behaviors on one axis. The schedule carries enough space against each item to second observation. After every three seconds a dot is recorded and so every minute almost 20 observed are recorded for each pupil. Like this the recording capacity of one sheet is of six minutes durations and for one pupil usually seven schedule sheets are required to record a lesson of about forty minutes.

The tool (PCLBOS) is given in the *Appendix* along with categories and their operational definitions.

Observer Training and Reliability

Keeping in view the needful reliable observation, intensive training in the use of observation tool under the guidance of an expert is required. The author (MBY) and 3 other were trained in using (PCLBOS) for observing pupil classroom behavior. The training in observation continued till inter-observer reliability using Scott co- efficient of agreement worked out to be *80 and above. The reliability indicated for the 4 observers were *80, *81, *85 and *87 (Yadav 1993). Intra observer reliability was worked through coding a tapped lesson with a gap of 2 weeks, ranged between *79 and *83. These indexes were considered reliable for coding the pupil's classroom learning behavior (Yadav 1993).

Validity of the Schedule

Validity refers to extent the scale measures what it purposes to measure. Six experts read the items and rated what it measures – thus indicating face validity of the test. All agreed that it measures classroom-learning behavior of students and teachers. It showed high face validity of the scale.

Context validity also is high. Since the pupil classroom learning behavior was defined to include "total verbal and non verbal learning from teacher instruction". Similarly teacher classroom behaviors include "all the verbal and not verbal behavior during classroom transactions by the teacher" (Yadav 1993, pages 16 and 19 respectively). As stated earlier, the items were constructional for each behavior area and rated separately. Each category was adequately and satisfactorily defined (Appendix–1).

Utility of PCLBOS

In his study, Yadav (1993) has shown that the hypotheses tested with regard to area wise prediction were by and large confirmed, for example listening attentively had positive correlation and looking fatigued had negative correlation with achievement in science, etc. similar studies are needed in other subject as well.

Usefulness of the PCLBOS

This tool can be used in all studies where improvement in classroom behavior of pupils, in qualities of education variables, school achievements, standards of education, etc are envisaged as a variable to be evaluated.

The tool can be and in fact, should be used in al educational institution particularly in education of teacher whenever the aim Is to improve the quality of life of students/teachers and the overall quality of education as such. This pupil classroom learning behavior and their outcome have important role to play in future as the future of nation, a society, a group or an individual depends upon progressiveness for which education acts as a major instruments.

The tool can help n queries asked by professionals, like;

a) What do pupil do in the classroom?

b) What are the instructional resources available and how they are make use of?

c) What are the ways, which can be suggested to teachers to exhibit teacher behavior pattern to generated the desired level learning in pupil?

d) Do pupils differ in their classroom learning behaviors? If so, do they differs in their achievement?

Limitations

The tool was developed and tried out in a couple of studies confined to one grade (Class -X) and one subject only (Yadav 1993). Inter grade, inter subject and even intra-subject variations need to be studied for developing further the scientific basis of the art of teaching. The tool need to tried out at different places, by larger number of observers and on larger number of subjects. There is a wide scope of further refinement and improvement.

Appendix

Pupil Classroom Learning Behavior Observation Schedule (PCLBOS):

Sl. No.	**Sources of Behavior**	**Behaviors Area**	**Category**	**Definition**
1.	Pupil	Attention	(a) Listening Attentively	Applying ones mind. Pupils giving watchful head to the wishes of other or pupils i.e. the teacher in the classroom. Looking towards the speaker showing listening gestures.
			(b) Looking Fatigue	Showing sign of weariness, resulting in yawning, dozing changing setting posture too often.
			(c) Looking Distracted	Diversion of attention, symptomised in looking away from the source of communication involved in unsolicited behavior.

Sl. No.	Sources of Behavior	Behaviors Area	Category	Definition
			(d) Involved Disruptive Behavior	The behaviors indicate of disruption like disturbing peer, speaking irrelevant a tone that takes away other pupil attention from the learning tasks.
2.		Response	(a) Volunteer Response	Showing eagerness to respond by raising hands or other gestures like partially raising the body. Asking the teacher for permission to respond verbally.
			(b) Volunteer Ideas	Using initiative, contribute ideas on his own without being called specifically by one teacher.
			(c) Does not Respond	Silence or withholding of reaction to stimulus from the teacher.
3.		Seat Work	(a) Reading Books Attentively	The action of pursuing written or printed matter, engrossed in reading.
			(b) Preten-ding to Read Book	Posing to read the book, showing sign of restlessness though keeping the book in front in ready position, looking away and often without any solicitation.
			(c) Coping from Blackboard	Writing and noting down the solutions of problems or points written on the blackboard.
			(d) Evades Seatwork	The act of being engaged in off task behavior poses as if doing seatwork but involved in disruptive behavior.

Sl. No.	Sources of Behavior	Behaviors Area	Category	Definition
4.		Soliciting Teachers Help	(a) Reaches the teacher for removing difficulties	In the case of difficulties in the assigned learning task or self-study, approaches teacher for help.
			(b) For help to complete seatwork	Solicit help for completion of seatwork.
			(c) For clarifying doubts	The act or processes of seeking clarification of ideas from the teacher.
			(d) For management of disruptive behavior	In the event of being disturbed by the peer, reaches teacher for help in the management of disruptive behaviors of the peer.
			(e) Waits for teachers help	Gap between the time reaching teacher for help and the time actually received.
5.		Pupil-pupil interaction	(a) Discussing a Point	Examination of matter by arguing for and against in a specific direction during classroom interaction.
			(b) Giving Help	To deliver, communicate, impart or render the necessary assistance to a pupil to fulfill his needs during classroom transaction.
			(c) Accepting Help	To take or receive an assistance to fulfill ones need for peers during classroom transaction.
			(d) Responding to pupils questions	Replying to question raised by peers in the classroom transaction.

Sl. No.	Sources of Behavior	Behaviors Area	Category	Definition
6.		Extends Help to Teacher	(a) In handling of Material	Help the teacher in the presentation of aids, teaching material during classroom transaction (as in case of demonstration).
			(b) On blackboard	The act of pupil writing on the blackboard as assigned by teacher or volunteering to solve a sum or problem on blackboard.
7.		Managerial Activity	(a) Teacher Directed	Managerial activities like organization of groups for different tasks, rearranging of seats etc. as directed by the teacher.
			(b) Self Directed	Managerial activities done on his own will without teacher direction.
8.	Teacher	Teacher Explanation	(a) Explains Plan	Refers to explanation provided according to previous plans of the teacher. Explanation involves a general pupil need but not as immediate pupil need. A scheme of action, project, design, explanation, the way in which it is proceeding i.e. details description of subject matter in a sequence of long range effect.
			(b) Explains Need	It refers to instructional explanation provided to the student to satisfy a clear and immediate student need for help. To unfold, interpret and open out to make one self-arising from facts and circumstances of a case or the state of extreme wants.

Sl. No.	Sources of Behavior	Behaviors Area	Category	Definition
			(c) Writes on Blackboard	Use of blackboard by the teacher for the purpose of academic instruction and explanation of the content.
			(d) Handles Materials	Use of material for demonstration or use of teaching aid by teacher in the classroom.
9.		Teacher Question-ing	(a) Teacher Asks Question	Stimulus or enquiry make by teacher in the order to attain required response from pupils in the classroom on the content taught or, to be taught.
			(b) Listen to Pupil Response	After posing a question or stimulus to a pupil, teacher gives a watchful head to pupils reply.
10.		Teacher Helping	(a) Providing Help to Pupils	To assist the pupil according to pupils need for solicited or unsolicited.
			(b) Encoura-ging Pupils	To provide reinforcement through encouragement.
11.		Teacher Super-vision	(a) Super-vising Seatwork	To go around the class to assist the pupils who are engaged in the seat-work and extend help where needed.
			(b) Corrected feedback	Providing informative unsolicited behavior or performance in relation to learning objective sets promote guidelines for prompting.

Sl. No.	Sources of Behavior	Behaviors Area	Category	Definition
12.		Teacher Management	(a) Management of Disruptive Behavior	Controlling people behavior to avoid disruption of normal classroom transaction.
			(b) Gives Direction	Providing direct guidelines to pupils for specific creativities.
			(c) Interruption by Outsider	The interference, halt or, break caused in the flow of teaching learning by institute in the class.

References

1. Cohan, L. (1976): *Educational Research in classroom and school: a manual of material and methods*. London : Harper & Raw.
2. Simon, A and Boyer, E. G. (Ed.) (1967, 1970): Mirrors for behavior; An anthology of classroom observation instruments. Philadelphia: Research for better School.
3. Yadav, M (1993) *Classroom behavior of pupils. The Academic Press*. Gurgaon, Haryana.

Chapter–24

Characteristics of Good Grammar Presentation

It is said that grammar is the essence and soul of any language learning. Therefore, it is all the more imperative that a good language teacher should be equipped with some of the basic features of a good grammar presentation which will make teaching learning experience fun, interesting and exhilarating both to the teacher and the taught.

Let's find out what should be included in a good grammar presentation.

1. **Is a surprise:** As strange as it might seem, a disbelieving look, a "No, really?" or most of the class getting what you are trying to elicit wrong are all good signs in a grammar explanation-signs that you have really got their attention, that you are teaching them something they don't know yet, and that it is something they are likely to be something they are still thinking about when they leave class and so remember for a longer time than usual. Ways to achieve this sense of surprise include contradicting their previous teacher or lower level textbook, contrasting with L1, contrasting spoken and written English grammar, and contrasting prescriptive grammar and how the language is really used nowadays. Something turning out to be much easier than they originally thought is also a nice surprise!

---

1. Dr Amita Puri, Lecture in Education Army Insititue of Education, Delhi Cantt.

2. Mandeep Bhalla, Teacher in Oxford Public School, Vikas Puri, Delhi

2. **Is Interactive:** Ways of getting students involved in the grammar explanation stage include: getting them to give you example sentences from their imaginations, previous conversations or the textbook; eliciting the names of grammatical forms; getting them to match grammatical names, example sentences and meanings; getting students to prepare grammar presentations for the class for homework; using guided discovery tasks they work through in pairs; and deliberately making mistakes they can correct you on.

3. **Is Copied Down:** After a student has understood your grammar explanation, the next stage should be copying it down. You can ensure that everyone has a chance to copy it down accurately by having the pause for copying written into your lesson plan, making sure nobody copies before you want them to so that they join in the eliciting and don't make others feel guilty for copying down later, and putting your OHP sheets etc somewhere students can see them after class to compare their own versions to.

4. **Is Easy To Copy Down:** You can make this easier by putting all the text on the board into a table (e.g. 3 columns for tense, example sentence and meaning, and three rows for the three past tenses), using very simple time lines and sketches, limiting the amount of text, and giving them a gapped version of the grammar presentation to copy the important things off the board into.

5. **Can Be Easily Referred To:** As well as something that is easy to understand and easy to copy down, you will want to make sure that the grammar explanation is something that the students and teacher can easily refer to during later grammar practice and error correction stages. To achieve this you will need to make sure that the grammar explained is exactly the same as is used later in the lesson. You can also make it easy to refer to by keeping it up on the board (in which case you will need to make sure when you write it that there is room around it to write other things that come up), saving it as an OHP slide you can put up when you need it, or by making students write it in a separate grammar part of their notebooks.

6. **Is Actually Referred To:** The easiest way of making sure that students actually do refer to the grammar presentation later in the lesson is to make some of the answers to the exercises you have given them exactly the same words as you used in the grammar explanation. The same thing can also be done with useful phrases for communicative activities, or for sentences from the homework. You can also encourage its use by getting students to refer back to it every time you do error correction on that grammar point in future lessons.

7. **Is At The Right Time In The Lesson:** There are two parts to thinking about this- making sure the students are alert enough when the grammar explanation comes to understand it and remember it, and making sure that it fits in with the rest of the lesson. You can make sure they are alert by making the grammar explanation near the beginning of the lesson, perhaps after a quick warmer. The end of the lesson is the second most alert period, with the middle being the worst. You can add to this alertness by making them need the grammar by getting them used to a lesson structure where practice always follows a grammar explanation, or by asking them to do a task where the language could be useful first as in TTT and some versions of TBA.

8. **Is At The Right Stage Of The Lesson:** This depends very much on what your teaching approach is and on the specific grammar point. For example, do you want to introduce the grammar point after the students have had a chance to use a task or text where it could be used and so know why they need the language, or will they feel "safer" if you introduce it from the start? Do you want to tackle it after revising the most recent or most similar grammar point, or is there the chance you will get bogged down in that and not be able to concentrate on the new point? Which stage of the lesson grammar explanations come in can often be a compromise with the timing of the lesson in other ways. For example, lots of revision and seeing the language in context might put the grammar explanation right in the middle of the class when students are least alert.

9. **Is At The Right Point In Their Language Development:** The difficulty of choosing to tackle a grammar point just by when the students are most alert is that their brains still might not be ready to take that particular grammar point in. This is often connected to the idea of Natural Order (the theory that both L1 and L2 language learners make progress with grammar points in a predictable fashion), but sometimes is more just simple logic of whether it is easier to explain the use of will for predictions before or after teaching the use of will for conditionals.

10. **Comes At The Right Interval Since The Last Connected Grammar Explanation:** Another factor worth bearing in mind when putting grammar into a syllabus is how long it will take students to really absorb a grammar point and therefore be ready for the next step with it. This factor can both shorten and lengthen the amount of time you wait. For example, students might be able to produce the first conditional at the end of the lesson but for them to really get a subconscious feeling for what it means and how it is used they will probably need at least another couple of weeks of chances to mull on it, use it in conversation and/ or see it in context before they will benefit from more conscious examination of this or a related grammar point (e.g. will for predictions or the second conditional). At the same time, the theory of Natural Order suggests that however much time and help we give students, they will still make errors with the Present Simple, so we shouldn't get stalled on that before we move onto forms we can contrast it with like the Simple Past or Present Continuous just because they are still making mistakes.

11. **Is For The Most Useful Language:** At That Point As well as looking at what language students are mentally ready to learn, we also need to look at what language they need. This can be defined by what they need for their work or studies, what they need for an EFL or other exam, what they need in order to cope with the next class they are going to go into, what they need to catch up with the better students in this class, what they need

in order to boost their motivation, what they need to be able to understand classroom instructions, what they need in order to be ready for the next grammar point, what they need in order to understand important functional language (e.g. Can for ability leading onto Can for requests), what they need in order to use a particular communicative skill (e.g. relative clauses for talking your way around a word you don't know), or what they need in order to benefit from English that is all around them (e.g. popular songs or station announcements in English).

12 . **Is Something Students Understand the Need For:** A teacher who has decided a particular grammar point is what students need will also need to make sure that students identify that need. This can be achieved by some explanation from the teacher ("With this grammar you will be able to..."), by doing a communicative activity where that grammar would be useful before you present it, or, even better, something that is obvious to students straightaway as something they can use inside or outside the classroom.

13. **Is The Right Length:** This usually means short, so that they can write it all down in their notebooks and there is plenty of time for practice. Sometimes, however, grammar presentations can be too short. You might need to plan for extra example sentences if they don't understand the ones you have chosen and/ or an extra little tricky bit of that grammar if they knew all the rest of it before you started the presentation.

14. **Includes Revision:** This could be revision of the form you are contrasting it with (e.g. Going to when presenting Will), revision of the grammatical forms it is similar to (e.g. Present Continuous or Past Continuous when presenting Future Continuous), or revision of a different meaning of the same form (Present Continuous for Present and Future).

15. **Gives The Students Something New:** One of the biggest criticisms of PPP is that the teacher often ends up presenting language that the students already know. You can make

sure that you are adding something new by gauging what students know as you elicit from them and then add one of the extra back up points you have prepared just in case. Possible back up points include exceptions (e.g. state verbs when presenting the continuous) and extra meanings (e.g. Present Simple when the word makes something true in "I name this ship" or "I do solemnly swear)".

16. **Gives The Students A Sense Of Anticipation:** From your own experience of being taught grammar at school, it might seem unrealistic that a class of students could be on the edge of their seats waiting to see how a grammar explanation turns out. There are, however, plenty of techniques to ensure that. One is to make sure that something about the grammar explanation is completely new to them (see other points). Another is to give them a spoken or written task they cannot achieve properly without the grammar and let them try it again after your explanation. In a similar way, starting a grammar presentation with a collection of real student mistakes from that class is great for getting their attention, Perhaps the most effective is to start with a statement that what they thought about the grammar before is (at least in part) wrong.

17. **Is Asked For By The Students:** This is an example of the point above. The important thing to aim for is the letter 's', i.e. students asking (or at least wanting to know) rather than just one student. If more than one student asks for the same grammar explanation, then that is the ultimate sign that you have planned the lesson perfectly. Again, the best way of achieving this is to give them a task where certain grammar is necessary to complete it. Please note that many tasks in textbooks and communication games books are perfectly doable with much lower level language than the level of the book, and research suggests that at least some of your students will be perfectly happy with having dealt with such a task in pidgin English and so will be unlikely to listen carefully to any further explanation. The secret, then, is to design an activity where it comes to an end without a successful outcome without

the language you are about to present, which as mentioned in a point above should be something that is in at least part new to them. It is very difficult to design a free communication task where particular language is absolutely vital, so this is generally easier with a comprehension question that most people will get wrong because of grammatical reasons (sometimes available in EFL exams like IELTS and TOEIC), or pairwork tasks where students try to achieve a language-based task together. Examples of the latter include grammar auctions and pair work grammar correction tasks where one student has the correct version for each pair of sentences.

18. **Is Something The Students Want To Use Straightaway:** Another advantage of giving students a task that stops half way through or comes to an unsuccessful end until they get the grammar is that they are likely to want to turn straight back to the task at hand and finish it off successfully with their new knowledge. As with anything students do unguided by a teacher, this is likely to increase how much they learn.

19. **Uses A Familiar Format:** In order to make sure that students can concentrate on the grammar being explained rather than the explanation itself, it is good to develop a familiar format of grammar explanations so that students instantly understand (consciously or unconsciously) what each part of your explanation means. Things to standardize include the colours of pens (red= name of tense etc), the layout of board (you always use tables and the right column is always the meaning of the grammar etc), the use of names and symbols (writing out "noun" or "subject verb" in full or just using first letters etc.), and gestures (hand over the shoulder to illustrate "past", always exactly the same hand positions to illustrate each preposition etc).

20. **Is Visual:** This makes a grammar explanation catch the eye more, cuts down on the amount of difficult language you need to explain the grammar, caters well to students who have a visual learning style, allows you to approach the same grammar for

several different directions, and can be easier to copy down and recall than the part of the grammar explanation that has words. Probably the most effective way of using pictures is to have a striking and memorable image such as a famous TV commercial or painting that the whole lesson is built around and students can use to recall the grammar point by picturing the image. Other techniques involving a visual element include the use of different colour pens to mean different things, time lines, simple stick man drawings and using flashcards.

21. **Is Active:** This can partly be a case of getting the students involved by asking you questions or joining in when you are eliciting, and partly a case of making sure the physical movement and noise you can easily build into a warmer doesn't die to be replaced by still bodies staring blankly at the board when this stage comes. This can be achieved by using gestures to illustrate grammatical forms (e.g. pointing forward = future), example sentences ("I was jumping when you shouted stop"), word and sentence stress, and right and wrong answers.

22. **Is Personalized:** As with many things in language learning, making sure the example sentences used in grammar explanations are personalized to the students can really help them understand more easily, and make the language more memorable and obviously useful. Ways of personalizing the language include statements about individuals in the class ("William is next to John"), statements about the teacher ("He is wearing a pink tie"), or statements about the class as a whole ("Most people live in a flat"). Another way of looking at personalization is telling students that the language covered is aimed particularly at their weaknesses, most common mistakes, upcoming test, jobs or studies.

23. **Is Topical:** Another way to make any language stick in the mind is to make it connected to the particular time and day it is being explained on. In a similar way to using a striking picture, many people find they can then help recall the relevant grammar point by bring back to mind the time it was explained. Ways of

making it topical include using recent news, celebrity gossip, weather, seasonal changes, natural events, national holiday etc. as an example sentence.

24. **Is Memorable:** The tips about being visual, physical, personalized and topical above can all really help with making a grammar explanation and therefore the grammar you are explaining more memorable. Other tips relevant to this dealt with elsewhere include making sure students are awake and ready to take it in. The use of humour and making sure you connect the grammar to things the students already know can also help a lot. Teaching grammar in context is also important.

25. **Is Easy To Understand:** Ways of ensuring this include the use of gestures and visuals, but you will need to make sure that you introduce even these simple techniques for the first time during easy grammar explanations and that you use the same ones consistently. The same is true of grammatical terminology such as the names of types of words and the names of tenses. You can also simplify this point by using grammatical jargon that is most similar to that used in the students' first language, school system or dictionaries. For example, many students know SVO without knowing the words Subject Verb Object, and the same is true of dictionary abbreviations such as (n) for noun and (adj) for adjective.

26. **Is Easy To Reproduce:** As well as being easy to copy down, a grammatical explanation should be something that students can easily repeat back to you when it comes to eliciting an explanation of the same grammar point for revision or to contrast it with another grammatical form. For example, you can make the grammatical terminology more memorable by explaining why an adverb is called an adverb and what the Simple in Present Simple means, so they can use those words the same way you do next time you ask them to correct their own or their partner's mistakes.

27. **Is Linked In Theme To The Rest Of The Class:** For example, you could make the character names and place names of your example sentences the same as in the textbook, use

example sentences straight out of a listening or reading text, use student mistakes from a previous speaking exercise, or give sentences that could be useful in a future speaking exercise. This not only makes how the language links to the rest of the lesson clear, but can make everything dealt with in that lesson sit together as one memory in students' heads and so make recall easier. You can consciously use this effect in future classes by eliciting error correction with comments like "What was happening when the Italian waiter Paolo came into the room? Can you remember?"

28. **Is Relevant To The Tasks In The Rest Of The Lesson/ Course:** The most well-known ways of tying in with the course is by choosing suitable practice tasks and (if you are using PPP) making free speaking tasks ones students could use that same language in. Other things you might want to look at is tying the grammar in with a present or future class graded reader, end of term student presentations, project work, a production (free speaking) task a couple of weeks later when they have had a chance to really get to know the language, a future reading or listening, or GTKY (getting to know you) tasks at the beginning of the course at the next level up.

29. **Helps The Next Grammar Explanation:** For example, explaining "going to" as "a plan i.e. something in your head" in today's lesson can help explain Present Continuous as "something in your diary" when you introduce it in next week's lesson.

30. **Stretches The Teacher:** Ways of making sure you are as interested in the grammar explanation as the students are and therefore pass on some of your passion include introducing new technology such as a video extract, teaching an exception to the rule that you have always tried to avoid before, dealing with the stages of a grammar lesson in a different way (e.g. TTT instead of PPP), teaching the same grammar but to a different level (all the uses of Present Simple to an Advanced class or Simple Past before Present Continuous to a Beginner class), using an explanation from a different book, finding the best explanation from

all the possible books, adding phonemic symbols to the drilling of the grammar, and copying the grammar presentation of another teacher you have observed.

31. **Looks At The Grammar In A Different Way:** As well as adding a little something to the understanding of the students each time they see the same point, looking at the same grammar in a totally different way in the hope that is suddenly clicks in a different part of their brain is always worth a try to maintain interest and boost learning. Methods include combining grammar points in unusual ways (e.g. a lesson on all the Continuous tenses to cover Future Continuous instead of a future tenses review) and teaching grammar just as sentence stems ("If I were you I'd...").

32. **Is Fun:** Hopefully the points above haven't made grammar presentations as daunting for the teacher as it was for the students before these kinds of things were taken into account. As with all parts of teaching, having a good atmosphere in class with smiling, joking and feeling like a group working together is at least as important as any more easily analysable technique like the ones described here.

Chapter–25

Relationship of Pupils Classroom Learning Behaviour of High and Low Achievers in High Schools of Delhi

Introduction

It was felt that the teaching process which did not receive the desired focus in the research on teacher effectiveness would be helpful in identifying effective teacher behaviours. In 1960's, tools with low inference categories of teacher behaviour with regard to teacher effectiveness could not yield expected results. Hence, the reviewers concluded that there were definite pattern of teachers pupil interaction between classroom and which can be objectively measured and characterized. It was seen that achievement perceptions and classroom climate were apparently related and that the relationship between teacher personality and teacher behaviour were uncertain.

The conceptual frame for research on teaching encompasses five sets of variables, namely presage, context, process – process and product variables. The presage variable relate to the characteristics of teachers like their formative experiences that is social class, age and sex and their cognitive and effective properties like their teaching experience, personality traits and teaching skills. Context variables relate to the conditions to which the teacher has to adjust, the characteristics of the school, classroom and pupil, school characteristics include the climate, community size, ethical

Dr Mahabir Yadav, Principal at Army Insititue of Education, Delhi Cantt.

composition of the community and buzzing school size; classroom characteristics include the class size, textbooks, educational hardware etc. While pupil characteristics include the pupils social class, age, sex, ability, attitude and knowledge. Besides these, the subject characteristics are also covered. Process variables concern actual activity of classroom teaching, teacher and pupil behaviours, while process-process variables deal with the interactive behaviour of teacher pupil behaviours. Finally product variables concern the outcome of teaching, the changes that occur in the pupils as a result of their involvement in classroom activities. The term pupil growth or pupil change can relate to cognitive, affective and psychomotor characteristics.

The quality and rapidity of social transformation, however, depends on the quality of education, which in turn depends on the quality on the quality of instruction. Research support is indispensable for improving effectiveness of teaching. Moreover, research on teaching, therefore, has assumed significance during the latter half of the last century. The classroom learning behaviour of pupils has been perceived as a missing link in the reviews on research on teaching. The present work is a modest attempt to bridge this gap in the area of teaching learning process.

Procedure

Pupils classroom learning behaviour of IX class students of schools of Delhi State has been observed with the help of the tool prepared by the authors i.e. Pupils Classroom Learning Behaviour Observation Schedule (PCLBOS).

Sample

The multistage sampling procedure was adopted comprising population of class IX students of science stream in senior secondary schools located in Delhi. At the first stage, 50 sections of class IX science subject were identified in 10 schools. At the second stage, the high and low achievers were identified in each class for observing the classroom learning behaviour.

Tool Used

Pupil's Classroom Learning Behaviour observation Schedule (PCLBOS) was designed and constructed by the investigators keeping in view the specific needs for the present study. The tool briefly described as under.

Pupil's Classroom Behaviour Observation Schedule:

There are seven pupil behaviours which were identified on the basis of the analysis of the process of instruction:

1. Attention
2. Response
3. Seatwork
4. Soliciting Teacher Help
5. Pupil-pupil Interaction
6. Extends help to Teacher
7. Managerial Activities

Observer Training

Inter an intra observer reliability were ensured for observing PCLB so that the data collection is reliable and valid. The tallies were recorded after every one minute in respect of high and low achievers – HA and LA, in a lesson of about 30 minutes.

Observation of Lessons

Pupils of high and low achievement were identified, who formed the sample of the study. Five classes of science section were selected randomly for the above observations. One pupil each of high and low achievement from each class were observed twice during he academic session. First, they were observed for two lessons (30 min. duration each) on consecutive days in the beginning of the session i.e. in July-Aug. Second time, the observation of PCLB of the same selected pupils was done towards the end of the academic session in Jan-Feb. when pupils were seriously preparing for the examination. The average to two consecutive lessons were taken as authentic percent occurrence of specific behaviours as BSL – Beginning of the session lesson and ESL – End of the session lesson.

Scoring and Tabulation of Data

The data analysis was done manually by the investigators. In the case of PCLB, the frequencies were to tallied and converted into percentages. These mean percentages formed the score for interpretation of the data.

Table – 1

Mean percentage of pupil classroom learning behaviour of high and low achievers in the beginning and end of the session – science theory teaching lessons:

Different Aspects of PCKB	High Achievers			Low Achievers		
	Beginning of the Session	End of the Session	Mean %	Beginning of the Session	End of the Session	Mean %
Attention	42.66	64.64	53.60	17.92	46	31.96
Response	14.66	15.98	15.32	4.04	11.32	7.68
Seatwork	14	12.66	13.33	12	10.66	11.33
Soliciting Teacher Help	5.38	3.32	4.35	8.66	8.66	8.66
Pupil-pupil Interaction	8.64	0.66	4.65	32.06	16.66	24.36
Pupil Helping Teacher	9.24	1.32	5.28	6	1.32	3.66
Managerial Activities	5.30	1.32	3.31	17.98	10.64	14.31

Table – 2

Mean percentages of each behaviour of PCLB of high and low achievers:

Sr. No	Pupil Behaviour	Mean Percentage
1	Attention	42.78
2	Response	11.50
3	Seat Work	12.33
4	Soliciting Teaching Help	6.50
5	Pupil-Pupil Interaction	14.50
6	Pupil helping Teachers	4.47
7	Managerial Activities	8.80

Results

Attention

The pupil attention behaviour has been revealed as maximum in terms of mean percentage behaviour of pupils. In high achievers, it is as high as 53.60 whereas in case of pupils of low achievement, it is 31.96. However, the overall mean percentage that is 42.78 shows that almost half the time pupils were quite attentive in the classroom. This is the only Pupil Behaviour which have gone over 40% as compared to the other behaviours.

Response

The response behaviour of high achievers is 15.3% as compared to 7.68% of low achievers. It reveals that the high achievers participation in more numbers as compared to low achievers. However, the mean value of response in 11.5% which is adequate time for involving pupils in teaching learning process in a classroom teaching.

Seat Work

The seat work of the class work given by the teacher is being handled by the pupils generally in the same proportion in about 12%. It has been observed that the high achievers are able to finish the seat work early as compared to the low achievers.

Soliciting Teacher's Help

The teacher's help is solicited more by the low achievers which is 8.66% as they need more and repeated explanation of the content, while the high achiever's frequency of soliciting teaching help is comparatively low, i.e. 4.35%.

Pupil-Pupil Interaction

The pupil interaction behaviour in relation to the content is much higher in case of low achievers as high as 24.36% as they want to discuss the matter at their level and are generally shy of asking teacher. The high achievers relatively discuss fewer points taught by the teacher and repent only 4.65% of their time.

Pupil Helping Teacher

The pupil helping teacher behaviour is higher in case of high achievers i.e. 5.25% as compared to low achievers i.e. 3.66% because they are more confident and are closer to teacher.

Managerial Activities

The low achievers have shown 14.31% of time being spent on managerial activities as compared to high achievers spending only 3.31% of time. It reveals that low achievers are more often distracted during the classroom transaction.

Discussion

The research paper has tried to answer questions; do pupils differ in their classroom learning behaviour? If so, do they differ in their achievement? Based on these questions, a new generation research on teaching involving several new variables have emerged. Like as we have seen above that attention behaviour of pupils has taken maximum time i.e. above 40%, which is quite significant, related to their achievement related efforts.

Secondly, pupil – pupil interaction variable has emerged as the next most dominant pupil behaviour in the classroom, which has covered about 15% of their time. It has been widely accepted that pupil interactions are more desired and helps a lot in keeping the pupil motivated in the class. If they are allowed more frequently to answer the other pupil's questions they show more enthusiasm and energy.

The next pupil behaviours are response and seat work, which has taken about 12% of their classroom time in the class transaction. These are also in consonance with the earlier research findings that pupil's response and pupil's seatwork variables are highly contributory to their academic achievement.

Soliciting teacher's help and pupil helping teachers are activities, which are about 5-6% of the total time. Hence they do not get much importance towards pupils achievement. Managerial activities generally consuming 9% of the time is also within the accepted norms as classes are distracted by the managerial work very often.

Conclusion

The pupil classroom learning behaviour and their outcome has emerged as an important area of research in teaching. The present survey findings are a modest contribution by initiating research in this area in schools of Delhi. It has provided results, which can be utilized for generating further studies in Delhi schools teaching learning process. It will provide practical guidelines for improving effectiveness of teaching when backed up by more researches.

References

1. Anderson, W. Lorin (1984). *Time and School Learning. Theory research and Practice*. Croom Helm London and Canberra.

2. Bloom, B.S. (1984). The Search for Methods of Groups Instruction as Effective as one to one tutoring, *Educational Leadership*, 41, 4-17.

3. Brophy, J. (1979). Teacher Behaviour and its Effects. *Journal of Educational Psychology*, 71, 753-60.

4. Donald, J. Veldman (1983). Type of Student Classroom Behaviour. *Journal of Educational Research*, 786, 4, 204.

5. E.C. Wragg (ed.), (1993) *Primary Teaching Skills, Routledge*, pp. 111-136.

6. Harrison, C. (1996). *The Teaching of Reading: What teachers need to know*, Shepreth, United Kingdom Reading Association, U.K.

7. Howe, M.J.A. (1999). Genius Explained, *Cambridge University press,* Cambridge.

8. Wragg, E.C. and Brown, G. (2001). *Knowing the Subject Matter*, pp. 43-52.

9. Yadav, M. (1993). *Classroom Behaviour of Pupils*. The Academic Press. Gurgaon, Haryana.

Chapter–26

Contextual Learning in Biology

The importance of knowledge lies in its use, in our active mastery of it—that is to say, it lies in wisdom. . . . Now wisdom . . . concerns the handling of knowledge, its selection for the determination of the relevant issues, its employment to add value to our immediate experience.

– Alfred North Whitehead (1929/1967, p.30)

Introduction

While teaching, it is not unusual to face questions from students like "Why do I have to know this?" or "Will I ever use this again?" You need to learn this because you will be tested over this material or this forms the basis for higher level biology, replies the teacher. Can we satisfy students by giving these replies? How to make teaching as well learning of life science interesting? Yes life science can be made very interesting by relating it to real life and real-life situations. Educators have an obligation to make the connection of what is being taught in their classes and the real world beyond. "Knowledge and information are best learned if the context is meaningful to the individual and if learning connects to some realistic and recognizable application" (Parnell, 2001). This is where contextual teaching and learning comes alive. Contextual learning is a phrase *to describe bringing applications to knowledge educators are teaching in their classrooms.* In

Dr. Bharti Dogra, Lecture in Army Institute of Education, Delhi Cantt.

contextual learning it is the major task of the teacher to broaden students' perceptions so that meaning becomes visible and the purpose of learning immediately understandable (Parnell, 1995).

What is the best way to convey the many concepts that are taught in a particular course so that all students can use and retain that information? How can the individual lessons be understood as interconnected pieces that build upon each other? How can a teacher communicate effectively with students who wonder about the reason for, the meaning of, and the relevance of what they study? How can we open the minds of a diverse student population so they can learn concepts and techniques that will open doors of opportunity for them throughout their lives? These are the challenges teacher's face every day, the challenges that a curriculum and an instructional approach based on contextual learning can help them face successfully.

What is Contextual Learning?

The dictionary meaning of the word is "significance or purpose" (Webster's New World Dictionary, 1968). Asked to learn something that seems meaningless, students seem invariably to ask, "Why do we have to learn this?" Rightly they look for meaning, significance and purpose in their schoolwork. According to the distinguished psychologist Victor E. Frankl, "Man's main concern is not to gain pleasure or to avoid pain but rather to see a meaning in his life". Frankl says that we can discover ... meaning in life in three different ways:

1. by creating a work or doing a deed;
2. ... by experiencing something (such as) nature and culture or, ... by encountering ... another human being in his very uniqueness—by loving him ...; and
3. by the attitude we take toward unavoidable suffering . . . Meaning is possible in spite of suffering" (Frankl, 1959/ 1984, pp. 134-135).

Contextual teaching and learning, an instructional system, is based on the premise that meaning emerges from its relationship between the content and its context. Context gives meaning to content. The broader the contexts within which students are able to make connections, the more meaning the content will hold for them. A great part of the teacher's job, then, is to provide context. The more students are able to connect their academic lessons to this context, the more meaning they will derive from these lessons. To discover meaning in knowledge and skills leads to mastery of knowledge and skills.

Contextual teaching and learning engages students in significant activities that help them connect academic to their context in real-life situations. By making these connections students see meaning in their schoolwork. When students formulate projects or identify interesting problems, when they make choices and accept responsibility, search out information and reach conclusions, when they actively choose, order, organize, touch, plan, investigate, question, make decisions to reach objectives, they connect academic content to the context of life's situations, and in this way discover meaning. The discovery of meaning is the central characteristic of Contextual Learning.

Contextualization of Curriculum in NCF–2005

1. The basic idea of a model curriculum at the national level should only be seen as a way to set uniform general standards of education throughout the country. A common syllabus (or small variations of it) and common textbooks are certainly not to be expected for the country as a whole.
2. School systems in different states must derive their own curriculum. The larger states particularly need to reflect their diversity in their curricula.
3. Within the broad guidelines of the curriculum framework the syllabi and the textbooks must allow space for contextualizing and variations at the local level for all stages of school education.

Theoretical Grounding

The grounding of the contemporary work on contextual teaching and learning is based in the writings of John Dewey, in the early 1900s, who believed that schools must create communities of learners emphasizing experience, scientific methods of investigation, and democracy in the learning environment. John Dewey advocated a curriculum and teaching methodology tied to a child's interests and experiences, blending mind and body, and linking academics to application. He believed that the most powerful learning would come from combining the intellectual and the practical and in situating learning in the vocations of adult life, whether in professions or trades, academics, or the arts.

Dewey advocated project based learning. Educators were to design contextual group activities in which students worked together, as they would in the work place, to problem solve. "School should be less about the preparation for life and more like life itself" (John Dewey). "He emphasized the social aspects of learning and viewed schools as places where students could practice democracy and have opportunities to work together to identify problems" (Bizar & Daniels, 1998). Projects that make connections between curriculum and the work place have been, "...a time proven approach for providing rigorous, relevant, contextual, applied learning in a manner consistent with how learning takes place in the adult world and is also compatible with how the brain learns more efficiently" (Blank & Harwell, 2001).

Other theoretical strands over the years that have contributed to theory and practice of contextual teaching and learning include experiential learning, cognitive apprenticeship, transformative learning, critical theory, constructivism, reflective practice, adaptive teaching, action theories associated with situated cognition, social learning theory, communities of practice, and the work on multiple intelligences and different learning styles. An important basis for CTL is the brain-based research that shows that learning occurs faster and more thoroughly when what is being learned is presented in meaningful contexts, rather than fragmented facts, and that skills are developed more easily if learned in the context in which they will be used. Retention of new information (learning) requires cognitive restructuring and the connection of new information to what is already known.

Assumptions & Hypotheses

In effect, Contextual Teaching and Learning (CLT) provides a unifying base for a constellation of educational theories and practices and tests several assumptions and hypotheses. CTL is based on the hypotheses that:

- students tend to retain higher-level knowledge and skills longer when their experiences occur in multiple contexts that are as close to real-life situations as possible. When teachers provide opportunities for students to learn in multiple contexts, they are drawing upon the theories of cognition and learning that suggest the acquisition of knowledge is situated in particular physical and social contexts and that learning is inseparable from the contexts and activities within which it develops.
- learning naturally occurs by all learners in a variety of contexts inside and outside of school, cyberspace, and even in one's imagination. These multiple contexts offer valuable, engaging, and meaningful learning sites that extend beyond the school's classroom, bring reality and illustration to the subjects being taught in school, and facilitate transfer of knowledge to contexts and situations with which the student may not currently be familiar. Effective use of context does necessitate complex interaction of teaching methods, content and standards, situation, and timing to enhance the use of workplaces and non-school contexts to enhance learning outcomes for students.
- contextual teaching involves a commitment to the learning of all students, regardless of age, ethnicity, gender, socioeconomic status, family background, or disability. It also extends the concept of diversity to students with varying learning styles, values, personality characteristics, educational experiences, language, culture, and other life experiences that represent the many ways in which

students are diverse. CTL implies a belief that all students can learn and that they usually learn more profoundly and deeply in classrooms that reflect diversity. Contextual teaching involves planning lessons and instruction in relation to the diverse beliefs, values, skills, and experiences that students from diverse backgrounds bring into classrooms. Because different students learn in different ways, CTL offers students a variety of ways to learn and to demonstrate that they have learned.

- another assumption underpinning CTL is that ultimately, students must take responsibility for their own learning and that they do aspire and can be motivated to become independent, self-regulated, lifelong learners. Self-regulated learners acquire the requisite academic knowledge and skills in self-control and planning that help them learn easier, and they are motivated to learn more. Self-regulated learners are assumed to be well equipped to acquire knowledge about the subject and the task at hand, and strategies to learn about the subject, themselves as learners, and contexts in which they will apply the learning. Furthermore, they are motivated to learn and find schoolwork and research in the real world interesting because they value learning and coming to know how knowledge is used and applied in context.

CTL affects several aspects of schooling. For example, as a curriculum strategy, CTL emphasizes concrete applications of abstract ideas using contexts that have meaning, engage students in their learning, create opportunities for students to experience applications of knowledge first hand, and may even organize an entire program of studies around a profession or theme (e.g., the arts, science, careers). CTL, as an instructional reform, affects how a curriculum is delivered and supplements traditional teaching methods by allowing students to design and carry out projects, engage in hands-on learning, and learn from complex problem solving involving cross-disciplinary knowledge and skills. Nearly all theory and research point to the result of CTL as students' ability to apply knowledge in real-world contexts, engage in problem solving and higher levels of learning by drawing on various disciplines and sources of knowledge, and retain knowledge and its applications over the long term.

Using Contextual Teaching and Learning Strategies in Biology

The CTL model guides teachers to incorporate the following six strategies as they design instructional units.

1. Base learning on an overarching problem, which is in the context of students' community.
2. Plan for learning to be in multiple contexts.
3. Draw upon students' diverse skills, interests, experiences, and cultures.
4. Build in strategies that support students in becoming self-regulated learners.
5. Plan strategies that stimulate interdependence among students and their learning groups.
6. Examine students' learning outcomes by incorporating authentic assessment strategies.

1. Unfortunately biology is usually taught as separate units of knowledge in courses that are isolated from each other and from the real world outside. Students see no connection between ecology, genetics and biochemistry. When a connection is made to the world outside in biology classes, nature provides an integrating focus for this knowledge and an authentic context for their understanding.

- While teaching cell biology, a teacher is expected to cover prokaryotic and eukaryotic cells, cell division, and role of mitosis in growth, repair, replacement of old and damaged cells and role of meiosis in formation of gametes. These important and basic aspects need to be related to stem cell research, storage of stem cells and its use in screening drugs, toxins and restoring functions of diseased organs and the ethical dilemmas surrounding oocyte donation, embryo termination and on cogenesis.

- While explaining different types of microbes and their uses and harmful effects, role of HIV in causing AIDs, difference between HIV+ and AIDs patient, modes of transmission, social and economic consequences of AIDs needs to be discussed.
- While explaining ecosystem, a teacher discusses interdependence of biotic and a biotic components, food chains, energy transfer in a food chain, recycling of nutrients. These fundamental concepts and principles are placed in social contexts: urbanisation, pollution, ozone depletion, global warming etc.

2. The switch from teaching to learning can only be accomplished when a meaningful context for learning biology is presented. Despite the adoption of student-centered approaches, learning can only be superficial if the student does not have a biological context to stimulate learning. All biology pedagogy should be grounded in the study of the natural world. Real biology (plants, animals and microbes) are outdoors, not in labs, textbooks or on television. Nature must be the starting point for learning biology at all levels of the educational system. When students are exposed to the natural world in their school and university classes the material they learn in classrooms is integrated, relevant, and immediate.

Disconnection from nature can lead to alienation and indifference to the fate of natural ecosystems. We believe that the connection to nature should be established early and based in the community in which the students live. Children are attracted to plants and animals and are innately curious about the world around them. This love of nature can provide a "hook" to give students a will to learn more about biology and develop investigative skills to study the natural world. A connection to nature can develop into a caring attitude from which springs not only the desire to know more but moreover a sense of responsibility and stewardship to the place where one lives.

Many simple but powerful learning experiences can be made on the life in the schoolyard or in the 1 km radius around the school.

- Plant and animal identification is a beginning. Studies on bird and other animal behavior (fish, insects, snails, etc.) encourage careful observation.
- Similar exercises can be based on plant growth, distribution and dispersal. Species counts provide an appreciation of biodiversity.

Biology education grounded in a study of the natural world will provide students with the tools to investigate the crucial issues that face them now and in the future. Most of the major problems that we face in the world today, whether economic or ecological, are rooted in biology. This fact requires biologists, teachers and the general public to be able to deal knowledgeably with issues based on a wide variety of data input and opinions.

3. Contextual learning theory focuses on the multiple aspects of any learning environment, whether a classroom, a laboratory, a computer lab, a worksite, or a wheat field. It encourages educators to choose and/or design learning environments that incorporate as many different forms of experience as possible– social, cultural, physical, and psychological – in working toward the desired learning outcomes.

In such an environment, students discover meaningful relationships between abstract ideas and practical applications in the context of the real world; concepts are internalized through the process of discovering, reinforcing, and relating. For example in a biology class students might learn basic scientific concepts by studying the spread of AIDs or the ways in which farmers suffer from and contribute to environmental degradation.

Instructional Strategies for Contextual Learning of Biology

CTL is described as including at least seven strategies or instructional approaches that help students make meaning out of their school subjects. The methods of teaching that are used are based on the professional judgment of the teacher, the age and developmental level of the students, and the subject being taught. Among the approaches typically cited include:

- ***Problem-based learning***: An instructional approach that uses real-world problems as a context for students to learn critical thinking and problem solving skills and to acquire knowledge of essential concepts of a course. Learners draw on prior knowledge to understand and structure the problem, encode specificity (the context) into problem solving to make transfer of learning more likely, and elaborate on solutions through discussion, answering questions, peer teaching, and critiquing.
- ***Project-based learning***: A comprehensive approach to classroom learning designed to engage student investigation of authentic problems, including an in-depth study of a topic worth learning. Typically, students are engaged in a relatively extensive project that involves considerable time and effort, is grounded in complex, real-world contexts, and is developed to require students to apply academic skills and knowledge. Learning further requires students to draw from many subjects and information sources to complete the project and manage and allocate resources such as time, materials, and technology appropriately.
- ***Inquiry-based learning***:This approach is used concomitantly with reflective teaching and engages students in "what if" scenarios and investigations to construct mental frameworks that adequately explain their research and experiences. This instructional strategy is based on the theory of the inquiring mind, which seeks an answer, solution, explanation, or decision to some sort of query. Teachers and students read about, share, observe, critically analyze, and reflect upon that which is being studied to improve it, change, it, and or predict results.
- ***Work-based learning***: An educational approach that uses work places to structure learning experiences that contribute to the intellectual, social, academic, and career

development of students and supplements these with school activities that apply, reinforce, refine, or extend the learning that occurs at a work site. By so doing, students develop attitudes, knowledge, skills, insights, habits, and associations from both work and school experiences and are able to connect learning with real-life work activities.

- ***Service learning***: An instructional method that combines community service with a structured school-based opportunity for reflection about that service, emphasizing the connection between service experiences and academic learning. Service learning is integrated into student's academic curriculum and provides structured time for students to think, talk, and write about the learning taking place. Service learning enhances what is learned in school by extending student's learning beyond the classroom and into the community and helps to foster a sense of caring for others.
- ***Collaborative/Cooperative learning***: Sometimes defined separately, but both are instructional strategies that emphasize small groups in which students work together to maximize their own and each other's learning, accomplish a specific goal, or develop an end product. Ideally, learners engaging in cooperative or collaborative learning highlight individual group members' abilities and contributions. They share authority and acceptance of responsibility among group members for the group's actions. In general, collaborative learning focuses more on the process or working together, and cooperative learning (to complete or get the work done) stresses the product of such work but often includes some assessment of the process as well.
- ***Authentic assessment***: Assessment is authentic when student performance is measured on achievement that represents accomplishments that are significant, worthwhile, and meaningful. Authentic assessments attend to whether the student can craft polished, thorough, and

justifiable answers, performances, or products. It requires use of higher-order thinking skills, mastery of disciplinary context, elaborated communications, consideration of alternative solutions, and performance for authentic audiences. Authentic assessments typically include demonstrations of accomplishment, oral and written project reports, detail and descriptions of problems solved, evidence of work-based activities completed, critiques of literary and technical work, criteria-referenced assessment (often aided with the use of rubrics) by teachers and others, case study analyses, and so forth. Typically, assessments are put forth in a portfolio of accomplishments that represents a history over time of learning, organized progress of accomplishments, direct and valid outgrowths of standards and objectives set for the curriculum or learning event, and input from multiple human resources.

Other terms, related descriptions, and strategies often used to illustrate contextual teaching and learning include hands-on learning, real-world learning, case based learning, simulation, active learning, role-playing, applied learning, interdependent learning groups, and internships and externships.

Summing Up

Contextual teaching and learning is a response to a continuing challenge that so many students find school irrelevant to their lives and seem to have difficulty using knowledge they are required to learn to solve diverse, complex problems in other settings, inside and outside of school. For far too many students, especially those in high school, academic subjects seem to be taught through abstract, didactic, "chalk and talk" methods and textbook reading and memorization – all of which culminate in end-of course or end-of-year test taking based on recall from class notes and the textbook.

If teachers can design projects based on the curriculum and model an adult work place contextual and project-based learning will take place. These students in future will not face any problems in coping with the expectations of the work place. Employers are looking for students who can work well with others and have problem solving skills. "Technology literacy, problem solving, and creative thinking are the valued skills of all modern careers" (Blank & Harwell, 2001). By having teachers create projects and a classroom environment where students are encouraged to work together educators will be preparing the students for the "real world".

References

1. Bizar, M. & Daniels H. (1998). *Methods that matter: Six structures for best practice classrooms*. Maine: Stenhouse.
2. Blank, William E. and Sandra H. Harwell (2001). *Promising Practices*. Waco, Texas: CCI Publishing.
3. Dewey, John *(1938/1997)*. Chapter 3, *Criteria of experience from Experience and education*. Macmillan.
4. Frankl, Viktor (1959). *Man's Search for Meaning: an introduction to Logotherapy*, New York : Simon & Schuster, (Revised 1984).
5. *NCERT (2005). National Curriculum Framework 2005 Retrieved on 24 Jan., 2009 from* http://www.ncert.nic.in/html/pdf/schoolcurriculum/framework05/prelims.pdf.
6. NCERT (2005). *National Focus Group on Teaching of Science*. New Delhi : NCERT.
7. Parnell, D. (1995). *Contextual Teaching Works! Increasing Students' Achievement*. Waco, Texas: CCI Publishing.
8. Parnell, Dale (2001). Contextual Teaching Works! Waco, Texas: CCI Publishing.

SECTION – IV

Reflections on the Current Curriculum

Chapter–27

Privatization and Secondary Teacher Education: Issues and Challenges

Introduction

The phenomenon of privatization is as old as the existence of human being and, education as one of the social sectors, began primarily with private initiative only. Today, education in general and teacher education in particular is facing numerous challenges which needs to be resolved by the apex controlling bodies like NCTE, NCERT, NAAC, etc. The major challenges to teacher education and especially to secondary level teacher education are the quality deterioration, inequitable access and commercialization[1]. Privatization has raised several issues before teacher education from mid of 1990s. On one hand, privatization has increased access, technological advancement and job opportunity whereas, on the other hand, it has deteriorated quality at large.

Universalization of schooling and entry of new socio-economic order in form of Liberalization, Globalization and Privatization have boosted the issue of quality in school education as well as of teacher education. As NCF 2005 reflects, '*Globalization and the spread of market relations to every sphere of the society have important implication for education, at one hand we are witnessing the increasing commercialization of education and on the other hand inadequate public funding for education and official thrusts towards alternative education*'. NCF 2005

Mr Bhanu Pratap Pritam, Research Scholar in NUEPA, New Delhi.

also silently accepted the malfunctioning of education system due to privatization and curriculum needs to be redesigned in such a way that it can meet the diversified demands of learners and also emphasized the needs of distinct types of teacher training.

There exist several types of privatization in teacher education at secondary level in India. On the basis of management and funding, privatization secondary teacher education can be categorized basically of three types; Government Aided in which partial fund comes from government and partial funds arranged through private bodies as well as from students; Private Unaided (Self-Financing) in which entire cost of education is bared by the students only in privately managed teacher education institutions and; lastly and newly emerged category is Government Self-Financing in which government teacher education institutions run B.Ed. Courses in Self-Financing mode and entire cost of education is bared by students only in such types of government institutions. In the name of private self-financing teacher education course, institutions are in the practice of commercializing teacher education on the other hand, in the name of government self-financing course in teacher education, government is trying to withdraw public funding to teacher education and creating ways for privatization which further leads to commercialization as well in teacher education.

As far as the issue of quality and efficiency in teacher education are concerned in teacher education especially in the era of globalization and privatization, creating a professional teacher through one year pre-service teacher education programme seems more a notional than empirical. A longer duration of pre-service teacher education programme can seen as an alternative model of teacher education to prepare a professional teacher who can diagnose and resolve educational problems unlike any other professionals; Doctors, Engineers, Management Graduates, etc. Such kind of teacher education programme which prepares professionals are required in teaching profession at school level as well which can meet the diversified demands of learners.

Within teacher education, secondary teacher education (B.Ed) programme visualizes the preparation of quality teachers for secondary schools to serve those children who are going to face the toughest competition for getting into good quality higher education (technical and professional) institutions and for vocational education as well. The rationalization of quality higher and vocational education depends upon quality school education and quality of school education depends upon quality of secondary teacher education.

The private participation and quantitative expansion of secondary teacher education in last few years have posed multiple challenges which have been also emphasized by Sudeep Banarjee Committee Report[3] . Hence, it is indeed an issue to retrospect the entire teacher education programme in general and secondary teacher education programme in particular in the realm of LPG. This is the contemporary requirement to give a holistic touch to empower the teachers to make school education responsible for all round development of the children around the four pillars of education suggested by Delors Commission (1996).

Now, government has also identified privatization as the temporal solution of public demand of higher education. In the view of the tremendous pressure on total knowledge enterprise for higher education and teacher education in particular, privatization is not just an option but a natural evolution because state has started withdrawing funding to the higher education which was called non-merit good as well. But it is still under a great debate whether privatization should be considered as the offshoot of the crunch of public funding to higher education? Government has found it difficult to finance and setting up of new institutes because of several demographic, cultural and financial complexities. So, privatization has been seen as a better available instrument through which the supply and demand of teacher education can be met. Although, privatization has not been formally accepted by the state as a policy but in practice, government has already accepted it and which can be seen in recent five year plans as well 11th five year plan and several other initiatives directly reflect the dependency of the government on the phenomena called privatization.

On the backdrop of above discussion and NCF 2005, the challenges faced by pre-service secondary teacher education are the major issues and concerns before the entire education system in general and teacher education in particular. Knowing the importance of teacher education, increasing demand of quality education and also increasing the demand of quality teachers as well as teacher-educators need to be addressed primarily by the apex bodies in its policy of teacher education, curriculum of teacher educators, adequate support from the concerned ministry to teacher education, correcting the norms and standards for the establishment of institutions of beginning the courses of teacher education and most importantly to create an awareness for quality and efficiency among the stakeholders of teacher education. Privatization with philanthropic motive improves quality in teacher education (Pritam, 2009) can be on of the alternative solution of the temporal problems and it must be substantiated with appropriate legal provisions. Philanthropy in teacher education must be encouraged and there must be some kind of mechanism which observe and supervise whether institutions are moving towards malpractice of privatization.

On the whole, privatization of education in general and teacher education in particular has both benefited upto large extant and fulfilled the public demand of teacher education which government alone was unable to. Although curriculum (NCF 2005 & NCTE 2006) has provided sufficient ways to improve quality of school education through pre-service training of teachers but it also lack in proper direction and translation of policy document in such a way that it becomes easy to implement in classroom teaching-learning situations. Finally, it can be said that privatization has both positive as well as negative impacts on teacher education but especially the challenges needs to be revisited by the apex bodies for successful achievement of aims and objectives of teacher education, which will improve quality in teacher education and successively quality in school education as well.

References

1. MHRD (2008) *Sudeep Banarjee Committee Report.*
2. NCERT (2005) *National Curriculum Framework.*
3. NCTE (2006) *Draft Curriculum Framework for Teacher Education.*
4. Pritam, B.P (2009) A Study of Challenges posed by Privatization to Teacher Education in India. An *M.Phil Dissertation.* New Delhi: NUEPA.
5. Pritam (2009) *M.Phil Research titled "A Study of Challenges posed by Privatization to Secondary Teacher Education In India".*

Chapter–28

Population Education:

Role of Teacher Education

1. BACKGROUND

Any curriculum remains a futile exercise unless it is put into practice. Teacher occupies an important place in the implementation of this area. It is the teacher who has to use the material, create learning situations in the classroom for his students and help them to learn. Orientation of teacher to the new curriculum is, therefore, absolutely essential. Both in-service and pre-service orientation should be organized. Population education being an educational area, need an imaginative teacher who could enable students to develop creative thinking and take action in relation to a number of problems and issues that surround them.

Teacher's quality is in turn a function of teacher's mastery of subject matter, use of appropriate teaching skills and positive professional attitude. At the early stage of educational expansion, it was assumed that such knowledge skills and attitudes were developed during general education. There is now however, evidences for the importance of professional teacher education, both pre-service and in-service for improvement of competencies required of a teacher for curriculum transaction.

In population education teacher plays a very crucial role particularly when it is not a separate subject rather its content are

Dr. Saroj Bala Yadav, Professor & Coordinator, National Population Education Project, NCERT, New Delhi.

integrated into different subject syllabi and textbooks. The quality and effectiveness of teacher education, therefore, is central to the quality of curriculum transaction in population education.

A number of basic concepts having universal applicability form a part of the content of population education. First concept is the importance of having respect of others especially persons of the opposite sex. If children can truly learn and understand what respect means and can hold it as a value then they will refrain from behaviour which is potentially harmful to others. The second important concept is that of self-respect and self-esteem. This is pertinent to both boys and girls, it is particularly important for girls. They should be given more opportunities of education, employment etc. The third important concept is that the children and young people should learn to understand that it is possible to plan the family size. The fourth to convey is that behaviour has consequences. If adolescents behave irresponsibly, for example, in the area of reproductive behaviour, they should understand that the consequences have life long implications. And finally children need to learn how to withstand and recognize the social pressure coming from peers, parents, relatives and help to deal with them in a responsible manner. Education of this type is complex and, therefore, largely depends on a through preparation of teachers. They need to be oriented into the content of population education, to be exposed to the techniques and skills of using the instructional materials in the classroom so that they are able to develop proper understanding of population related issues among themselves and in turn in the students. Population education being a value-laden area, it is more demanding on teachers. It is not just a question of mastery of new content, but also of new values, attitudes and behaviour

2. POPULATION EDUCATION: FRAMEWORK

Population education has been introduced with the objective to help the learners to understand the interrelationships of population and development and other factors of quality of life and to make informed and rational decisions with regards to population related behaviour with the purpose of improving the quality of life of individual, family, community, nation and the world. Over the period of time, several important developments have taken place in population education. New contents have been incorporated into it, such as responsible parenthood, adolescents' reproductive health, prevention of HIV/AIDs, family its roles and responsibilities, gender equity and equality, and sustainable development.

2.1 Meaning of Population Education

Population education is defined "as an educational process which develops among learners an understanding of inter-relationships between population and development, causes and consequences of population change, and the criticality of the essential conditions for population stabilization. It inculcates in them rational attitude and responsible behaviour, so that they may make informed decisions in respect of population and development issues" (NCERT, 2004). Accordingly the objectives of population education are: Making learners aware of the interrelationships between population and sustainable development;

- Developing in them an understanding of the criticality of essential conditions of population stabilization for better quality of life of present and future generations.
- Inculcating in them rational attitude and responsible behaviour towards population and development issues.
- Making them understand the crucial aspects of adolescent reproductive health, focusing on the elements of process of growing up, and implications of HIV/AIDs and drug abuse.

Inculcating in them rational attitude towards sex and drugs and promoting respect for the opposite sex; and Empowering them to take informed decisions on issues of population and development including those of reproductive health.

2.2 Broad Content Outline

With a view to attaining these objectives, the Reconceptualised Framework focuses on six major themes and selected contents relating to these themes. These contents belong to the existing subjects being taught at the school stage, such as, Environmental Studies, Social Studies, Economics, Geography, Civics, Political Science, Science, Home Science, Biology, Chemistry, Physical and Health Education, Psychology, Sociology, History and others. The contents have been placed under the six basic themes in the following manner.

Theme I: Population and Sustainable Development

A. Population Growth and Structure: Implications for Population Stabilisation: Population Growth, Fertility, Mortality, Age and Sex Structure– Implications in terms of the interrelationships between population change and the pace and quality of economic and social development; Infants, Children, Youth Elderly People and Persons with disabilities - health, educational and special needs and well-being in the context of population stabilisation.

B. Population, Sustained Economic Growth and Poverty: Integration of population issues in the development strategies–Interrelationship between eradication of poverty and population stabilization; Sustainable patterns and levels of resource utilisation, production and consumption.

C. Population and Environment: Interrelationship between population, development, natural resources, use of technology and quality of life Socio-economic dimensions of sustainable development; Sustainable management of resources– Unsustainable pattern of consumption and production and their impact on environment; Environmental Pollution Impact on health and quality of life; Use of technology in agriculture, Industry and other aspects of life styles– Impact on the sustainability of resources and environmental degradation; Women and environmental issues- Interrelationships.

Theme II: Gender Equality and Equity for Empowerment of Women

A. Gender Equality and Equity: Fulfillment of women's potential through health care, education, skill development, ability to earn beyond traditional occupations, employment opportunities outside the household, and making them self-reliant; the role-stereotypes and the social worth of women; discrimination/violence against women.

B. The Girl Child: Need for change in the perception of the social worth of the girl child; health care, education; role-stereotypes and discrimination within the family and society.

C. Male Responsibilities: Appreciation of the key role of males in bringing about gender equality; Shared parental responsibilities.

Theme III: Adolescent Reproductive Health (Adolescence Education)

A. Process of Growing Up: Physical change and development during adolescence; Socio-cultural development; Gender Roles.

B. HIV/AIDS: Basic information on HIV/AIDS; prevention and control; care for the affected.

C. Drug Abuse: Causes of drug abuse; drug addiction; drug dependence, effects of drug abuse; prevention and responsibility.

Theme IV: Family: Socio-cultural Factors and Quality of Life

A. Family as Basic Unit of Society: Importance of institutions of marriage and family; Impact of rapid demographic change and socio-economic development on patterns of family composition and family life.

B. Socio-Economic Support to the Family: Basic needs: housing, food, clothes, health, education, social security and work; Need to promote social environment against domestic and sexual violence; Problems of old and handicapped members.

Theme V: Health and Education: Key Determinants of Population Change

A. Health, Morbidity and Mortality: Interrelationship between health, morbidity and mortality, population change and quality of life.

B. Child Survival: Linkages between child survival and timing, spacing, number of births and reproductive health of mothers.

C. Health of Women and Safe Motherhood: Health of women as a key factor for the quality of life in family and society.

Theme VI: Population Distribution, Urbanization and Migration

A. Population Distribution: Interrelationship among patterns of population distribution, socio-economic development, environment and quality of life.

B. Population Growth in Urban Agglomerations: Continued concentration of population in primate cities/mega-cities and economic, social, civic and environmental challenges.

C. Migration: Causes of migration, especially related to poverty; Impact of migration on socio-economic development of rural areas.

3. STRATEGIES OF INSTITUTIONALISATION

The overarching objective of concerted efforts being made under the National Population Education Programme in India has been the institutionalization of population education in the content and process of the education system. Although in some other countries this new educational area was introduced as a separate subject area, the strategy of integrating population education elements in the on-going subject areas of the school curriculum was adopted here.

3.1 Integration Strategy

In India population education, therefore, has been accepted as a critical curricular area in the national policy document, and its elements have been integrated in the selected subjects being taught at different school stages. It has not been treated as a separate subject in the school curriculum. Moreover, attempts have also been made to include a separate paper on population education, over and above integrating its elements in existing papers in the courses prescribed for pre-service elementary and secondary teacher education.

3.2 Co-curricular Approach

Co-curricular activities have always been an integral part of the teaching-learning process. Their significance particularly for an educational area like population education, which aims primarily at influencing attitude and behaviour of the learners, can hardly be over-emphasised. However, for population education co-curricular activities are considered important not only for reinforcing the classroom teaching but also for initiating the teaching-learning process without waiting for a number of its elements to become an integral part of school syllabi and textbooks. The activities are expected to be organized in schools on such a scale and so frequently that both students and teachers, and in certain cases the parents also, are thoroughly exposed to the new population education contents.

4. ROLE OF TEACHER EDUCATION

Adoption of appropriate strategies for curriculum transaction is crucial for achievement of the objectives of population education. It is very often presumed that when there is teaching, learning takes place automatically, and that learners learn only because the teacher teaches them. But this is not always true. There can be no learning in spite of teaching, and the learners can learn even without teaching. As a matter of fact whether learning takes place, whether things learnt are retained and whether the learning process leads to desirable attitude formation and behaviour change depend largely on the teacher and the system that prepares them. The system can prepare the teachers through **Pre-Service In-service Teacher.**

4.1 Pre-Service

Population Education has been incorporated into the pre-service teacher education courses of elementary and secondary levels. A study by MHRD was conducted to know the status of adolescence education elements in the syllabi/courses of elementary and secondary stages is as follows:

(A) Elementary Teacher Education Courses

The elementary teacher education courses are prepared generally by State Council of Educational Research and Training (SCERTs) or Directorates of Education in respective States on the basis of broad guidelines stipulated in the National Curriculum Framework of Teacher Education developed by National Council for Teacher Education (NCTE). These are generally transacted through District Institutes of Education and Training (DIET). The elementary teacher education courses being transacted in other elementary teacher education institutions are also patterned on that prepared by SCERTs/Directorates of Education. The courses of pre-service elementary teacher education prescribed in twenty States and Union Territories were procured from the Population education Cells of SCERTs /SIEs of respective States and content analyzed.

The courses of pre-service elementary teacher education prescribed in 20 States and Union Territories were content anlaysed. The courses of sixteen states were found to contain some or the other elements of adolescence education. The courses of 13 States have topics related to process of growing up but those related to HIV/AIDS are included only in the courses of 2 States. The topics on drug abuse are present in the courses of a very small number (6 only) of States, and that too combined with the other components of adolescence education.

(B) Secondary Teacher Education Courses

The syllabuses of teacher education for secondary stage are framed by Universities and prescribed for pupil teachers opting B.Ed. and M.Ed. courses and students of M.A. in education course. These syllabuses are prepared on the basis of the broad guidelines delieated in the National Curriculum Framework of Teacher Education developed by National Council for Teacher Education (NCTE).

The syllabuses of only 37 Universities belonging to 20 States and Union Territories were content analysed Out of these, 37 syllabuses belong to B.Ed. course, 4 to M.Ed. course and 3 to M.A. in Education course.

The study shows, the elements related to one of the three major components of adolescence education, viz., process of growing up are incorporated in the B.Ed./M.Ed./M.A. in Education courses of all the 37 Universities in one way or the other. But independent topics related to HIV/AIDs are included in the syllabuses of only 3 Universities and those related to drug abuse in the syllabuses of 5 Universities. The syllabuses of 8 Universities have topics that jointly reflect the contents of two or three components of adolescence education.

The integration of adolescence education elements in the pre-service elementary and secondary teacher education courses is urgently needed to prepare teachers who can transact this curricular area competently. At present, these elements are very inadequately, sparsely and sporadically integrated in the teacher education courses at both the levels.

The first step in this direction would be to integrate this curricular area in the National Curriculum Framework for Teacher Education which is being finalized by the National Council for Teacher Education (NCTE). It may be noted that this area is quite comprehensively integrated in the National Curriculum Framework 2005 developed by National Council of Educational Research and Training (NCERT) and approved by the Central Advisory Board on Education (CABE).

It may appear that the contents related to one of the components of adolescence education, i.e., process of growing up are integral part of the existing elementary and secondary teacher education courses. But in fact, the topics included in the courses focus on the psychological dimensions, and not on the reproductive and sexual health. There is a need to incorporate topics that focus on adolescent reproductive and sexual health concerns. A separate unit on process of growing up containing physical, physiological, psychological and social developments may be included in the existing relevant papers.

HIV/AIDs and drug abuse are the most neglected areas in the present elementary and secondary teacher education courses.

The integration of these elements in relevant Papers of both elementary and secondary teacher education courses are urgently needed.

It is also equally important to lay emphasis on the Effective Transactional and Evaluation Strategies that have the potential to actualize interactive experiential learning and development of life skills among the learners.

The General Framework of Adolescence Education including the Life Skills Development and the Scheme of Contents of Adolescence Education developed by NCERT under the National Population Education Project may be made the basis for integration of these elements in the teacher education courses.

4.2 In-Service Teacher Education

Training programmes needs to be organized for the staff of these institutions to enhance their capabilities for integrating population education in the classroom delivery. For In-service Teacher Training integrated approach can be used to train various categories of teachers. Independent training may be organized for teacher educators for capacity building and for organizing integrated training programme.

Teacher Training in the context of Population Education needs to be focused on the following three things:

I. Planning;

II. Implementation;

III. Evaluation.

4.2.1: Planning: The success of any training programme depends to a considerable extent on efficient planning. For proper planning the following things need to be taken into account:

1. **Training for whom?**

The most important aspect is to identify the target group/groups who should be trained in population education. The different personnel who are involved in the implementation of various aspects of the programme would require training/orientation. The target groups can be classified as follows:

(i) **Target-group that need Orientation:** This group includes administrators such as head of the institutions/ schools,education officers, supervisors and trained teacher etc.

(ii) **Target-group that need Training:** Project personnel, curriculum developers, textbook writers, teacher educators, key/resource persons, and teachers.

(iii) **Target-group that need Advocacy:** Policy Makers, Educational Administrators, Educational Officers, Media persons, Non-Governmental Organizations, Parents and Panchayati Raj leaders, Opinion Leaders. Advocacy is generally organized to create an enabling environment for a new programme or for an area like adolescence education, which is sensitive in nature.

Identifying Training Needs

After identifying the target group or groups that need training, their training/orientation needs should be determined. The identification of training needs of different target groups is important in order to plan a need based training programme. Time, money, efforts and other resources could be put to the best possible use only if the training is based on their needs that are clearly identified. Below are given some factors which could be considered in identifying training needs:

Base-line Information of the Target Group

To make the training need-based, steps should be taken to acquire information about the profile of the target group in terms of background current level of awareness/knowledge, attitude with reference to the reconceptualized framework of population education knowledge and skills related to population education in which the target group need training local cultural and social norms, values and attitude particularly on the sensitive areas of population education the environment, urban or rural in which target group will implement the activities.

Training needs could be identified through: *Administering questionnaire to trainees before the actual training base-line surveys available interview, etc.*

Training Objectives

The next important issue is to define training objectives for the category of personnel to be oriented/trained or advocacy is organized. Objectives are basically statements that define a programme's tasks, targets and desired outcomes. The exact determination of a programme's objectives is a precondition to any subsequent plan of action. The objectives should be based on the identified training needs which will also help in determine the content and methods of training. The objectives should also be specific, measurable, achievable, relevant and time-bound (SMART).

Coverage in terms of number of persons to be trained

The orientation of administrators and key/resource persons does not pose any serious problem, but the problem gets complicated when it comes to decide the number of teachers. This question is bothering since the inception of the project and also in adolescence education whether all teachers of all subjects of all stages or selected number of teachers of selected subjects and of selected stages. The decision as to the number of teachers who should be trained will depend on many factors like the status of integration of population education in various subjects, availability of resources etc.

Time Frame for Completing Training Programmes

The funding of Population Education Programme is provided for a specified period of time by the funding agency – UNFPA, for competing all aspects of the programme including training. Population education including adolescence education focus also changes from time to time, there should be a minimum of time lag between training of teachers and implementation in schools, otherwise the trained personnel would replace into illiteracy complacency and dilution so far population education is concerned.

The teacher trained in the first year, if not oriented again, relapsed into a stage of untrained teachers in population education and adolescence education. The training programmes has thus to be designed in a way that training in these areas can be provided to the maximum number of teachers within the specified time-frame. Planning is also required for reference programme for those who have been trained earlier.

Available Resources

The training programme has to be decided in the light of the human, physical and financial resources available. Along with the financial support for population education/adolescence education programme being provided by the external agency the States should have their own resources for designing the training programmes.

Coordination among different departments

Because the training at different levels demands interdependence within and between institutions, the effectiveness of any training model will depends upon to the extent to which proper coordination and support of various sectors of the educational system is available. The coordination also becomes important in view of the availability of limited resources and covering of large number of target groups. Many of the related departments organize their own training programmes for teachers and other personnel which some time overlaps. It is, therefore, essential that a workable mechanism of coordination among different agencies involved in training of different kinds of personnel should be worked out. For example efforts at the national level have been initiated by jointly organizing Training Programme for the Project Personnel of three education sectors, namely, Directorate of Adult Education, University Education and School Education.

Duration of Training

Duration of the training programme influences the effectiveness of the training. Duration will depend on the category of personnel to be trained, nature of the programme, (whether orientation/advocacy or fresh training) availability of resources, number to be covered and many such issues. For example, advocacy in Adolescence Education for policy makers, administrators require one or two days, whereas training of teachers in reconceptualised framework of population education or in Adolescence Education would require an intensive training of five to seven day duration.

Modalities of Training

The training activities at national and state levels have been conducted under the project by adopting two broad modalities –

(i) Independent; and

(ii) Integrated.

(i) **Independent**

Independent training programmes exclusively for population education have been organized at national and state levels. At the national level these programmes have been of seven to ten-day duration. Some orientation programmes have also been organized for only three-day duration. At the state level, training programmes for teachers and teacher educators have been of two to three day duration and for key and resource persons for three to five day duration. In States more than one tier strategy has been adopted for training of teachers. These training programmes have been of three different categories – (a) Single-period, (b) Multi-period, and (c) School-complex/school based.

Single-period

This training modality has been adopted by one State that organizes programmes for specific group of teachers of the entire State within single-period. A large number of teachers are trained at different centres within the fixed time-frame. The most striking feature of this modality is that educational infrastructure of the entire State along with the relevant agencies involved in developmental, environmental, health and family welfare programmes are associated with the training programmes at the lower levels. The Panchayati Raj institution and members of local communities are also involved and media is widely used throughout the State.

Multi-period

This modality has been adopted by most of the States. They organize training programmes for different categories of teachers throughout the year at multiple points of time. This gives flexibility to the organizer in terms of selecting resources and also to trainees to decide the time period suitable to attend the programme.

School-Complex/School based

This modality has been adopted an experimental basis by some States. The Population Education Cell organizes training programmes for Principals/Headmasters of selected schools as resource persons and they in turn orient the teachers of the school complex or of the particular schools. These days independent training programmes are organized only in adolescence education and for resource persons of teacher training institutions.

Integrated

This training modality has been adopted more regularly since the second cycle of the National Population Education Project. Under this modality, efforts have been made to make the training in population education an integral part of the on-going teacher training programme. It is being done in two ways: (a) Teacher Training Programmes Based, and (b) Teacher Training Institution Based. By Teacher Training Programmes Based means that any training programme organized by SCERT or SIE/SIERT/Deptt. of education should have component of population education. Teacher Training Institution Based means other related institutions other than those implementing the Project should also incorporate the components of population education in their on-going programmes.

10. Training Strategies

Before the trainees actually arrive at the training centre, it is imperative that the training strategies have been fully worked out.

In particular, one should consider whether the training which is being organized is pre-service or in-service. It is equally necessary to consider the levels at which the training take place – national, regional or local levels as this will influence the choice of training modalities and the duration and timing of training. The way adults learn also varies quite a lot. Trainers should also take into consideration the institutional setting in deciding what methodology to employ. Thus, in deciding which methodology/methodologies to use, one can consider several factors as shown in the diagram below:

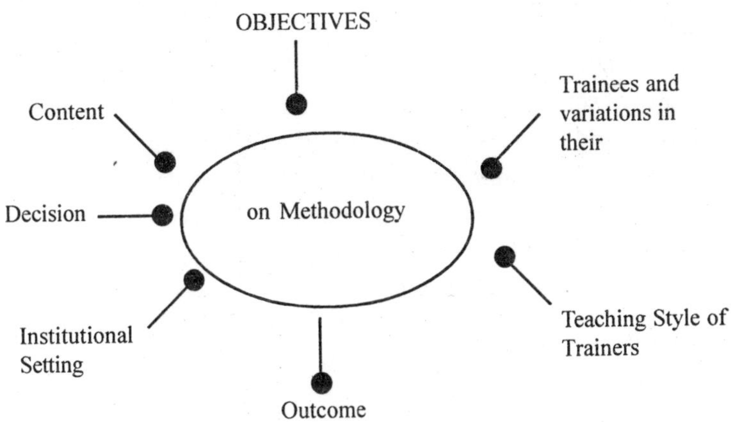

A range of modalities are given below for training the teachers in population education. Selection of a modality or a combination of modalities for effective training will depend on the objectives of the training programme.

Face-to-Face Training

In this mode, training is given face-to-face either independently or in an integrated way. Under independent category, the training programmes are organized for varied duration exclusively in population education, whereas under the integrated category, the training programmes are dovetailed to the existing teacher training programmes. Under his modality, if training is organized for different levels of functionaries in the descending order of hierarchy and, therefore, is also called hierarchical Face-to-Face training. Different strategies such as one tier or more than one tier are used for training the teacher educators and teachers. In India, this modality is used more commonly for training the teachers in population education. Under integrated face-to-face training, population education is made an integral part of the on-going teacher training programme, being organized by any other institution.

Peer Group

In this modality, the principals or subject heads or coordinators in each secondary school are trained through face-to-face modality and they, in turn, are given the responsibility for training teachers in their own schools. Peer training also involves a pattern wherein the trainer and trainees are both teachers at the same level. Each school is provided training material and it prepare its own schedule of training the teachers. Under this modality, supervisory team also visits the school and provides on-the-spot assistance, guidance as well as evaluation of the programme.

(iii) Mobile Training

In this modality, a mobile team consisting of trained, competent and experienced trainers conduct teacher training programme in schools. These teams are equipped with a variety of instructional materials, teaching aids, and equipments. The team member can be rotated during the course of the training. Thus, minimizing the absence of members from respective posts for a long period.

iv) Module or Self-Learning Model

In this modality, the training material/modules are prepared at a central place and are provided to teachers for independent and direct training. Being self-contained learning package, modular learning requires minimum supervision, easy to administer and require the trainee to manage his or her own learning. The crucial need in using the modular approach is to ensure teacher's motivation. It can be supplemented with peer group training modality.

Training via Correspondence

Under this modality lessons and other learning materials are sent to the trainees through postal service. A correspondence phase is supplemented with some kind of face-to-face training sessions at the local level either by the peer training or by the head of the institution.

Training Through Radio and Television

In this model specific educational/instructional programmes are developed for radio/television transmission. These programmes are transmitted regularly at predetermined schedules, indicating time and date. The schools are provided through radio and TV programmes and teachers are expected to listen/view the programme. This model can be supplemented with a peer training model and modular training model.

There are also other modalities like field base preparation, team work inviting teachers in workshops and seminars. During such activities teachers are exposed to population education.

It is evident that the modalities of training teachers vary in terms of approach, tasks and subtasks, supportive services, teaching learning instruments, managerial efforts, cost and coverage of target group and expected intensity of learning. A survey of literature reveals that countries are using one or a combination of more than one modalities for training teachers in population education. In some case under one modality, different strategies are adopted. For example, under face-to-face training modality in India, strategies like independent training, integrated training, massive orientation, tier system, etc. are used.

11. Teaching Strategies

The choice of a particular method/methods is crucial for successful training. Methods used and the training should be close to the field situations as well as provide to the trainees with experiential learning for their new responsibilities.

- In itself no particular training method is superior to all other possible methods. The desirability of a particular training method or a combination of methods is a question to be determined in relation to a number of factors.
- Specific Training Objectives and Content.
- The Situation in Which Training is to Take Place.
- The role and involvement of trainees are expected to play in the training process.
- The extent of support available in terms of learning materials; and
- The level of familiarity and mastery of various methods on the part of trainers. A description of various teaching methods is given below in brief. The trainer should select a method or combination of methods. The focus of methods should be on life skills development particularly dealing with the topics of adolescence education.

Lecture Method

In this method, the trainer does most of the talking with very little participation from the trainees. It may be supported by the use of teaching aids. This method is suitable when there is a large number of audience. Trainer through this method can present a large amount of information in a shorter time. But this method provide limited participation and stimulation to the trainees.

(a) Group Discussion

Under this method, there is free exchange of knowledge, ideas and opinions among trainer and trainees. It is less formal than lectures and trainees usually do more talking than the trainers. The role of a trainee is more of a facilitator It can be used to examine issues in depth, explore alternative opinions and develop life skills. Active role of trainers enhances improvement of knowledge, changing attitude and forming opinions. But this method is more time consuming and chances of deviating from the subject matter are also more.

(b) Role Play

Role plays are short narratives or cases especially developed to suit the theme or topic for which a life-skill or attitudes are to be developed towards behaviour change in learners/trainees. The whole situation is described and played as realistically as possible. Trainer along with trainees enact the role of a certain person in a particular situation. It is used to practice real life situations. Role play helps the learner to develop confidence to trainees when faced with the real situation. Due to high level of involvement, it is useful in strengthening the skills of human interaction, planning, decision making and thinking. However, role playing require special skill, experience, proper guidance and time for implementation. They are the best means for developing attitudes where the trainer is trying to indicate behaviour change.

(c) Case Study

Under this method, a short description of a situation is given. The trainees are asked to reflect upon the given case. After the enough reading of the case, the case is thrown open for discussion. Questions are framed so as to direct the trainees to come up with possible solutions, which are then discussed in the group. The benefit of this method is that trainers participate actively. It helps in developing problem solving skill, but this method is time consuming.

(d) Assignments

Commonly called 'homework', assignments include reading, writing, viewing, or listening tasks given to trainees as conditioning for a topic to be presented or as a follow-up to a presentation. Trainers are expected to review the assignments and to give trainees feedback where possible.

(e) Audience reaction team

An audience reaction team generally consists of two to five trainees who react to a trainer's presentation. Members of the team are expected to interrupt the trainer to seek immediate clarification of points that are not clear, and otherwise help the trainer to meet the specific needs of the trainees.

(f) Brainstorming

Brainstorming is a technique where creative thinking is more important. The format is to have trainees spontaneously present ideas on the topic without regard to how practical the ideas might be, to jot down the ideas on the blackboard, and then to edit the list. An atmosphere must be created which will cause the trainees to be uninhibited. One key factor to be emphasized by the trainer while using this method is to inform participants not to ridicule or reject any idea as no idea is bad or wrong.

(g) Buzz Sessions

The buzz session is a method involving all members of a training group directly in the discussion process. The group is divided into very small group (3 members) for a limited time (about 5 minutes) for discussion to which each trainee contributes his ideas.

(h) Critical Incidents

Critical incidents are contrived educational experiences in written, audio and/or visual which stimulate real life events. They generally require to make decisions and perform acts in a "laboratory" setting moments in behavioural situations. The technique is used, to teach supervisors how to handle workers, interviewers and how to obtain information.

(i) Demonstration

The demonstration is a presentation to show how to use a procedure or to perform an act. It is often the trainee carrying out the activity under the supervision/trainer. It is basically a visual presentation and accompanies discussion where psychomotor skills are taught.

(j) Field trip or tour

These are purposefully arranged where a training group visits a place of educational interest, direct observation and study. Field trips usually involve less than four hours while tours include visits to many points of interest and require from one day to several weeks to complete.

(k) Forum

A forum is an assemblage of trainees used to facilitate discussion after a topic has been introduced by a speaker, panel, film, or other technique. A moderator is used so that everyone has a chance to voice his views in an orderly manner.

(l) Interview

An interview is a presentation in which one or more resource persons respond to questioning by one or more trainees (interviewers). It is used to explore a topic in depth where a formal presentation is not desired by either trainees or resource persons.

(m) Listening Team

A listening team listens, takes notes, questions and/or summarizes a training session. The team is used to provide interaction between a speaker and the trainees and is especially useful where the speaker is not especially knowledgeable about an agency's unique problem.

(n) Panel

Panel is a dialogue between a group of four to eight experts on an assigned topic in front of a training group. A moderator ensures that order is maintained, that each resource person gets equal time, and that the topic is covered in depth.

(o) Question Period

The question period is an organized follow-up session to a lecture or speech in which trainees ask questions than the speaker. It is during this time that trainees ask for clarification of points made in the formal presentation, and take the opportunity to ask for information, which was not covered by the speaker but which is of interest to them.

(p) Seminar

A Seminar consists of a recognized expert leading a discussion among a group of trainees engaged in specialized study. The leader generally opens a seminar with a brief presentation, often covering provocative issues, and then guides a discussion in which all trainees participate.

(q) Simulation

Simulations are contrived educational experiences, in audiovisual or model form, which have the characteristics of a real life situation. Simulations allow the trainee to make decisions or take action in a 'laboratory' setting prior to interacting with people and things.

Skit

A skit is a brief, rehearsed dramatic presentation involving two or more trainees on a specified theme with an objective to clearly initiate behaviour change in trainees through presentation of skits. Working from a prepared script, the trainees act out an event or incident, which dramatizes a situation taken from on-the-job experiences. It helps in internalizing the attitudes into realistic setting and within a situation which is more or less real.

Symposium

The symposium is a series of prepared lectures given by two to five resource persons; each speaker presents one aspect of the topic. The presentations should be brief to the point, and generally not exceed 15 to 20 minutes.

Workshop

The workshop is a training method, which permits extensive study of a specific topic. It usually gathers 15 to 30 people who meet together to improve their proficiency, collectively develop new operating procedures, or to solve problems.

13. Development of Prototype Training Material

Once the objectives and framework of the programme have been determined, the need of prototype material arises. This proto type training material should cover the core content of the reconceptualized framework of population education. Six broad themes identified in the context of Post-ICPD should be elaborated as per the learning needs and expected future tasks of the trainees be accurate and up-to-date provide scope for interaction with the immediate social-cultural environment encourage interest and involvement of the trainees include activities which helps in the acquisition of skills related to population issues.

This material can be in the form of a self-learning material, training package, etc. Before being widely used, it should be tired out.

14. Designing of Training Programme

The training programme should be organized keeping in view the "Systems Approach to Designing Training Programme". The Training Programme design must have following 5 components:

i) TNA (Training Need Assessment).

ii) Framing objective.

iii) Designing Curriculums.

iv) Implementation of training.

v) Evaluation.

A training programme reflecting the above be prepared. It should be as per availability of time and resources. Appropriate learning activities (group work) and field visits should be reflected in the Training Programme in the light of the objectives to be covered. At the same time, some flexibility to include any changes should be there in the training programme design.

Implementation Stage

An effort should be made as far as possible to follow the training design that is decided upon. A favourable social climate should be provided during the training so that both trainers and trainees feel free to interact and express their point of view. Such a climate would help to generate an eagerness to pursue learning. Satisfaction during the programme about various aspects lead to better achievement. Steps may be taken to get continuous feed back from the participants for improvement.

Evaluation and Follow-up

Evaluation of training programme is an integral part of the process of training. It must develop information about both trainees and trainers, about what the trainees are able to learn during training and how training affects their subsequent performance. Evaluation of training, therefore, is basically conducted to access the planning, implementation and outcome of training with a view to improving it. It is used to determine the success or failure of the objectives set for the programme, particularly the effectiveness of the training programme. Thus, evaluation will be participatory in nature and emerge from the desire of the trainees and trainers to know their respective achievements as related to the methods employed, objectives set and their own capabilities.

Evaluation of training actually starts before the training programme, during the training and after the training including the follow-up. Thus, it can be divided into three stages : I) Pre-training evaluation or context evaluation; ii) In-training or process evaluation also called formative evaluation; and iii) Post-training evaluation or product evaluation, also called summative evaluation.

(i) Pre-Training Evaluation

Pre-training evaluation includes gathering baseline data of the knowledge, attitude and skills of the future trainees, an analysis of their training needs and of the organizational requirements of the training programmes including strategies, learning activities and the management. Pre-training evaluation provides basis for designing of a training programme.

(ii) In-service Training Evaluation

This is the process of assessing the training programme itself as it progresses. Some basic questions which should be answered are:

- Is the programme being implemented as planned?
- What improvements should be made to attain the objectives.

The purpose of this evaluation is to decide what changes in the programme are necessary. These changes may take the form of additional learning activities, more participatory sessions etc. There are three basic dimensions in relation to which the effectiveness of the training may be assessed:

- The knowledge and understanding that the trainees acquire
- The attitude, opinions and reactions they show.
- Skills they acquire during the training.

Evaluation during the training programme can be done through short tests, informal talks with the trainees to get their opinions, observation of trainees. The purpose of this evaluation is to identify the problems of the trainees in terms of learning the content, changing or reinforcing attitude, demonstrating expected behaviour and providing feedback for improvements.

(iii) Post-Training Evaluation

At the end of the training programme some basic questions which should be answered are:

- Have the training objective been achieved?
- Has the original training scheme been implemented?
- Do the trainees show measurable gains in knowledge and understanding, attitude and skills?
- Should the training programme or any parts of the programme be revised, continued or terminated for future?

The data to be used for answering the above mentioned questions may be obtained by the use of tests, impressions of the trainers and trainees comments of observers, etc.

An important point to remember in gathering data for evaluation purpose at all stages is timing. Test should not be given when the trainees are tired or already to go home or to do some exciting activities such as before or after the field trip.

(iv) Follow-up Activities

The follow-up activities will be more meaningful and interesting if the trainees and trainers plan and work them out before the training programme is over. The trainees have the knowledge of his role before and after the training, while the trainers have the experience and expertise needed in follow-up. Some follow-up activities are given below:

a) Using a two-way communication system

A regular two-way communication through newsletters, reports, seminars, workshops etc. could be maintained to remind the trainees about the activities conducted, the problems and their solutions available.

b) Field Visits

The visit to the trainees should be well planned and ahead of time. Some of the visits should not be known to the trainees, so that the trainers could have first hand information. Some information which could not be collected through questionnaire and some answers to questions not considered in the training programme may be discussed. Field visit could be made effective, if they are visited, especially when persons from other agencies or other countries are brought along. Field visits also help in verifying some of the evaluation results.

c) Conducting refresher courses or inviting them in some programmes

Refresher courses of shorter duration covering emerging areas or new strategies may be organized. Some of the trainees may be invited in some workshops, seminars etc.

Chapter–29

Reflection on Teacher Education and NCF–2005

Introduction

The changing role of teachers and the changing definitions of teacher effectiveness have been increasingly studied and analyzed, with research undertaken and the outcomes being fed back into the system to facilitate the process of education reform. The current focus of researchers, policy makers and practitioners with regard to teacher education is on the development of professional competencies, and on the most effective ways of achieving higher levels of commitment and motivation for higher-level performance on the part of teachers. In addition, important possibilities are arising with regard to current developments involving the new information and communication technologies. As a result, teacher education in India is on the brink of a major transformation.

The paramount duty of schools is to provide quality education through a curriculum frame work. Quality education is comprised of dimensions like enriching the innate potential of learners, inculcation of self-discipline, enabling the students to assimilate the best learning experiences in every subject and creating interest in learning among students.

Rubina Shahnaz, Anjum Ahmad, and Aftab A. Ansari, Research scholars in Department of Education, AMU, Aligarh.

Curriculum is revised from time to time based on the changing needs of learners and their environment. NCERT, New Delhi has designed National Curriculum Framework–2005 (NCF–2005) bearing in mind the contextual and professional needs of all the stake holders of education.

The following five cardinal principles of NCF–2005 have been assimilitated into teacher education curriculum and in the source books of Elementary Teacher Education which are to be introduced in 2008-2009:

- Connecting knowledge to life outside the school.
- Ensuring that learning shifts away from rote methods.
- Enriching the curriculum so that it goes beyond textbooks.
- Making Examinations more flexible and integrating them with classroom life.
- Nurturing an over-riding identity informed by caring concerns within the democratic polity of the country.

What is Curriculum and the Need for New NCF

Few can distinguish between the terms 'curriculum' and 'syllabus'. The tendency to view both in the context of examinations is rampant. For teachers, the prescribed textbook serves as the *de facto* curriculum. As for the National Curriculum Framework (NCF), hardly anyone outside the limited world of professional pedagogues and planners can recall what role the National Policy on Education (1986) intended to assign to this invention. It was designed to bring systemic coherence and parity in quality standards across the country. It is widely misconceived as an instrument of uniformity; in reality, it was meant to serve as a reminder of core national values and priorities around which diversity and flexibility in curriculum and syllabus could be structured to meet the needs of a rapidly expanding system.

The 1986 policy stressed the need to make education child-centered. Nearly two decades after the policy was approved by Parliament, the school-going child's life continues to be afflicted by rote methods and the chronic fear of doing badly in examination. Yes, there are plenty of people who feel unmoved by this reality. But R.K. Narayan did succeed in touching the nation's heart when he made his maiden speech in the Rajya Sabha in 1991, inspiring the Ministry of Human Resource Development to set up a committee under Professor Yash Pal to prescribe remedies. Its 1993 report gathered dust while the problem got increasingly worse. One terrible symptom is the increasing number of children who contemplate or actually commit suicide during examination time.

The 1986 policy assumed that India would universalize elementary education before the end of the century. That did not happen. Today, as high proportions as 53 per cent of our children are eliminated by the system before Class-8. Not many could recall that the National Council of Educational Research and Training (NCERT) had set up a large steering committee, chaired by Professor Yash Pal, and as many as 21 National Focus Groups. It also invited public opinion through advertisements in 28 national and regional dailies, organized regional seminars, and meetings for consultation with the States and rural teachers. And now the document is with CABE (Central Advisory Board of Education), where the previous NCF was never discussed.

This recent history of intensive nation-wide deliberation among professionals and other stakeholders appears to have been drowned by weightier subjects such as Ambani's inheritance, Jinnah's role in Partition, and the difficulties in tracking black buck shooters. Suicide by farmers arouses no one's interest. So why should we be surprised that Gokhale's move to make primary education free and compulsory evokes no awkward memory or enthusiasm 94 years later? The children that Gokhale's legacy asks us to worry about are poor and mostly rural. Their high dropout rate, as it is officially called, is a key symptom of the system's inability to reform itself. If an intrinsic urge for reform is a measure of systemic quality – as a recent UNESCO report suggests – then we deserve to be rated poorly. Indeed, resistance to reform is so high that you are forced to wonder why the system attracts any criticism at all.

Perspective on National Curriculum Framework and Issues Related to NCF–2005

The new NCF discusses quality in terms of the resources available for infrastructural needs, professional training of teachers, and provision for monitoring. It relates quality to the experiences provided to children to enable them to construct knowledge. This approach calls for the recognition of children's creativity and motivation to learn. The belief that every child has a personality and a unique potential is fundamental to the development of a democratic system of schooling.

Four decades have passed since the Kothari Commission recommended a common school system. That vision is a shambles today and cannot be resurrected magically in the middle of sharp socio-economic contradictions. What is possible and important is to initiate long-range reforms, starting with steps to improve systemic efficiency and accountability.

The new NCF focuses attention on two sets of challenges for reform: pedagogic and systemic. The first set includes rational designing of syllabi and textbooks, teacher training and examination procedures. The second set calls for more resources for school infrastructure, and a change in roles and power relations from the ground level upwards. Both sets of reforms have been appreciated for long, and in stray pockets – usually with NGO involvement – have been successfully tried out. Numerous innovative projects have established that school functioning can be improved with community involvement. NCF recommends that the approach used in such experiments be mainstreamed. Among pedagogic reforms, an important one recommended is the involvement of school teachers in the preparation of textbooks, not merely in reviewing them after they are written.

The most urgently needed pedagogic reforms are those related to teacher training and examinations. Institutional structures available for these two sectors need to be strengthened, which means that the National Council for Teacher Education and the various examination boards need to be given considerable academic support. NCF proposes deliking competitive entrance tests from school-leaving examinations. A nodal agency is suggested for the former so that children are saved from the ordeal of endless entrance tests and to discourage coaching. In Tamil Nadu, the Government has already taken an important step towards reducing the role of coaching in children's lives. Hopefully this step will lead to greater consensus on ways to select the most creative, rather than the most expensively coached, for professional courses.

Isn't it a fact that NCF–2005 goes only to elite schools, mostly English medium? Kendriya Vidyalayas, Navodaya Schools and private schools? And there, too, it is only after the eighth standard that CBSE [Central Board of Secondary Education] schools are required to use them? What is being done to promote these curricular guidelines and model textbooks in State-run schools?

The NCF is certainly not meant only for elite schools. Its approach and recommendations are for the entire system. A number of its recommendations, in fact, focus on rural schools. It is true that the syllabus and textbooks based on it are being used by all the CBSE schools. But several States, such as Goa, Sikkim, Himachal Pradesh and Uttarakhand, have already sought copyright permission to reprint them. So, NCF-based material is also being used in many State schools.

More significantly, quite a few States are currently preparing their own plans for syllabus and textbook reforms. Kerala, Bihar, Mizoram and Punjab are examples of this kind. Within the next few years we expect to see an NCF-oriented curriculum design in these States.

The NCERT had given a one-time grant of Rs.10 lakh to each State in the country to promote NCF in the language of the State and to compare its current syllabus with the syllabus we have proposed, so that a plan for future reforms can be made. Several States have taken up this challenge. This exercise is being carried out with the involvement of State Councils for Educational

Research and Training [SCERT] and District Institutes of Education and Training [DIET]. The most recent experience is that of Uttar Pradesh, which organized a seminar in Lucknow and invited all the DIETs to participate in the process of analyzing the NCF and its relevance for the State.

Which are the areas in which change is not up to the expectations-such as examination reform and teacher education, both of which will impact the implementation of NCF–2005?

These are two sectors that need urgent attention. A modest beginning has been made in examination reforms. The Council of Boards of School Education [COBSE] has made an effort to build consensus among the 42 school boards in India, on some basics like improving the quality of questions. This is no small matter, the CBSE has taken some concrete steps to include at least some questions of a reflective nature in the examinations to be held in March. It is not clear whether all the subjects will show evidence of this effort. Among other boards, Kerala has taken some measures. Evidently, examination reform is a complex exercise and India has a long way to go before its children can benefit from an improved strategy to assess them. The NCF's recommendations on other aspects of examination reforms have received scant attention. For instance, it recommends a staggered examination calendar, offering children the freedom to take some papers in March, and the remaining later on.

Similarly, the NCF says that children who repeat Class-X should have the option of taking a school-based exam for Class-X rather than the Board exam if they wish to do so. Schools have welcomed this recommendation, but no Board has moved in this direction. The NCF's focus group on exam reforms talks about several other measures to reduce stress and to make examination an educative process.

If progress in examination reform has been slow, the case of teacher education is worse. The sector is facing a grim situation, with rampant commercialization on the one hand and a lifeless, uninspiring B.Ed. curriculum on the other. We need drastic reforms in B.Ed. and other teacher training programmes for primary and pre-primary classes. We are currently designing a new course structure for our own Regional Institutes of Education. It will be a modest beginning. The real power to bring about major changes in this sector lies with the National Council of Teacher Education.

Critical Overview on NCF–2005

At the outset a searching question needs to be asked, has the new NCF followed this fundamental Constitutional Mandate? Has the NCF in its present form emerged without an inadequacy of procedure that the previous regime's NCF followed or has it also short-circuited dissent by a lack of transparency in mode of procedure? Has the NCF–2005 even addressed the question of severe and serious criticisms of the former regime under NCF–2000's textbooks? Do we even want to remember at this historic juncture what the previous regime had succeeded in destroying when we wish to revive and reconstruct India's national educational policy?

The NCF–2005 is confused, with no direction and systematic approach. It avoids the harsh reality on the ground and the ideological erosion that outfits and organizations that are antithetical to the Indian Constitution have successfully made over the past two decades that was also the periods when the Indian state chose to withdraw from its basic constitutional mandate of providing good quality, free and compulsory education to all.

What can the NCF–2005 do to ensure equity in access across class, caste community and gender of a curricular framework? Moreover as rightly pointed out "this NCF–2005 barely touches upon poverty (and discrimination be it based on caste, community or gender) and does not encourage children to wonder how a country of millions of tones of buffer food grain stock can also have millions of hungry people".

The overemphasis in the NCF–2005 on decentralization and diffused local knowledge is downright dangerous. It is no wonder that the BJP-NDA ruled opposition states have merely a problem that yoga is not included. They know that if implemented in the current form, the NCF–2005 would be a continued invitation to dubious, hugely-funded non-governmental organizations to continue to operate freely in the area of mass education and even draw government funds where politically sympathetic regimes exist. So while the Ministry of HRD directly initiates a move to stop funding of outfits like the Ekal foundation who run Ekal Vidyalayas because of the curricular framework that they are adopting that is downright unconstitutional, and while of the CABE Committees on regulatory Mechanisms actually has recommended scrutiny of all texts and textual materials being taught in all schools, the NCF fights shy of acknowledging the huge corrosion that a combination of privatization (driven by neo-liberal policies and a withdrawal of the State from education) and downright communal and sectarian schemes and agendas in education.

The error in fundamentals in the NCF–2005 apart from those outlines above also mean that inequities due to caste, class, community and gender are not treated as violations of basic human rights and dignity but cloaked in syrupy phases such as "minority sensibilities" etc. This is downright dangerous for a rational national curriculum. For instance in the five major concerns outlined in the forward to the NCF–2005 (pg vi) not one reflects the non-negotiable Constitutional right of every Indian to have access to quality education based on the principles of egalitarianism, non-discrimination and therefore, democracy. The distinct approach that hopes to convert itself into national policy appears to be to offer the disadvantaged poorest of India's poor sops and comforts but not the basis inalienable right to a good, free and quality education.

Adivasis, Women, Muslims and Dalits have together suffered these systemic denials. The largest private player in education that used to be the Church is today the RSS driven Vidya Bharati or the VHP inspired Ekal Vidyalaya. Within the minorities, a combination of brutal assault and resultant ghettoisation has meant that the madrassa and the private minority Institution-that by the way also needs to be monitored in terms of adherence to

Constitutional principles–is today the major supplier of education. But what we deliberately want to fail to see, it appears that all official and other studies show, that where there is a good quality State Education, no Muslim parent wants to send his or her child to a madrassa. By failing to state and draw from this reality we are also contributing to the further demonisation of the ordinary Muslim citizen who is being denied a Constitutional stake in quality education.

The link between access to all and quality of education needs to be articulated sharply in the NCF–2005 if it claims to be a National Policy of Education that comes after Huge and Deliberate Aberrations have Used Hatred within the Educational Sector. Our schools and textbooks have been used as laboratories for hate and division. Why are we today historically shying away from outlining this historic moment?

Teacher Training Colleges

The effects in the dimension of teaching-learning processes is on a large scale appreciated as the expected effects of globalization. Teacher Training Colleges are generally closed to the effects of globalization in terms of teaching-learning processes. The conclusion made started out from these findings is that level of awareness towards effects of teaching-learning processes is remaining limited within the academic life practices of the instructors. Once internationalization, quality development, strategic planning operations in Teacher Training Colleges began to increase, and once managing administration–in which activity and efficiency is a priority-is fundamental, standardization, homogenization, international control mechanisms and understandings of quality are results of this process, and their effects on the nature, the scientific and autonomous character of academic education must be deeply interrogated and explored. According to research findings. Teacher Training Colleges have difficulties about these subjects concerning with global effects on educational and instructional level:

- Developing multicultural and interdisciplinary programs,
- Implementing interactional and multi-dimensional teaćhing and learning,
- Developing individual learning processes,
- Developing skills which are facilitated to adapting global interaction and relations,
- Developing learning processes which are based on research,
- Expand and bringing in the practice international quality standards, lifelong learning and to become a learning center for university environment.

As a result, this research is considered to be a commencement in determining the effects of globalization over Teacher Training Colleges in our country and will bring important contributions to the field and to reconstruction of Teacher Training Colleges according to the international inclinations and principles.

Conclusion

An unusual development is that within a short span of five year two curriculum frameworks for school were brought out by the NCERT. The recent national curriculum framework (NCF-2005) has advocated the need for creating constructivist-learning environment in schools and for this it visualized some basic changes in the role of a teacher. In the constructivist paradigm the role of a teacher has shifted from an information provider or an instructor to a facilitator and a guide who can create such an environment where learners themselves create their knowledge. In this paradigm the concept of learning as well as its assessment has drastically changed. The role of a teacher is not now confined to that of curriculum transactor but she has to be actively involved in the process of curriculum development which includes development of the learning resources and curriculum evaluation. Since the relationship between the school education and teacher education is a synergic one so the teacher education curriculum must be responsive to such changes that are taking place at school level that is why NCF–2005 envisages a paradigm shift in teacher education programme. In response to this suggestion the NCTE in collaboration of NCERT has brought out a draft curriculum framework for Teacher Education 2006. There is an immediate need to critically and thoroughly look into this draft curriculum too. Given the centrality of a curriculum for school education, the National Curriculum Framework (NCF) could have been more extensively discussed in public. A curriculum framework has to address educational programmes as well as acquainting society with what the next generation is being taught and why. At the present point in the history of India, this particular NCF has a more than routine relevance. It has to concern itself with how we can prevent the hijacking of the curriculum of the kind that was experienced under the previous government.

References

1. Menon Mohan, Rama. K., (2006) "*Quality Indicators for Teacher Education*" National Assessment and Accreditation Council (NAAC), Bangalore.

2. NCERT Team (2005) *"National Curriculum Framework–2005"* National Council of Educational Research and Training, New Delhi. Draft Curriculum Framework for Teacher Education (2006) retrieved on 17th January 2007.

   1) en.wikipedia.org/wiki
   *National_Curriculum_Framework_*(NCF_2005).

   2) www.*solutionexchange*-un.net.in.

   3) www.*indiatogether.org*/2005.

   4) www.ncert.nic.in/html/*schoolcurriculum*.

Chapter–30

Teacher Education Curriculum in the Context of Globalization, Liberalization and Privatization (GLP)

Introduction

Education plays a very crucial role in shaping the character and quality of people. A new born infant is a helpless human being. He is neither a friend nor an enemy. But as he grows older, education in him is able to instill sense of maturity and responsibilities likes elders. Education bestows in child immense benefits.

India is a developing country. We have thousands years of tradition and culture. Different types of people are living in India. In olden days educational institutions were called as "Ashram" and teachers were called as "Guru". Guru was respectable as father and mother in the society. According to Vedas, "Guru" is our third God.

Now we are living in the technological world. Vast changes are occurring in day to day life of human being. Even today also teachers are role model for students in the society. Teaching profession is a respectable job in the society but because of process of globalization and privatization, enormous changes have occurred in the system of education.

Western culture is at fast pace. Due to globalization and liberalization, we see everything in form of commercial, but it is

---

Shineh Suri, Lecture in Trinity Institute, Mansarover Garden, New Delhi.

not good as teacher is nation builder and development of any country lies upon educational system.

The concept of curriculum can be perceived as a connective link between teacher and student. Curriculum should be organized in such a way to achieve goals set by teachers or curriculum specialist.

Teacher Education

When India attained freedom, the educational system including teacher education largely remained isolated from the needs and aspirations of the people. During last five decades efforts have been made to improvise it but the gap are still wide and visible. The imperatives for building the bridges may be as follows:

- To build a national system of teacher education based on India's cultural ethos, its unity and diversity.
- To prepare professionally competent teachers to perform their roles effectively as per the needs of society.
- To upgrade standard of teacher education, enhance the professional and social status of teacher and develop sense of commitment.

According to Cunninghum, "It (curriculum) is a tool in the hands of the artist (teacher) to mould his material (pupil) according to his ideal (objectives) in his studio (school)".

"Curriculum" is everything that goes on within the school including extra-class activities, guidance and interpersonal relationship.

In India there are large number of communities living in the dessert, the hilly areas, the plateau area, the plain area and the costal area all having their own peculiar individuality ,environment, custom and needs, therefore same curriculum cant be forced upon all irrespective of their needs and environment. It must differ from locality to locality and society to society.

Further Teacher Education and Curriculum has to be modified in the context of Globalization, Liberalization and Privatization.

Teacher Education Curriculum in Context of Globalization

Globalization is a qualitatively new phenomenon of multi dimensional nature possessing variety of complex trends in economic, social and cultural fabrics of all societies. Globalization impacts on all conceivable facts of life including education. Rapid development in technology and communication are forcing changes with educational system across the world. In the changed context of globalization and privatization human labour became a commodity like all other commodities and is exchanged for wages.

Consequently education service would naturally be commercialized, privatized and capitalized (CPC). Education would soon wear a new face-modernized for knowledge, economy based on information technologies, its value, preferences and taste would be different.

In the global market where industrial based economics are giving ways to knowledge based industries, the education in the post industrial society of present is preparing the learner to acquire knowledge and skills and intellectual capacity in order to cope up with the demands of emerging global society's needs.

As this being the age of techno scientific revolution and the pace with which changes at work are taking place, it requires the people to re-group themselves as new skills and knowledge is needed to compete, survive and prosper. Hence their should be clear perception in the minds of the curriculum maker of what competencies, professional skills and knowledge do learner need for successful performance in the user system.

India has thousand years of tradition and culture. As explained earlier, educational institutions were used to be called Ashrams and teachers were called gurus. A tremendous change has occurred due to globalization, liberalization and privatization. The education system is affected in totality.

Now educational institutions give lot of importance to technical education. Teacher is a national builder and has capacity to change the society. By knowing the importance of technology and communication skills, National Council of Teacher Education (NCTE) introduced a separate subject on Technology known as "Educational Technology" at ETE, B.Ed and M.Ed level.

Also, we are facing many negative problems in form of terrorism, poverty and over population. We want such type of curriculum, which teaches peace, non-violence, positive attitudes and values in the society.

Our National Educational Policy (1986) and other education committees and commissions have given importance for quality teacher education. Now it is our duty to follow such type of curriculum by conducting national seminars, workshops and conferences. It is important to collect imminent scholar's attitude towards importance of curriculum change in the present scenario.

Issues and Concerns in School Education

- **Stalling the social divide– Privatization and concerns of equity**

Low efficiency and effectiveness of the public schooling system, coupled with inadequate financial resource allocation has tended to push more and more people to seek even primary education through privately managed institutions. However, there is no reason to believe that people are voluntarily moving away from the public system which is free, towards private education.

It is important to note that this trend is likely to lead to further increase in inequity.

In fact, one can observe that in urban areas this divided system of school education has contributed to a vertical division in the society on the basis of economic status of the parents. Can the state silently watch this phenomenon of education becoming an instrument of division and perpetuation of inequality in the society? Is it desirable to throw open the education system to the vagaries of the market when a large majority of the population are still deprived of even the basic levels of education?

• **Bridging the male-female disparity**

Recent statistics show that even though GER for girls has risen to more than 90 per cent at the primary stage, it has remained practically static around 50 per cent at the upper primary stage for the last several years. In fact, even at the primary stage, the male-female disparity remains not fully bridged.

School education has to address this issue by designing special strategies to overcome the barriers and bridge the gap between boys and girls on a priority basis.

• **Vocationalise or not to Vocationalise—at what stage, how and how much?**

It is a well-known fact that millions of children in the country are forced to enter the labour market instead of pursuing education in the schools. Even among those who begin attending the school, a large number as indicated by high dropout rates and low transition rates, enter the workforce at a very early stage of life.

It is in this context that the school curriculum that remains academic in nature has come under repeated criticism for not being able to add any value to the lives of such children and rather making education a drudgery and burden. Notwithstanding deliberations by several committees and commissions, we have yet to establish a meaningful structure of schooling which can benefit both streams of students—those who terminate at elementary or secondary stage and those who continue their education to the tertiary level.

• **Linking school education with the changing economic scenario**

School education cannot be impervious to the fast changes taking place in the economic sector through liberalization and globalization of the market.

Demands on the school, particularly with regard to those who enter the production sector straight from the school are two-fold. On the one hand, school education, particularly at the secondary stage has to keep pace with the needs of a competitive market, dependent on continuously improved knowledge and skill levels. On the other hand, school education has to recognize that the liberalized market framework directly affects the micro-economics of the poorer sections of the population, often corroding their fragile occupational base.

The school education system has to become pro-active in preparing the curriculum and processes not only as a matter of social concern, but also to meet the basic needs of those entering the emerging economic framework.

- **Interface with Technology**

Information Technology (IT) presents an excellent opportunity for making a quantum jump in the provision of school education in a need-based manner. Unfortunately, very little attention has been given in the country for exploring the tremendous potential of IT in school education, both for its quantitative expansion and for improving its quality.

It is, therefore, urgent that immediate attention is given in school education to imparting basic IT skills to all learners. Learning from the past efforts, it is important that adequate provisions are made for development of software and capacity-building for teachers in order that it does not remain only as an additionally to the existing subject areas, but becomes an integral part of the learning experience of all children.

- **Quality is the heart of the matter**

Examination statistics show that about 60 per cent of children routinely fail in the public examination conducted at the end of the secondary school; and of those who succeed and join higher secondary; only 40 per cent succeed in the higher secondary examination.

Curriculum reforms, examination reforms and large scale efforts for introducing progressive pedagogy and so on, are being made in almost all the states. However, given the large size of the school education system, these system level reforms seem to be making very little impact on the functioning of the school. Direct actions for changing the functioning of people and institutions operating at the grassroots level have not received adequate attention.

The situation demands a total reversal of perspective so that school occupies the centre stage and improvement in the quality of the school becomes the major agenda of all reform processes.

- **The question of alternatives and plural avenues**

Non-suitability of a standardized model of full-time formal schooling to create a universal mass education system in the country was emphatically pointed out by Mahatma Gandhi much before we embarked on the task, fifty years ago.

It is now fully realized that a monolithic approach to delivery of school education cannot meet the legitimate demands of the people for provision of educational facilities of a reasonably acceptable quality. Yet, it has been difficult to break the monopolistic hold of full-time formal schooling on the education system. Interestingly, society has begun adjusting its expectations to the limitations of formal schooling, instead of more actively pursuing the task of designing alternatives.

Prospects and Propositions

Elaboration of issues and problems of school education confronting the country should not be construed to imply that we are saddled with an impossible situation. Rather, it points to the need for acting with a sense of purpose and determination. What are the priority areas in which well-planned action holds promise for taking the school education system in a progressive direction? Some of these are indicated below.

- **Liberalizing the curriculum framework**

An important area that needs immediate attention is the introduction of a flexible and dynamic curriculum framework that meets the varying needs and aspirations of the diverse profiles of children entering school education. This is essential, if school education is to be made more joyful and relevant to the lives of the people. Actions have to be initiated, therefore, to avoid increased standardization of the curriculum and allow for more decentralization. This again requires curriculum development to be a participatory Endeavour of the direct stakeholders replacing the high bureaucratization that characterizes the current scene.

- **Harnessing advances in information technology to the advantage of school education**

In India, use of technology has invariably been identified with prosperity and affluence. With the relatively under-endowed state of the public education system, technology is seen as an alien element, which has no place in the school education programme. This perspective has failed to fully grasp the potential of technology to overcome some of the very barriers arising out of inadequate resources. It is important to take positive steps for building a more meaningful interface between modern developments in the field of information technology and school education programmes.

It is paradoxical that whereas the national leadership harbors aspirations of making the country a global leader in the IT sector, there has been no plan at all to make even basic computer literacy a part of the larger school system. It should be worthwhile that a national taskforce examines all the issues involved and comes out with a pro-active and futuristic framework for creating a sustainable interface between IT and school education.

It is essential that the task of quality improvement in school functioning is addressed in a more holistic manner by viewing teacher capacity-building and managerial skill development in an inter-related framework. Without bringing substantial improvement in the managerial efficiency of the schools, no amount of investment in pedagogy training will make an impact.

There is a need, therefore, to abandon the traditional concepts and practices of training the school teachers and managers through centralized arrangements involving the use of generic packages of training inputs. These have to be replaced by more localized and sustainable support mechanisms and delivery modes that are capable of providing contextualized learning inputs directly at the workplace.

If efficiency and quality improvement are our concerns, there appears to be no alternative, but to go for more local initiatives within a participatory framework and move towards the creation of more easily manageable organizational arrangements.

In spite of the hyperbole created with regard to decentralization under the banner of recent Constitutional Amendments on Panchayati Raj institutions, no perceptible change has come in most of the states with regard to the educational management scenario.

The benefits of ushering a decentralized system of management are enormous. The most important one is that smaller systems built through participatory processes are in a better position to remain sensitive to the local needs and aspirations; they allow for creative alternatives to emerge; and they are more likely to bring in a sense of ownership as well as accountability.

Conclusion

We have a very large army of scientifically trained manpower; we also have, perhaps, the largest number of illiterates. As many scholars have pointed out, we seem to be unwittingly nurturing a fractured system of school education. One part of the system is keeping pace with the most advanced systems of the world and the other, which serves the poorer and disempowered sections of the society, is remaining inefficient to reach out effectively and provide meaningful education.

The challenge is to invest more energy and resources to improve the system, both in its outreach capacity and quality. We have to act on this with a sense of urgency and earnestness, lest education itself becomes a means of promoting social inequality and a source of increasing chasm between those who can pay for their education and those who cannot. It is necessary to strategies actions so as to make real improvement in the lives of the people.

References

1. Tyler, R. (1949). *Basic Principles of Curriculum and Instructions,* the University of Chicago, Press Chicago.

2. Gertzel Cherry, *The Internationalization or the Globalization of Education* in the 1990's and paper presented to HERDSA, August 1997.

3. Lyons Tanya, *"Globalization and Education, Survival Guide* to a Global World Lecture, 12th August 2000.

4. Axford Barrie (1995). *The Global System, Economics, Politics & Culture,* Cambridge, UK Polity Press.

5. *National Curriculum Framework for Teacher Education-NCT 2005,* Published by NCERT.

6. Burbules, N.C. and Torres, C.B. (2000). *Globalization and Education: A critical perspectives.* London: Routledge.

7. Ilaiah, K Ancha (2003). Cultural Globalization. *The Hindu,* 22nd February 2003.

8. Stewart, Frances (1996). Globalization and Education. *International Journal of Educational Development*, 16 (4), 327-333.

Chapter–31

Need for Change in Roles and Perceptions of Teacher Education with Reference to NCF–2005

Introduction

"The ill trained teacher or substandard teachers would be detrimental to our educational system if not a punishment to our children. The government and the university must, therefore, take care to see that inadequacy in the training of teachers is not compounded by any extraneous consideration" (Hob'ble Supreme Court).

Education all over the world have agreed that the training of the teachers is of utmost importance in any educational endeavor. From Vedic times, ashrams and gurukuls have insisted on the primacy of the teacher and the utmost importance of teacher. The great Indian Universities of Taxila and Nalanda were real centers of knowledge via training. Recognizing the significance of teacher education Kothari Education Commission (1964-66) pointed out that the essence of a Programme of teacher education is "quality" and in its absence, teacher education becomes not only a financial waste but also a source of overall deterioration in educational standards.

Professional competencies of teacher educator at various levels are crucial to ensure quality both in teacher education and school education. There is a need to develop well designed

Dr. J.N. Baliya, Assistant Professor in Department of Education, University of Jammu, Jammu.

mechanics, for content enrichment, augmentation and renewal. Steps are also to be taken for their professional growth and development on continuous basis to enable them to keep abreast with the changes and developments in their respective fields besides developments in pedagogy and related disciplines. Expertise to be developed through short term attachments and carefully devised courses conducted in selected institutions and university departments.

The NCTE after becoming a statutory body in 1995 brought out a discussion document on Curriculum Framework for quality Teacher Education (1998) in order to give a new look to teacher education by brining out a cosmetic change in the system. But these suggestions have not been converted into some radical transformation or the overhauling of the teacher education Programme as envisaged by NPE (1986, 1992). The teacher educating Programme today is far from a satisfactory position and quality. It is undergoing a severe turmoil leading to a considerably low quality of products i.e. trained teachers. The quality issues of the teacher education Programmes can be examined by analyzing the quality of inputs, quality of processes and the quality of outputs. This can also be stated in terms of quality of content and techniques of teacher education, quality of teacher educators, the quality of infrastructure and the quality of teacher trainees.

The metamorphic changes in terms of growth and expansion influenced by the plans and policies pertaining to teacher education programmes and the major shifts in India's economic policies-liberalization, privatization and globalization have also affected the equilibrium between Quality and quantity of teacher education institutions. In J&K State alone, we have around 150 Colleges of Education with at least 2600 teacher educators. The quality of teacher preparation is closely related to the professional competencies of teacher educators. Therefore, there is a constant need for specialized professional development Programme for teacher educators to refine and improve their professional competencies as desired to train the teachers to follow the basics of National Curriculum Framework (2005). In fact NCF (2008) recommended that teacher education Programme to be recast to reflect professionalism in the process of training and teaching. It must become more sensitive to the emerging demands from the school system. But unfortunately, the programmes of professional preparation of teacher educators are not relevant and satisfactory to consider them as "Skill" or "Professionally competent" teacher educators.

Therefore, there is need to adopt a more rational approach to teacher development in India by developing desirable professional competence among teacher educators. We need to take up the issues regarding initiating a permanent and productive mechanism for developing *"Professional Competence"* of approximately 50,000 teacher trainers who are working in various teacher training Institutes in the country. There is a constant need for specialized professional development programmes for teacher educators both at pre-service as well as in-service level to refine and improve their professional competencies. The teacher educator of the current era has to be a curriculum designer and analyst, internet user, placement officer, educational consultant, support services provider and also a master trainer in computer education. We also need to devise a proper policy for creating some resource training centre among some leading teacher education institutes where teacher educators may be imparted the continuous and comprehensive training to make them more productive and effective teacher trainers.

The teacher educators who are assigned the task of imparting training to the in-service or pre-service teacher trainees need to be fully equipped with all essential knowledge and professional skills pertaining to the discipline of Education and science of pedagogy. In addition to that he should have in depth understanding about innovative methods of teaching. Techniques of conducting applied and action research and appropriate methods of guidance and counseling. In the contemporary emerging "knowledge society" every teacher educator has to perform an integrated role for which a well designed policy needs to be framed and implemented to ensure qualitative teacher education Programme, Some of the reformative steps have been listed below :

- Evolving a permanent mechanism for a qualitative and productive pre-service training of teacher educators i.e. at B.Ed/M.Ed/M.Phil/Ph.D level.
- Conducting workshop/seminar on the issue pertaining to professional skills such as lesson planning , methods of teaching, techniques of guidance and counseling, curriculum designing, methods of conducting research, techniques of evaluation, maintenance of in signing records etc.
- Establishing a Cluster Resource/Training Centres (CRC / CTC) for teacher educators where senior teacher educators and experts may impart training to new generation of teacher educators on the existing /new trends of teacher education.
- Introducing a Continuous Comprehensive Performance Appraisal (CCPA) system for teacher educators for monitoring and strengthening their professional competencies by taking corrective measures.
- Involving on mandatory basis the teacher educators in the task of applied/action research on the specific issues of teacher education.
- Engaging the teacher educators in the process of curriculum design and book review.
- Conducting periodical conferences / conventions of all teacher educators where they may share the experiences and observation of their training fields.

If above cited measures are widely acknowledged and implemented with due promptness sincerity and motivation, we can certainly lead towards quality assurance as envisaged by every one associated with quality teacher education Programme.

References

1. Government of India (1986), *National Policy of Education–1986*, New Delhi, Ministry of Human Resource Development.
2. Government of India, (1992). *National policy on Education-1992, Programme of Action-1992,* New Delhi, Ministry of Human Resource Development.
3. Mavi, N S (2005). *The Emerging Role of Teacher Educators in the Knowledge Era, University News,* 43 (18), December 2005.
4. National Council for Teacher Education (1998). *Curriculum Framework for Quality Teacher Education.* New Delhi, NCTE.
5. Nisha Singh, (2001), *Teacher Education-Changing Perception* for the Next Millennium, Frontiers in Education, 31 (3).
6. Zayapragassarazan, Z (2005), *Encountering Emerging Challenges in Teacher Education, University News,* 43 (18), December 2005.

Chapter–32

Beyond Cognition

The emotions are not "a state within a state". They cannot be understood outside the dynamic of human life. It is within this context that the emotional processes acquire their meaning and sense. – Vygotsky

Introduction

School reformers too often underestimate the relation between optimal learning conditions for students and similarly supportive working conditions for their teachers that is, anytime we want students to adopt a new practice, we must first ensure that such practices are integrated into the system as a whole, characterizing as well the way teachers approach their daily tasks.

Tharp and Gallimore (1993) have argued that whereas, it is widely recognized that students need both caring sensitivity and intellectual challenge, school reformers, theorists and researchers alike have been slower to recognize that the same can be said of teacher's work and on the job learning. Even as burgeoning qualitative studies on teachers and classrooms are providing countless portraits of the cognitive and affective nature of teaching and learning, seldom is this integration explicitly identified or conceptually framed.

1. *Sushma Sharma, Pupil-teacher in Army Institute of Education, Delhi Cantt.*

2. *Dr. Amita Puri, Lecture in Army Institute of Education, Delhi Cantt.*

Emotions

Emotional catharsis plays a very important role in literary appreciation. there is a dynamic relationship among emotion ,thought, and motivation. Vygotsky wrote "thought, is engendered by motivation, i.e. by our desires and needs ,our interests and emotions .behind every thought there is an affective-volitional tendency, which holds the answer to the last 'why' in the analysis of thinking ".

He condemned the tendency to separate intellect and affect into district fields of study, believing that this separation had created the false illusion that thinking is some how segregated from the fullness of life and from the needs and interest of thinkers, Such misleading binaries had legislated against close attention to emotion's role in stimulating thought, as well as to "the influence of thought on affect and volition". Popular attention to teacher's professional lives has long been preoccupied with competence and expertise, most recently manifest in proposals for test of teachers knowledge and for linking of pay to indices of student achievement. Such proposals are causing distress, eliciting, strong responses, and attracting new attention to the ways that affect permeates the lives of teachers. But teaching has always been an emotional work. If all learning is imbued with emotional meaning and influences, all teaching is too. Teacher must be learners, after all, as they negotiate the multiple demands of their workdays, restlessly seeking more effective and satisfying paths. In doing so, they draw not only on distributed cognition, but also on the distributed emotions that are scattered across the terrain of work place and profession.

Feeling, Thinking and Teaching

We embark here on a bit of detour, turning from reflection on other ideas to reconsideration. Let us consider the case of Sonia's first hand experience with stress and burn out in her 7th year in class room.

Sonia's teaching career began and ended in a small town in rural area, enrolment in the K -12 schools was 400, and Sonia was the only English teacher for grade 10 to 12. Socio economic class divisions tended to be keenly felt by Sonia's students some of whom growing up on prosperous farms, other in rural poverty.

Whether her student's plans included going to college or managing a local gas station, Sonia wanted to ensure that each found her classes engaging, challenging, and meaningful. Whenever some asked about her long term plans, Sonia always said that she saw herself putting in several decades of dedicated work here, retiring one distant day from these very districts. She had initially been hired just a few days before the start of New Year, entering her class room to find scant materials and virtually no curriculum, which was all developed as well as doubled by her. Over time she would struggle to meet the demands of her work with a gathering sense of personal inadequacy. As she watched her less passionate colleagues move through the days and weeks with seeming ease, she was increasingly troubled by her own lack of time and sagging spirits. She began to experience frequent headache, bouts of fatigue, and feelings of failures, symptoms she would recognized only later as classic signs of stress.

At times, Sonia fully believed that she was alone responsible for the loss of her old intensity and commitment–in usual metaphoric short hand that she had failed to "manage her stress", and though once "on fire", had unfortunately "burned out". When teachers like Sonia failed to tends their own fires – failing, that is "to manage" their professional stress – they face the personal embarrassment of careers in gulfed.

For Sonia's former administrator and colleagues, this "burn out" problem was hers, and the problem was wholly emotional Sonia's story serves to underscore the need to move from an individual, behavioristic view of teacher's stress to a social – cultural conception that acknowledges the importance of work place traditions, conditions and norms.

Emotions and the Dynamic of Teacher's Lives

It is hard to imagine a life in teaching truly devoid of emotional charge. Dicken's Gradgrind comes to mind, embodying the familiar head-heart dichotomy and the strong western tendency, often traced to Plato and later Descartes, to celebrate the head and distrust the heart. And yet one somehow senses that by novel's end comeuppance will be had, the heart given its due, hearts and minds put in a rightful relation. We know this only in parts because we know Dickens; we know it too, because we recognize that teaching is human work and that both teachers and students are indelibly human creatures.

The choice is not whether to feel or not; what emerges in the extended vygotskian framework sketched here as well as in the more recent neurological and psychological work, is that emotions are inevitably present in any teaching learning event. As key strands in the "web of meaning" (Vygotsky, 1982) our emotions are intimately connected to our thoughts and actions and shaped in important ways by the institutional, cultural and historic contexts in which we live and labour. We act on the basis of socially constructed thoughts and emotions which ,"gone inward" become what we tend to regard as our private sensibilities and understandings.

We clearly need a more developed and politically viable theoretical base in order to argue for enhanced attention to emotion in teacher education, in teacher development and in empirical research on teacher and learning. Work on narrative ways on knowing seve to enrich vygotskian conception of teacher's professional lives in several ways. First, it can provide a better framework that can help us better understand how intellectual and emotional understandings are internalized and developed – that is, through a process of narrativising experience and continually revisiting and refining these narratives that they might reflect more robust conceptions of teaching and learning. Secondly, this work provides more concrete examples of relationship between teacher reflection and student learning.

Emotion as Vygotsky emphasize, cannot be usefully imagine as a "state within a state" in educational research, as in fictional narratives, emotions are best explored as integral thread in the larger web. If we acknowledge that teaching is a politically charged work involving both emotional and intellectual investments and challenges, we must also recognize that threats teacher's professional wellbeing undermine the very core of their labors. The affective aspects of teacher's professional lives tends to be filled away in separate categories- "morale", "stress", even "emotional intelligence" – and made just for facile workshops.

We see the role of emotionality as an untapped vein in this generative and still developing theoretic base, represents a conceptual challenge that holds key implications for research, policy, and practice. ensuring the vitality of our nation's teacher's demands these still-richer theoretic conceptions-conceptions that might empower our efforts to understand and support teachers like Sonia as they strive to understand and support students who are (as we all are) at once feeling and thinking beings.

References

1. Tharp, R. & Gallimore, R. (1988) *Rousing minds to life: Teaching, learning, and schooling in social context.* New York: Cambridge University Press.
2. Vygotsky, L. (1987) Lecture 4: *Emotions & their development in childhood.* In R. Rieber & A. Carton (Eds.), *The collected works* of L.S.Vygotsky. (N.Minick, Trans.) *(Vol.1,* pp.325-358). New York: Plenum Press.
3. James. (1950) *The principles of psychology*. New York: Dover.
4. Brunner. (1986). *Actual minds, possible worlds*. Cambridge, MA: Harvard University Press.

Chapter–33

Enhancing Understanding of the Terms Commonly used Clinically

Many a times, most of us get stuck into the web of terminology used by the doctors/clinicans while they try to decipher the behaviour of our precious children to us. And its important for us as parents and teachers to know little bit more about them to be able to help our children for their better future tomorrow.

This article is an attempt to demystify the frequently used but misunderstood words especially used while trying to describe the behaviour of the children.

Here are some of the few:

Achievement Age: Another term for educational age. It is established by standard achievement tests comprising a series of educational rather than intelligence tests.

Acute Psychotic agitation: impaired state, characterized by severely increased psychomotor activity, often associated with or produced by psychotic experiences such as delusions and hallucinations.

Affect: It includes inner feelings and their external manifestations. Affect and emotions are often used interchangeably. It is also described as experience of emotion that is expressed by the patient and observed by others.

Dr Amita Puri, Lecture in Education at Army Insititue of Education, Delhi Cantt.

Affective flattening: A disturbance of affective response, expressed as emotional blunting and indifference.

Aggression: Behaviour both physical and/or verbal that has potential for actual harm. Aggressive behaviour ranges from normal assertiveness and coping behaviour to acts of violence. It may be expressed overtly (abusing, cursing) or covertly (defiance, no cooperation, gossiping), directly (physical assault) or indirectly (planned, systematic hostile acts). Aggression includes diverse motivational, emotional and behavioral aspects.

Agitation: Inability to sit still, pacing, fidgeting, movements of legs or fingers, wringing hands and / or pulling at clothes, along with a feeling of uneasiness or restlessness.

Agoraphobia: Intense anxiety with a feeling of being trapped in a situation, a public place or fear of losing control in a public place leading to embarrassment.

Anger: Strong feeling elicited by real or supposed injury that is often accompanied by a desire to take vengeance.

Anhedonia:Inability to derive pleasure from situation and stimuli that usually induce pleasure. It is a pathogenic feature of a major depressive disorder.

Anorexia Nervosa: Eating disorder that occurs commonly in pre-pubertal adolescent girls and young women. Distortion of body image is considered central to the diagnosis characterized by morbid fear of becoming fat, refusal to maintain normal body weight and obsession with dieting.

Anxiety: Subjective, unpleasant feeling or emotional state of apprehension, dread or foreboding ranging from excessive concern about the present or future to feelings of panic, accompanied by a variety of autonomous signs and symptoms – palpitations, dry mouth, panting, pupil dilation, shortness of breath, sweating with skin pallor, abdominal discomfort, dizziness etc.

Apathy: Lack of feeling. A symptom found in severe depression, schizophrenia and brain injury.

Aphonia: Loss of voice, not caused by laryngeal or neurological abnormalities.

Assertiveness: Affirmative and confident behaviour that allows a child to meet his/her needs.

Astasia-Abasia: Gait disorder characterized by bizarre staggering with abortive falls or collapse. Neurological examination confirms the absence of paralysis, ataxia or sensory loss. Its generally a manifestation of hysteria or conversion disorder.

Attention: Ability to focus in a sustained manner on one activity.

Attention-Poor: Lack of focused alertness and is manifested by poor levels of concentration, distractibility from internal and external stimuli and difficulty in harnessing, shifting or sustaining focus to new stimuli.

Autism: Behavioural syndrome characterized by poor social interaction, impaired communication and language, poor display of emotions, lack of empathy and atypical responses to people, objects and events. It is also associated with hyper-arousal state (e.g. hyperactivity, repetitive/stereotyped behaviour). Autistic children often exhibit ritualized body movements, repeated touching and sniffing of objects, ritualistic ordering, checking and collecting and insistence on following routines precisely.

Autistic Fantasy: A mechanism by which the child substitutes excessive daydreaming for the pursuit of human relationships, more direct and effective action or problem solving.

Automatic Behaviour: Stereotyped repetitive actions that apparently occur without the individual's awareness.

Automatism: Repetitive stereotyped sensor motor or verbal phenomena which occurs episodically, associated with clouding of consciousness over which the individual generally has no control and cannot remember. It can occur in epilepsy and sleep disorders,

Behaviour disorder: Deviant or maladaptive behaviour of a child inappropriate for its age or social expectations, causing nuisance or distress to people around it, not to itself.

Biological rhythms: The cyclical changes occurring in the physiological, psychological and emotional functioning and the level of activity of an individual at regular intervals ranging from minutes to months.

Bulimia: Eating disorder manifested by insatiable hunger resulting in compulsive or excessive eating of large quantities of calorie rich food, followed by self induced vomiting, excessively restricted dieting or prolonged periods of fasting.

Catalepsy: It is a state of generalized unresponsiveness in which parts of a child's body are held rigid for prolonged periods.

Cataplexy: It is a transient sudden loss of tone of the skeletal muscles which can result in a fall and injury to the patient. It generally manifests as a buckling of knees, sagging of head or complete collapse of the body. It is precipitated by a variety of emotional stress.

Catatonia: It is a syndrome characterized either by a state of stupor with marked muscular rigidity/flexibility or over activity with verbal/motor stereotype. It is found secondary to various medical, neurological and psychiatric disorders.

Catharsis: Relief due to release of pent up emotions. It occurs when a child releases feelings (anger, affection, sorrow, grief) about past or present experience that have previously been difficult or impossible to discharge.

Child-Physical Abuse: Acts that cause or could have caused physical injury to the child.

Child-Psychological Abuse: Acts or omissions that caused or could have caused emotional state or trauma that is inappropriate for the developmental age of the child.

Child Abuse: Physical abuse and neglect causing harm to children – usually infants, toddlers or preschoolers – generally by those who are responsible for their care. Caregivers may bring in children with minor or major injuries with explanations that do not fit the injury.

Child Neglect: Failure to provide care and nurturance to the child as is appropriate and necessary for his/her age.

Child Sexual Abuse: Acts in which dependent, developmentally immature children are involved in sexual activities that they do not fully comprehend, are unable to give informed consent to and that violates the sexual taboos on family roles.

Clanging: Speech in which associations are determined by sounds, rather than the meaning or the concepts of the words. It may include rhyming and punning. The term is applied only when it is a manifestation of the pathological condition e.g. schizophrenia or manic episodes.

Clinging: It is the inability to end appropriately or unnecessary prolongation of an interaction or conversation.

Clouding of Consciousness: A state of impaired consciousness representing mild stages of disturbance on a continuum from fully awareness to coma. It is found in the early stages of organic brain disease.

Cluttering: Disorder of speech fluency in which the rate and rhythm of speech are affected and speech intelligibility is impaired, There are alternating pauses and bursts of speech that produces groups of words unrelated to the grammatical structure of the sentence. Cluttering varies in its severity in individuals and is distinct from stuttering.

Communication Disorder: Form of speech or writing that impairs communication because of aberrant use of terms, content or form.

Compulsion: Repetitive, seemingly purposeful behaviour performed according to a specific or stereotyped fashion. The child may not recognize the senselessness of the behaviour.

Confabulation: Inventing stories and producing fast and fluent answers to any questions without regard to facts.

Delinquency: A term applied to various forms of antisocial behaviour and conduct of children that constitute legal offences.

Delirium: Transient, organic mental syndrome characterized by global impairment of cognitive functions including memory and perception.

Delusion: Unfounded, unrealistic, idiosyncratic belief that is firmly held without supporting evidence.

Developmental disability: Severe and chronic mental handicap ? Physical handicap occurring in children, for example mental retardation, autism, cerebral palsy etc.

Developmental disorder (pervasive): A group of disorders with deviant and delayed development, abnormalities in reciprocal social interactions, patterns of communications and restricted stereotyped , restricted behaviour involving child's functioning in all areas. These are severe disorders with poor prognosis.

Dyslexia: A form of difficulty in reading, writings or spellings despite having been taught to read and write in the absence of defective vision/hearing, mental handicap or brain damage.

Dysphoria: Unpleasant quality of mood with acute transient changes in it (e.g. feelings of sadness, sorrow, anguish, misery, mental malaise) accompanied by verbal complaints of feeling depressed, sad, blue, gloomy, empty etc.

Dysthymia: It is a mild form of affective disorder where symptoms of depression persist for a longer time and may fluctuate from day to day or on hour to hour basis.

Dystonia: Neurological condition characterized by slow, tonic, sustained muscle contractions often of the tongue, jaw, eyes and neck and frequently causing twisting and repetitive movements or abnormal postures.

Echolalia: Automatic and persistent repetition of words or phrases uttered by others.

Elective mutism: A condition exhibited by children who although being able to talk and comprehend language , remain silent in the presence of particular individuals and environments, usually related to school.

Emotional incontinence: Involuntary, sudden expression of feelings such as weeping, grimacing, laughter over which the person has no apparent control.

Emotional withdrawal: Lack of interest in or involvement with events and happenings. It may range from mild to extreme.

Reference

1. Savita Malhotra (2002): Child Psychiatry in India. Macmillan India Ltd.

Chapter–34

Digital Language Laboratory and the Teaching of English in India

Introduction

Language is the tool of expression and communication. Although English is taught as a Second language in India, it is seen as a preferred academic language by both parents and students alike. Today, most schools are opting for English as a medium of instruction, as English is seen as a language for social mobility. Teaching of English, has undergone a lot transitions and today there are numerous approaches to tackle the teaching of English. Teachers are trying to develop a support system that could help in transacting the English Curriculum with ease.

Teaching of English and NCF–2005

The NCF–2005 talks of a curriculum framework that enables schools and teachers to make choices and move towards greater autonomy. Such a movement towards school autonomy is seen in a positive light by all major policy and curriculum documents. It has also been recognized that the choices at the level of school and teacher could be made possible only within an accepted framework of basic principles. NCF–2005 has talked about these principles in connection with the general aims of education (nationally accepted), stage specific objectives (accepted state and district level in agreement with the national level standards for the

---

Pranita Gopal, Lecturer in Education at Army Institute of Education, Delhi Cantt.

final stage of school education), and selection of content (at district and school level), in guidance of, perhaps, a state level syllabus.

A national curriculum can aim for a cohesive curricular policy based on guiding principles for language teaching and acquisition, which allows for a variety of implementations suitable to local needs and resources, and which provide illustrative models for use.

Input rich communicational environments are a prerequisite for language learning. Inputs include textbooks, learner-chosen texts, and class libraries allowing for a variety of genres: print; parallel books and materials in more than one language; media support; and authentic materials. The aim should be to identify delivery systems for comprehensible inputs to the child, whether in the classroom or outside it; for example, the school can serve as a community resource centre for children after school hours. Research has shown us that greater gains accrue when language instruction moves away from the traditional approach of learning definitions of words (the dictionary approach) to an enriched approach, which encourages associations with other words and contexts (Fawcett and Nicolson, 1991). Materials used or available as texts in class libraries may be in print as well as multi-media formats. Children must be exposed to a whole range of genres.

A package of teaching-learning material that relates with the child cannot be developed only with the child's context in mind. No single package, however well and professional designed, can address all the contextual situations in a country as large as India. Therefore, a large number of packages should be developed at state and district levels with adequate provisions for cluster and school-level modifications and supplementary materials.

In addition to squarely contextualizing the educational processes, the production of teaching learning material package at local levels will also increase avenues for teacher participation at a hitherto unprecedented large scale. This should significantly enhance the quality of local level educational discourse, and is likely to improve upon the ownership of material and methods by the teachers.

Each school or teacher should be able to choose the package of her liking, given that she is committed to achieve the required learning levels and all available packages are of proven quality. Freedom to choose methods and materials is likely to enhance the teacher's self image and responsibility.

Technological Options in an English Language Classroom

Around the world English Language Teachers especially Teachers of English as a Second Language have been using technology resources in their classroom. Listed below are various technological options that can be used in the language classroom.

Radio: The radio is a low cost teaching aid in the language classroom. It can be used for listening comprehension activities and also help students to improve their own speech and intonation patterns. Radio changed the face of the distance language learning classroom. The basic disadvantage of the radio programs are timing issues, inability to replay and the fact that it caters to a larger audience, but not a local audience.

Television: In the language classroom, television is capable of bringing out the essence of communication. Communication concerns itself not only with verbal expressions but also non verbal cues and gestures. Students can see, learn and reproduce these communication patterns in their behavior. The major problem with using a television as a teaching learning tool in the language classroom, is that it is expensive to make programs for the television that cater to the local needs.

Tape Recorder: has had probably the single greatest impact on language learning. Its introduction meant that the teacher could play recordings of authentic native speech. This device has two options that make it useful in the language classroom. One, it can replay programs over and again and second it can help students record their own language usage. When students are able to record and listen to their own language usage, they can learn language more effectively.

VCR: (Video Cassette Recorder): The video cassette recorder was an expensive option, in the language classroom. But, it was capable of playing, replaying and recording situations that could be used as input in the language classroom. Like, the television, language was in totality meaning apart from verbal dimension, the non verbal dimension was also learnt by the language learner.

CD/DVD Player: Like the VCR and the Tape, the CD/ DVD Player allows the teacher in the language classroom, to integrate, authentic language samples from native speakers. The only advantage is that the output using a CD/DVD player is clearer as compared to a Tape player. Also, the CD and DVD have longer shelf life as compared to the cassettes or tapes.

Computer: The computer revolutionarized the language classroom. A single machine was capable of creating, editing, sharing, recording and storing language samples in both audio and video format that could be retrieved at any place and anytime with the Internet connection.

Language Laboratory

The language laboratory is an audio or audio-visual installation used as an aid in modern language teaching. They can be found, amongst other places, in schools, universities and academies.

Functions of the Language Laboratory

The language laboratory can serve the following functions:

1. **The Aural Objective**: The language laboratory can provide samples native speakers of the language to be learnt. These samples can be played repeatedly and can help the learner gain an understanding towards the tone, intonation pattern and stress while speaking the language.

2. **The Oral Objective**: The language laboratory with its various tools can help the learner record sample of her voice and replay it again to either identify errors or monitor progress.

3. **The Grammar Objective**: The language laboratory is useful in teaching grammar as it is in instilling good pronunciation habits. It copes with two of the major problems of grammar instruction: the need for more exercise material than the instructor

usually has available, and the need for a transition from a theoretical mastery of a grammar point to an ability to apply the point orally with ease. The student who gets an opportunity to learn grammatical concepts in this manner, is assimilating grammar without passing through the well known cycle of remembering the rule, applying it as though on paper, and then trying to stammer it out orally.

4. **The Remedial Function**: Most language teachers feel the existence in the classroom is a constant struggle between the needs of the class as group and those individuals who make up the group. The language laboratory can function as a remedial education centre for students who take time in learning and those who require more practice sessions.

5. **The Evaluation Function**: Testing of English in majority of the classroom situations is in the form of paper pencil test. The language laboratory can be exploited to evaluate a learner's progress in the aural, oral, writing and reading dimension of the language. This adds to the authenticity of learning experience.

Foreign language learning lends itself naturally to the use of media. Linguists stress the primacy of speech over writing in language: children can listen and speak before they learn to read and write and all languages of the world are spoken, but not all have a writing system. Accordingly, foreign-language educators have been heavily involved in the use of audio equipment. They welcomed the first audio device, the phonograph, and have immediately adopted other advances in audio technology such as magnetic tape and digital media. (Delcoque, Annan, & Bramoull´e, 2000). The language laboratories flourished during the 1960s, with the changing methodologies in the teaching learning process and the decline of behaviourism, language laboratories began a period of decline.

With the technological boom in the horizon, the Teachers of English as a Second Language, began exploiting the computer as a tool in the English Classroom. The computer, has the distinct advantage of being a single machine capable of *creating, sharing, editing and saving* language projects, assignments, lessons and modules in the language classroom.

Digital Language Laboratory

A digital language laboratory is a network of computers (or even stand alone computers) with appropriate software that provides the functions of the language laboratory along with the integration of video, word-processing and other computer applications.

Dedicated digital laboratories can provide:

- **Versatility:** Texts, images, audio and video can easily be integrated, and the teacher can remodel and tailor-make the materials to fit the needs of different language learners.
- **Ease of movement** between different applications: like a word-processor, a presentation software, the internet or a computer assisted language learning module.
- **Interactivity**: the computer can help students learn at their own pace, allow them to choose the activities they wish to do and essential record, edit and share their own voice samples or writing samples with others.
- **Teacher intervention:** The teacher can not only intervene in the language learning process of the students, but also keep track of the learning curve of the language learner.
- **Self Learning**: is made possible, as the material in the digital laboratory can be transferred easily as most students today own a PC themselves. This allows students to learn at their own pace and sometimes repeat the lessons after the lab hours.

Setting up a Digital Language Laboratory

In principle a digital language laboratory can be set up in the computer laboratory of the school, in the computers that are multimedia enabled. Multimedia enabled computers can play, record and share audio and video files that can be seen and heard by the language learner. Table 1 describes the Digital Language Laboratory Component (Hardware and Software) and the Language Skills in Learning a Language.

Table 1: The Digital Language Laboratory and the Language Skills in Learning a Language

Language Skill	Hardware Component	Software Option
Aural Skill	· Speakers: for a larger audience · Headphone: for a single	· Media Player that comes with operating System (for example Windows Media Player in the Windows OS, Songbird in Ubuntu)
Oral Skill	· Microphone: to record oral speech sample · Headphone or Speakers: to hear the recorded samples	· Audacity or any Sound Recording Software that comes with the operating system. Such software also allow editing the recorded sample
Writing Skill	· Key board: to type data · Monitor: to view the typed data · Memory Disk: to save and transfer the data · Printer: to print the data	· Word Processing Software like MS Word, Open Office Writer etc can help language students record their writing samples in the language they are learning · Desktop Publishing Software like MS Publisher, Scribus for Linux etc. · Presentation Software like MS PowerPoint or Open Office Impress, to make Presentations on content areas.

Language Skill	Hardware Component	Software Option
Reading Skill	• Monitor: to view the samples • Printer: to take print-outs of the sample	• Reading comprehension activities can be conducted using the Internet Browser, where the students can read the passage and then attempt to answer questions based on that.

Communication in the Second Language involves the four skills mentioned above. While learning a second language like English, it is important that the learner is not only exposed to four skills separately but also as a whole. It is here where the digital language laboratory can provide maximum benefit. Communication in the digital world could be either Synchronous or Asynchronous.

• **Synchronous Communication** involves communication at the same place-same time mode; as in chatting or video conferencing. This mode of communication asks for immediate language use. If a Webcam is attached to the computer, it is capable of acting as a relay station for video conferencing (an expensive option) or video chat (an inexpensive option). Using synchronous communication in the Language classroom provides for authentic language learning environment where the learners can also simultaneously record their language use. *Instant messaging* (IM) is a text-based synchronous form of electronic communication. It requires two or more people to be online at the same time and these participants communicate via the instant messaging software. In most instant messaging software, the user has a window on the computer screen where an anticipated question, response, or comment can be typed before sending. This allows the user to edit the message before sending it to the user on the other end.

• **Asynchronous Communication** involves communication at the different place-different time mode.This mode of communication, necessitates, that the language user *think, plan* and respond to situations. It is very useful to teaching English via content or context mode. In the classroom, *email* exchanges can take place between teacher and student, student and teacher, student and student, or student and any outside classroom person, including a keypal. Keypal is the word coined for penpals who communicate using email; it is the digital equivalent of a penpal but email is used as the mode of interaction instead of the traditional paper and pencil letters that were once exchanged.

Teachers as Material Developers in the Digital Language Laboratory

An ongoing debate in the arena of Materials in English Language Teaching is, whether, English Language Teachers should use published materials or develop their own *tailor-made* materials. Published materials (or commercially available materials) originate from and are written for particular situations and learners; thus, it is impossible to have "all-embracing" textbooks or software, as those published materials often claim, ready for use in all English Language Teaching situations. Second, since published materials aim for a large and largely unknown readership, they don't take into account the level of English proficiency and expert knowledge of any particular group of learners. Consequently, even if the linguistic level of the materials is appropriate for a given group, they may still either become bored with the content they already know or feel helpless with the totally unfamiliar content. Also, most published textbooks or software are not based on empirical research or theoretical work. They fail to provide the rationale underlying the approach to language learning they propose or to explain how the particular language items were selected. Furthermore, published materials, for the purpose of appealing to a large market, do not consider the appropriateness for classroom use in a local learning situation. In other words, they may lack cultural and social appropriacy. In spite of general opposition to published materials (Jones, 1990; Robinson, 1988); Swales (1980) reminds us that pubiished materials have their potential virtues, and "a reconsideration of the role and structure of ESP textbooks would allow them a restricted but legitimate place... ". In his opinion, published textbooks have a clearly discernible shape which can create predictability for the students about the course plan and content. Besides, a greater degree of internal coherence can be expected from published textbooks than from teacher-generated materials, especially if the latter are developed hastily under time pressure. In addition, Swales (1980) indicates that it is not cost-effective for each institution to produce its own tailor-made materials. Sheldon (1988) also explains why some English Language teachers use published materials. Teacher generated materials often have less credibility than published materials, especially under the pressure of heavy timetables and the highly restrictive nature of most teaching situations. Sheldon (1988) goes on to talk about the 'cruel paradox' that students often prefer slickly produced commercial course books *or software* to materials made by teachers themselves. The argument here seems to be that teacher developed materials will seem ragged and unprofessional next to those produced by professionals.

Block (1991) states three reasons why English Language teachers should replace the commercial course books with a contribution of their own:

1. **Contextualization**: Contextualization with real examples which are of real interest to the learners will make them active participants in the process of language learning.
2. **Timeliness**: Commercially available textbooks are revised after a long duration due to various economic factors.
3. **The Personal Touch**: Block (1991) has found students appreciating teachers who prepare their classes and materials that give a clear tangible evidence of preparation.

Block (1991) presents a six phase process, to help teachers prepare teaching material for English Language Teaching:

- **Phase 1**: The teacher finds an interesting article in a news magazine.

- **Phase 2**: The teacher spends over an hour putting together a reading exercise, a language activity derived from the text, and a discussion activity.
- **Phase 3**: The teacher uses the text and activities in class, and then makes a few adjustments in the activities.
- **Phase 4**: The teacher posts several copies of the text with the activities on a board in the teachers' room.
- **Phase 5**: Several teachers use the text and activities in their classes.
- **Phase 6**: At some point, the text and activities are either put in a long-term bank (in which case, they are considered to be relatively 'timeless') or thrown away.

Davies (2002) states that the use of teacher generated materials is important, because whilst learners may wish for more cultural content, they do not always want to deal with the kind of '*issue-based'* topics which typify many course books, preferring instead to experience their culture in more accessible ways.

In view of the above arguments, teachers can become material developers to suit their local classroom needs. They can use the following software options to create material for their English Classroom:

- **Hot Potatoes**: Hot Potatoes is a program that you can use to create cloze exercises, crossword puzzles, multiple choice, matching, and mixed form activities. Research (Chapelle, 2001; Ellis, 2005) points to the need for providing English Language Learners with opportunities for language input, making language salient and focusing on form. Through the use of Hot Potatoes English Language Learners can work with language they understand while creating and using quizzes, games and activities to make the language real for them.
- **MS PowerPoint or Open Office Impress**: This presentation software can help the teacher create interesting content rich teaching aids or interactive games.

- **Movie Maker Software**: This software can help the teachers of English, develop their own videos, that they could use in their English Classroom to help students learn the language.
- **Audacity**: This software can help the teacher create, record, edit and share language samples; to teach the students correct pronunciation and intonation patterns in English.

Using the digital laboratory has another distinct advantage for the English language teachers, as they can share and store all their work in formats that can be transferred easily from one computer to another. Secondly, the teachers with a little bit of training can develop material to suit their local needs. These materials could provide remedial education to the learner; it could provide instant feedback and reinforcement to the learner so that learning English is an interesting process.

Some thoughts...

Although the traditional concept of a language laboratory may be questioned, the digital language laboratory presents a unique opportunity to integrate technology in the teaching of English Language, especially in a country like India. In India, we are often faced with the problems of large classroom, lack of teacher support, absence of authentic language learning environment and even poor language skill in the language teacher itself; a digital language laboratory can help students get individual attention, get immediate feedback, get enough exercises to practice the usage of language, learn correct pronunciation and intonation patterns of the language, learn verbal and non-verbal communication aspects of the language (here English). But, it also calls for a certain amount of discipline from the learner, a bit of dedication from the teacher and infrastructural support from the school authorities. This infrastructural support need not be in the form of latest branded computers or expensive proprietary software, it could be assembled computers with Free Software Programs.

The learning of English can be interesting for most students provided the content is presented in a manner that is interesting and interactive. A teacher may fail to cater to these demands owing to a number of factors, but a computer, with its multifaceted options, can come the to rescue of the teacher as an aid to enhance the teaching and learning of English. Let it not be forgotten, the computer cannot replace the teacher, for ultimately, it is the teacher who will decide how, when and where the language learning material will be presented. It will just make the journey of language learning interesting.

Reference

1. Block, D. (1991). Some thoughts on DIY materials design. *ELT Journal,* Volume 45; No. 3 July 1991.
2. Davies, A. (2002). Using teacher-generated biography as input material. *ELT Journal,* Volume 56, No. 4.
3. Delcolque, P. Annan, N. & Bramoull'e, A. (2000). The history of computer assisted language learning web exposition. *http://www.history-of-call.org/*
4. Jones, G. M. (1990). ESP Textbooks: Do they really exist? English for Specific Purposes, 9.
5. NCERT (1996): Position Paper National Focus Group on Curriculum, Syllabus and textbooks, New Delhi.
6. NCERT (2006): Position Paper National Focus Group on Educational Technology, New Delhi.
7. NCERT (2006): Position Paper National Focus Group on Teaching of English, New Delhi.
8. Robinson, B. (1988). Review of 'Writing Laboratory Reports'. English for Specific Purposes, 7.
9. Sheldon, L. E . (1988). Evaluating ELT textbooks and materials. *ELT Journal*, Vol ume 42; No. 4.
10. Swaies, J. (1980). ESP: The textbook problem. The ESP Journal, 1, 11-23.

The Contributors

Prof (Dr) N K Jangira: During half a century of professional life, Dr. Jangira worked as teacher in schools, headed teacher training institute, served as Head Department of Teacher Education and Special Education as well as Dean Coordination in NCERT, shouldered responsibility of secretary education in Sikkim, and rounded of as Senior Education Specialist in the World Bank. He provided consultancy to UNESCO, UNICEF European Commission, DFID, OECD, CIDA and World Bank. He has published scores of papers in India and abroad.

Also published scores of professional books. Some of these are: Rethinking Teacher Education in UNESC published Perspective, Effective Teacher Training: A Cooperative learning Based Approach, Effective Teacher Training: Child Centred Approach, Responsive Teaching: Innovative Experiments in Teaching, Technology of Classroom Questioning, Core Teaching Skills: Microteaching Skills, Teacher Behaviour and Teaching Effectiveness, Special Education Scenario in India and Britain: Theory Research and Practice. Email: jangirank@yahoo.co.in

Ms Aashim, Army Institute of Higher Education, Pathankot

Ms Afshan Anees, Research scholar, Department of Education, Aligarh Muslim University, Aligarh, Uttar Pradesh. Email: afshan.anees1@gmail.com

Aftab A Ansari is Research Shcolar in Dept. of Education, Aligarh Muslim University, Aligarh, Uttar Pradesh.

Dr Amita Puri is Lecture in Education at Army Insititue of Education, Delhi Cantt., New Delhi.

Anjum Ahmad is Research Shcolar in Dept. of Education, Aligarh Muslim University, Aligarh, Uttar Pradesh.

Dr Arti Srivastava, Lecturer in Education, Army Institute of Education, Delhi Cantt., New Delhi

Ms Bandita B Mohanty, Lecturer, DIET, Daryaganj, New Delhi

Dr. Bharti Dogra, Lecturer, Army Institute of Education, Delhi Cantt., New Delhi. E-mail: bhartidogra1@yahoo.co.in

Mrs Bhawna Sharma, Vaishno College of Education , Thapkaur (H.P)

Mr Bhanu Pratap Pritam, Research Scholar, National University of Educational Planning and Administration, (NUEPA), New Delhi. Email: bhanupritam@gmail.com

Prof Gouri Srivastava is Professor in the Department of Women's Studies at NCERT New Delhi.

Dr J N Baliya, Asst. Professor, Department of Education, University of Jammu, Jammu (J&K)

Dr. K. Kalyani is Asst. Professor at Dept of Education, LSR College, University of Delhi, New Delhi.

Prof L C Singh Formerly with the Department of Teacher Education, NCERT, New Delhi.

Dr Mandeep Bhalla is Teacher in Oxford Public School, Vika Puri, New Delhi.

Dr M.S. Chhikara is the Proffesor in Education at Surajmal Institute of Education and Technology Janakpuri New Delhi.

Dr (Mrs.) Nasrin, Reader, Department of Education, Aligarh Muslim University, Aligarh, Uttar Pradesh. Email: mhsiddiqui50@rediffmail.com

Dr Nakhat Nasrin is Reader, Department of Education, Aligarh Muslim University, Aligarh.

Dr P S Jamwal, Education Department, J&K State Govt., Udhampur (J&K)

Dr Pranita Gopal is at Army Institute of Education, Delhi Cantt, New Delhi. E.mail: pranitagopal@gmail.com

Ms Rekha Rani, Research Scholar, Department of Education, Aligarh Muslim University, Aligarh.

Rubina Shahnaz is Research Shcolar in Dept. of Education, Aligarh Muslim University, Aligarh, Uttar Pradesh.

Mr Rudra Narayan Sahoo, Senior Consultant, National Council of Educational Research & Training, New Delhi.

Dr S K Mohanty, Sr. Lecturer at R.C Institute of Technology, Nazafgarh, New Delhi

Mrs Sarwat F Usmani is Lecturer in Education at Aligarh Muslim University, Aligarh.

Ms Shineh Suri, Lecturer, Trinity Institute, Sector-9, Dwarka, New Delhi.

Dr Sudarshan Mishra, Lecturer in Education, Army Institute of Education, Delhi Cantt., New Delhi - 110 010. E-mail: sudarshanmishra@yahoo.com.

Dr Sushil Dhiman is Lecture in Central Institute of Education, Delhi University, Delhi.

Prof Subhash Chandra, Assistant Professor, Department of Education, Lady Irwin College, New Delhi.

Mr Susanta Kumar Pathy, Lecturer, Lingaya's College of Education, Faridabad, Haryana

Dr Sudarshan Mishra is Lecturer in Education at AIE Delhi Cantt since Apr 2004. He was the convener of the National Seminar held at AIE Delhi Cantt on 02 Apr 2009.

Dr (Mrs) Saroj Bala Yadav, Prof. & Coordinator, National Population Education Project, NCERT, New Delhi – 110 016.

Ms Sushma Sharma is student in Army Institute of Education, Delhi Cantt., New Delhi.

Dr S K Yadav is Professor in Deptt of Teacher Education and Extension NCERT, New Delhi.

Ms Talat Jamil, Research Scholar, Institute of Advanced Studies in Education, Faculty of Education, Jamia Millia Islamia, New Delhi. E-mail: talatjamil-2006@yahoo.co.in

Dr Vandana Ghai is Lecture in Army Insitiue of Education, Delhi Cantt., New Delhi.

Index